Invoking Lakshmi

Siddhalakshmi: Goddess of Power

Invoking Lakshmi

The Goddess of Wealth in Song and Ceremony

Constantina Rhodes

Dev Publishers & Distributors
New Delhi

Published by:
DEV PUBLISHERS & DISTRIBUTORS
2nd Floor, Prakash Deep,
22, Delhi Medical Association Road,
Darya Ganj,
New Delhi-110002
Phone : 011-4357 2647, 98102 36140
e-mail: devbooks@hotmail.com
website: www.devbooks.co.in

ISBN 978-93-81406-14-4
This edition, 2012
The publication of this book in India is made possible by
permission of the State University of New York Press © 2010,
and may be sold only in Indian Sub-continent.

Printed in India.

For my beautiful daughter, Alexandra

Contents

Acknowledgments

I wish to express heartfelt gratitude to Sri Swami Chidvilasananda Gurumayi, for it was she who first suggested that my increasingly unresolved questions about the enigmatic goddess Lakṣmī might be turned into a book. The challenge to unfold even a small portion of the goddess's mystery could not have been undertaken without great support on many levels, seen and unseen.

I am extremely grateful to Nancy Ellegate, senior acquisitions editor at the State University of New York Press, both for her creative sensibility and her steadfast support of this project from seed of thought to fruition. Many thanks also to Laurie Searl, senior production editor at SUNY Press, for her excellent guidance throughout the production process. I gratefully acknowledge Eckerd College, the Sheva Arts Foundation, and the Muktabodha Indological Research Institute for their generous financial support in the form of research grants during the two sabbaticals that were required for the completion of this book. My sincere gratitude goes to the individuals in each of these institutions for believing in this project so wholeheartedly, most especially to Dean Lloyd Chapin at Eckerd, Janice Burney of Sheva Arts, and Hema Patankar of Muktabodha, who has lovingly held this project close to her heart from the beginning. I would also like to acknowledge the Rubin Museum of Art for granting permission to use the image of Siddhalakshmi, with special thanks to Helen Abbott for her gracious facilitation of the process.

Many colleagues have contributed to my ideas and evaluated numerous drafts of my translations and their interpretations as this book has taken shape. I am grateful for the Works in Progress sessions at the conferences of the Society for Tantric Studies, most especially to the generous collegiality of Loriliai Biernacki, Marcy Braverman, Douglas Brooks, Glen Hayes, Jeffrey Lidke, William K. Mahony,

June McDaniel, Paul Muller-Ortega, Charles Orzech, Bruce Sullivan, Sthaneshwar Timalsina, and David Gordon White. I am grateful for the opportunities to have presented lectures and workshops at Sri Muktananda Ashram during the early phases of this book's development; feedback from workshop coordinators as well as participants has been particularly helpful in making connections between theory and practice.

Many other friends and colleagues have contributed to this project as it has developed over the years. For reiterating the value of a book on the goddess Lakṣmī, as well for sharing their scholarly wisdom, inspirational conversations, and practical advice, I wish to thank Elisabeth Benard, Edwin Bryant, Carol P. Christ, Saraswati Clere, Thomas B. Coburn, Paula Christine, Barbara D'Angelis, Janet Dobrovolny, Laura Duggan, Mark S. G. Dyczkowski, George Franklin, John Friend, John Grimes, Rick Jarow, Angana Jhaveri, Sally Kempton, Valerie Leeds, Peggy Lipton, Rachel Fell McDermott, Patricia Monaghan, Beverly Moon, Vasudha Narayanan, Suze Orman, Tracy Pintchman, Carlos Pomeda, Diane Rhodes, Sujata Ringawa, Steven J. Rosen, Deepak Sarma, Graham Schweig, Miranda Shaw, Rita DasGupta Sherma, Frederick M. Smith, H. Daniel Smith, and Demetri Tashie.

At Eckerd College, I extend warm thanks for the congenial support of Victoria Baker, Jewel Spears Brooker, David Bryant, Julienne Empric, Davina Lopez, Carolyn Johnston, Jared Stark, and Robert Wigton. At Hunter College of the City University of New York, I gratefully acknowledge Barbara C. Sproul, Director of the Program in Religion, for her foresight and generosity, as well as fellow linguists Vishwa Adluri and Alice Hunsberger for delightful explorations of ancient phraseology. Thanks also to my many students whose astute questions and comments have contributed to a richer understanding of the goddess. I am deeply grateful to Stephen C. Robinson, founder and director of the Holistic Studies Institute of New York, for creating new avenues to explore the ideas in this book, as well as for his wise counsel and continuous encouragement. Many thanks as well go to my amazingly gifted friends at H.S.I. for generously sharing their insights as this project has progressed.

Countless others who have contributed their thoughts, insights, and inspiration remain unnamed. I am grateful to all, though of course any oversights or inaccuracies in this book are entirely my own.

Constantina Rhodes
New York City

INTRODUCTION

The Goddess Arrives in Delhi

It was autumn in Delhi, that majestic time of year when the sky sparkles a bright blue and evenings resonate with a gentle coolness. A season of delightful reprieve from the summer's heat, autumn is a time to celebrate life's bounty. As its refreshment mediates against all kinds of torpor, many experience this season as an expression of the goddess. Even the name *Autumn* is one of her names.[1] This is a time of movement and excitement, a time of visiting and of receiving guests. It is therefore no wonder that this is the time to receive the most desirable guest of all, for this is when the gracious goddess visits her earthly devotees and infuses them with her blessings. In particular, autumn is the most auspicious time for invoking Lakṣmī, beloved goddess of beauty, wealth, prosperity, and abundant good fortune.

In every neighborhood, people were cleaning house, some of them also scrubbing the exterior walls, applying fresh coats of whitewash or paint. They were preparing for Dīvālī,[2] the Festival of Lights celebrating Lakṣmī. Everyone and everything seemed to be in on the celebration. Temples, homes, shops, taxis, and the streets themselves were decorated and made ready for the goddess's arrival. In the marketplaces, strings of tiny electric lights sparkled in the trees and from awnings. When night fell, firecrackers would compete with the sound of devotional music on public loudspeakers.

On the day of the new moon, women decorated the steps leading to their doors with beautiful designs in bright-colored powders, tracing footsteps for the goddess of wealth to find her way into their homes. Alongside the footsteps they placed rows and rows of small clay lamps, and at nightfall, they lit the lamps, their cotton wicks saturated with *ghee*,[3] which emitted an exquisite, golden brilliance. These small lamps were also placed up on the flat rooftops, so that the entire house was lit up in a kind of landing pattern for Lakṣmī to follow as she descended from the heavens. With an invitation of such beauty and luminosity, how could the goddess resist gracing these homes with her presence?

I had been invited to attend my first *pūjā*, or ceremonial worship of the deity, in a private home on the outskirts of Delhi. Veena, the woman of the house, was performing a Dīvālī *pūjā*, for which she had set up a temporary altar in a corner of the bedroom. Having spent the past few days in cleaning and preparation, she appropriately began the actual ritual at dusk, when lamps are lit to dispel darkness. The central image of worship was a small framed lithograph print of the goddess Lakṣmī, which had been set into a large stainless steel bowl filled with puffed rice. Veena lit several sticks of sweet, highly fragrant incense and began to recite prayers and make offerings as she waved a small brass lamp fueled with *ghee*. Here again was that exquisite golden light. She was invoking the goddess, inviting her to enter the home and impart her blessings.

Despite the steadfastness with which she performed the ritual motions, however, there was an impression of mild disorder, imprecision, and distraction: some of the liquid offerings spilled out of their containers, while powdered offerings blew away and onto the nearby bed, staining the bedcover with indelible vermilion and turmeric splotches. Children (hers and the neighbors') were running through the house and out into the lanes. Her husband would chase after them and bring them inside, after which they would wriggle free and resume their gleeful romping and attempting to get into the box of firecrackers. Despite the distractions and having to stop and start several times, Veena continued, nonplussed. It was clear from her relaxed demeanor that all was proceeding well. Although as a visitor I could only perceive the ordinary messiness of life that would somehow stand in the way of drawing down the divine into that house on that night, the hostess proceeded with a calm certainty that this *was* the *pūjā*, with spills, color, ringing bells, and interruptions, for as Veena sang supplicatory prayers to the Mother of the Universe, her own children were beseeching her to please hurry up and give them their sweets and sparklers. This jumbly melange of activities struck me as what the goddess of abundance must stand for—life, bright and awake, burgeoning, and despite all distractions and possible encumbrances, was ever moving in and around the human realm. This was certainly a far cry from the peaceful feeling of stillness I had expected. But the ceremony was not yet complete.

Toward the close of the ceremony, Veena lit another lamp, this one with camphor, which sent out an initial blaze of sparks and then settled into a diamond-like, piercingly brilliant white light along with an astringent and pungent fragrance. Very suddenly things got quiet. Of their own accord, the children gathered close to the altar, standing still and with an attitude of expectation. I noticed that the street noise had subsided, and the darkening room seemed to spread with light. Within an instant, everything had changed. A deep and peaceful fullness settled over the house. That yogic point of perfect quietude flooded the heart and stilled the mind. I let go of compulsive, dualistic queries: Is Lakṣmī a goddess of the worldly realm? Or a goddess of transcendence?

In that moment when the *pūjā* imploded into perfection, when the supplications from the human realm seem to have succeeded in drawing the goddess into our space, crowding out mundane restlessness with a deep and abundant tranquility, existence within the world and transcendence beyond the world seemed as one. The *pūjā* elicited a point of perfect suspension, a window into the infinite that exists between the movements of coming and going, of past and present, of mundane and holy. What was the cause of that glorious hiatus? When that splendid moment subsided and we began to move about, the first words out of anyone's mouth came when Veena's son Ramesh, all of three or four years old, announced: *"Devī ā rahī hai!"* That is, *"The goddess has arrived!"*

What Does It Mean to Invoke a Goddess?

The goddess had arrived. What exactly did that mean? What exactly is *a goddess*? Who is the goddess Lakṣmī? And if she had arrived, where had she come from? How had Veena convinced her to come? Certainly, there were preparations, ceremonial actions, and singing to the goddess, which, I later discovered, were conceptualized as invitations extended to a magnificent guest. Invitations, however, do not always guarantee arrivals. What was in Veena's invocation that seemed to spell success?

Invoking Lakshmi: The Goddess of Wealth in Song and Ceremony addresses these questions. The answers—or perhaps, speculations—are based upon songs of praise that are offered to the goddess and that constitute the essence of her worship in its countless variegations. All of the songs in this volume are originally in Sanskrit. None but a few of these verses has ever appeared in translation. This is, to my knowledge, the first English-version collection of devotional songs dedicated entirely to Lakṣmī. With this volume, we offer an entirely new resource for the study and the invocation of the goddess of prosperity.

Lakṣmī is by far the most popular and the most widely worshiped goddess in all of India. Her shrines appear everywhere—in homes, along roadsides, in most shops and places of business, and of course in the great temples across the entire subcontinent. For centuries, her devotees have invoked her in song and ceremony. Authorship of many of these songs is attributed to the gods themselves, and their words are said to have been imparted for the benefit of humankind, so that they may be used to invoke the goddess with efficacious results. All of these songs are invocations—the tradition holds that if a worshiper sincerely invokes Lakṣmī with these words, she will listen and respond to the call.

Why do people invoke the goddess Lakṣmī? A better question might be: Why would they *not* invoke her? Who does not have at least some concern for physical and emotional well-being, material comfort, harmonious relationships, and spiritual insight? Not everyone may be focused entirely upon all of these, all of the time, and some may insist that they have no need for any of them. It is no secret, however, that when people seek the advice of spiritual, psychological, or religious counselors, their most pressing concerns overwhelmingly involve health, career, love, or existential crisis. The labels placed upon these issues vary, of course, according to cultural, religious, and historical frameworks, but they remain a constant in one form or another. The songs to Lakṣmī in this volume give voice to these concerns, and they also provide insight into the nature and personalities of this goddess as she is envisioned both by her human devotees and by the gods themselves. As we shall see, Lakṣmī's devotees have turned to her again and again for blessings of good fortune in every aspect of life, for she is recognized as the limitless source-energy of all abundance, prosperity, and power, and her wealth takes infinite forms.

Ancient India was renowned as a land of bounteous splendor, majesty, and wealth: It was an abundant source of precious metals and gemstones; of exquisite spices and condiments and gorgeous fabrics; of sophisticated medical sciences and equally sophisticated arts of sensual pleasure; and of a multitude of philosophical schools and spiritual traditions whereby one could contemplate how to integrate these many ways of being or simply abandon them altogether in pursuit of spiritual liberation. India's majestic confluence of material and spiritual prosperity reflects the nature of this goddess who embodies the rich and diverse ways of experiencing one's walk though this world. This explains why her devotees extol her as *bhukti-mukti-*

pradāyinī—"bestower of material enjoyment and spiritual liberation." By worshiping the goddess of abundance, one is free to experience the fullness of *all* of life's blessings.

Invoking Lakṣmī, Invoking Divine Luminosity

Before moving forward with our study, we pause to address the question: What exactly is a goddess? The Sanskrit word for *goddess* is *devī*; the word for *god* is *deva*. Both derive from the verbal root *div*, which means to shine, to play, to sparkle, to rejoice. In English as well as in Sanskrit, luminosity and playful movement are two ways of verbalizing a singular phenomenon, as when we say, for example, that sunlight *plays* upon the waters. The verbal root *div* also means to gamble, to cast dice. The term, then, also conveys the excitement of uncertainty, the expectancy of luck, and the vibrant sensation that anything can happen—all of these as opposed to the frozen stagnancy of absolute certainty. Of course, depending upon perspective, playful uncertainty may be experienced as a chaotic abyss, and absolute certainty, a tranquil haven. This dichotomy is not lost as we move through this book and consider the many gradations of meaning in Lakṣmī's name, how she expresses herself, and what happens when she is forced into hiding. We shall see that Lakṣmī is the epitome of luminous energy in action: without a doubt, the goddess of prosperity is the quintessential *devī*.

The *deva*s (gods and goddesses collectively) are "luminous beings." When a worshiper invokes any of the *deva*s, he or she is first calling upon their essence—divine, undifferentiated luminosity. Every impulse toward invoking Lakṣmī begins with a desire for that source of delight, splendor, and source-energy. When the energy of that source is aroused, then one may consider a particular focus, of which there are infinite expressions. These expressions may be seen as moods or personalities of the gods, making them perceptible to the world qualified by name and form. This is why the particular avenue of expressing divine energy to break past obstacles, for example, is embodied in the form of Gaṇeśa, lord of obstacles. So too does that luminous essence take form as the lovely one who shapes sound into eloquent speech, and artistic impulse into glorious refinement of artistic expression, as Sarasvatī, goddess and patron of the fine arts. When that luminosity expresses itself as bounteous beauty, delight, harmony, abundant wealth, and spiritual liberation—in short, prosperity of every kind—then it is recognized and called upon as Lakṣmī, goddess of abundance. To invoke and draw forth the luminous source of all abundance and prosperity is the purpose of the songs in our collection.

On the Format of This Book

We offer this book as a source and resource for various types of readers. Scholars and students of Indic religion will find that this collection of original sources greatly enhances the study of goddess worship, devotional poetry, and, above all, the rich complexity of the goddess Lakṣmī herself, about whom surprisingly little has been written. Spiritual seekers will find that these songs are indeed conversations with the goddess, and that the words to these songs may give voice to their own joys and concerns as they navigate their way through the material expression of this world. And finally, devotees of the goddess in any of her forms will find in this volume a worship manual—a compendium of invocatory songs and the text of a worship ceremony—to use as a guide in their own worship, much as the original Sanskrit volume containing the texts of these songs was compiled as a guide for worshipers of the goddess in India.

The heart of this book is a corpus of texts invoking the goddess Lakṣmī, both in song and in ceremony. I have organized this volume into four parts, as follows.

In Part One, I portray the divine personalities of Lakṣmī as they emerge in the Vedic, Purāṇic, and Tantric texts—three major areas of Sanskrit sacred literature. In Part Two, I discuss the power of poetry in summoning the goddess, that is, I explore how each genre of song is understood to "work" in invoking the goddess. In Part Three, I present my translation of a complete Lakṣmī *pūjā* text. Here, in systematic detail, we revisit our impressionistic description of the Lakṣmī *pūjā* performed by Veena in her home in Delhi. I introduce this with a discussion of the nature of *pūjā*, explaining how to appreciate what *pūjā* is and how it "works." Then I present the translation of the *pūjā* text, accompanying each verse with additional analysis and commentary specific to that aspect of the ceremony. In Part Four, I present what I consider the heart of this book—my translations of Vedic, Purāṇic, and Tantric songs invoking Lakṣmī.

For scholars and for those devotees who wish to address the goddess in the original Sanskrit, I include, at the end of this volume, the texts in transliteration.

Three Categories of Song, Three Emerging Portraits of the Goddess

When viewed sequentially, the songs invoking Lakṣmī reflect an increasingly complex portrait of the goddess as she is envisioned by her devotees. Each "divine personality" of the goddess builds upon and enhances the nuances of the previous one. In order to get a glimpse into the nature of the goddess we are about to encounter, we offer here the highlights of our first three chapters (constituting Part One of the book), as follows.

Chapter 1, "The Awesome Power of Auspiciousness: Lakṣmī of the Vedic Traditions," introduces the goddess in her form as the lotus and the lotus goddess, as well as an embodiment of *śrī*—splendor and majesty. The Vedic hymns invoke the goddess to come to the earthly realm, specifically to assist the king, whose sovereignty ensures the well-being of the kingdom. The realm of the goddess's blessing, then, is this earth, this world that we inhabit as embodied beings and as social creatures seeking abundance and prosperity.

Chapter 2, "Living the Good Life: Lakṣmī of the Purāṇic Traditions," opens to a wider universe and engages the presence of the goddess not only across the fertile earth and propitious kingdom, but throughout the three worlds of heaven, earth, and the netherworlds. Prosperity expands in time and space, and, thematically, the goddess's blessings are now expressed through the more subtle and complex avenues of pleasure (*kāma*), material wealth (*artha*), virtue (*dharma*), and spiritual liberation (*mokṣa*). These songs engage both the king and the householder, and many of their verses are said to have been uttered by the god Indra, king of the heavenly gods, in gratitude to the goddess for restoring harmony among the three worlds.

The Purāṇic songs address the goddess as Lakṣmī, majestic goddess of wealth, and consort or wife of Viṣṇu. Together they embody the divine couple that preserves harmony in and among the worlds. These songs reflect the concerns of householders—whether the "house" is that of one's immediate family, the larger community, or the entire three worlds. The petitioners may be seeking prosperity or they may be expressing thanks to the goddess for having restored prosperity that had been lost and regained. The goddess is also addressed as Mahālakṣmī, or "Great Lakṣmī," the expansive form of the goddess who creates, preserves, and destroys the universe, as well as obscurs and reveals supreme reality. Most of the songs use the names Lakṣmī and Mahālakṣmī interchangeably, with little technical distinction regarding the divine attributes of the goddess.

Chapter 3, "Living the Powerful Life: Lakṣmī of the Tantric Traditions," moves into the esoteric realms of interior worship and the transformation of consciousness. Whereas the Vedic songs elicit the goddess's presence as the display of wealth and glory in this world, and those of the Purāṇas seek her presence as the harmonious blending of all types of wealth throughout the three realms of heaven, earth, and the netherworlds, the Tantric songs locate the power of the goddess in even more subtle universes embedded deep within the multiple strata of the human body and consciousness. Some of the Tantric songs invite the goddess's blessings by requesting that the goddess's powerful aspects come to dwell upon and within the practitioner. Most of the Tantric songs, however, reflect a monistic viewpoint: Here, the essence of the goddess is the ground of all being, inviting the Tantric worshiper to engage in her worship not only through external means but internally. The songs of the Vedas as well as those of the epics and Purāṇas invoke the goddess by *drawing her down* from her heavenly realm; the Tantric songs invoke her presence by *waking her up*, for she is the divine power that lies within us all.

The songs throughout our collection seek the "favor" (*prasannā*) of the goddess, or for her to grant a boon (*vara*). The Tantric songs seek also to generate *siddhi*—the spiritual power of attainment and perfection—within the practitioner's own body and consciousness. The Tantric poets invoke the goddess in her most subtle forms, for not only do they seek those blessings that make their mark in the material world, but they seek to live in complete alignment with the source energy of those blessings.

Sources: Sanskrit Texts and Popular Worship Manuals

My intention with *Invoking Lakshmi* is to present a collection of devotional songs and ceremonies that most closely replicates what a Hindu worshiper would use to invoke the goddess. I have therefore drawn upon a compilation of Sanskrit worship texts presented in a *paddhati*, or manual for popular worship. The *paddhati* is an intriguing popular genre that has received relatively little attention by scholars, especially as a source of Sanskrit texts. Although basing my selection of songs upon a *paddhati* has not been without some scholarly problems (mostly concerning the origins and lineage of the texts as well as some variants in language and spelling), I have found that presenting a body of work based upon the indigenous category of the *paddhati* offers an exciting new way to experience Sanskrit texts in translation.[4]

Most of the texts in this book are taken from *Śrī Lakṣmī Upāsanā* [Adoration of the Glorious Lakṣmī], edited by Pandit Rajesh Dixit. This manual contains Sanskrit texts dedicated to Lakṣmī that originate from a variety of sources and worship traditions. Since the main purpose of a *paddhati* is to facilitate ritual, it is therefore not surprising that the texts included in such a manual have not been categorized in any way, nor has much information been given concerning their original sources.

Some of the texts provide source information in the colophon, although this is not always reliable. Such disparity is a feature not only of the *paddhati* but of the textual traditions themselves, which, as they developed with complexity across time and region, may have come to exist in varying recensions and editions. For example, the colophon of the *Song for the Lakṣmī of Spiritual Power* (*Śrī Siddhalakṣmī Stotram*) indicates that it is found in the *Brāhma Purāṇa*, although inspection of that *purāṇa* has not revealed that text. Clearly, the very first questions often asked by scholars about the specific origin of a text may never be addressed within the tradition. However, this should not deter us from translating these texts, listening to what they have to say, and allowing them to increase our appreciation of how worshipers and deities communicate with each other.

Sanskritists may find interest in the slightly nonstandard forms of the language exhibited in some of the Tantric selections. The text of the *Song-Amulet of the Lotus Goddess* (*Kamalātmika Kavacam*), for example, suggests an Eastern transmission of Śākta literature (as in Assam or Bengal), employing the doubling of consonants instead of consonant clusters (such as (*samāttam* for *samāptam*), or the doubling of the semivowel *v* (such as *sarvva* for *sarva*, *purvva* for *purva*, and *pārvvatī* for *pārvatī*).

Locating the Heart of a Text

It is not always possible to ascertain the exact origin of some devotional texts, for a couple of reasons: First, the tradition itself does not always provide the types of answers we are looking for. Even the most easily identifiable songs—our first two, which are from the Vedas—are actually *appended* to the Vedas. We do not know where they "existed" before that. Second, the nature of Sanskrit devotional poetry is fluid and malleable. When a text is said to be found within a larger work, it is never entirely clear whether that text was *derived from* the larger work or whether it was later *inserted into* that work. Two well-known examples of this may be seen when we consider whether the *Bhagavad Gītā* was inserted into—or derived from—the *Mahābhārata*, or whether the *Devī Māhātmyam* was inserted into—or derived from—the *Mārkaṇḍeya Purāṇa.*

This feature—whereby entire segments may be inserted into or extracted from larger texts—actually begins with individual verses comprising the texts themselves. As I note throughout *Invoking Lakshmi*, certain verses in one song appear verbatim in other songs. Sometimes, these are the initial verses that establish a visualization for meditation on the deity. Perhaps the most striking example of this malleability is in the final song of our Tantric section, the *Secret Lakṣmī Incantation That Yields Immediate Results* (*Sadyaḥ Phaladā Lakṣmīstava Hṛdayam*); eleven of this song's sixteen verses also appear within the 108 verses of *The Secret Heart of Lakṣmī* (*Śrī Mahālakṣmī Hṛdayam*).

Another example of this feature may be seen when some songs, such as the two earliest texts in our collection—The *Hymn to Śrī* (*Śrī Sūktam*) and the *Hymn to Lakṣmī* (*Lakṣmī Sūktam*)—may appear as either two separate texts or as one blended text. And again, when they appear separately, they may vary in their number of verses. Some editions of the *Śrī Sūktam* contain fourteen verses, whereas others contain fifteen, and yet others, sixteen. The differences between these numbers are significant according to the tradition that employs the text in its ceremonial worship.[5]

The narrator of a Purāṇa or Tantra may shift into song to express the heart of a passage, for the richest, most memorable essence is always with song. We may not be too far from this concept if we think of the devotional hymns in these texts as akin to the musical interludes that punctuate the story lines of a Broadway show or a Bollywood musical. The songs accentuate the movement of the story, and so too they may be extracted to be sung and cherished independently, existing as memorable works that resonate with viewers long after the prose-dialogue has receded into the background of one's consciousness.

Worship Texts Versus Worship Traditions

Although the *Śrī Lakṣmī Upāsanā* does not divide these texts according to any specific lineage or origin, I have presented them in three broad categories: Vedic, Purāṇic, and Tantric. It is not my intention here to document the precise schools and subschools that may claim these texts as their own. Even the earliest of our songs, the *Śrī Sūktam,* while acknowledged as an appendage of the *Ṛg Veda,* is also incorporated into the worship texts and traditions of various sacred lineages. Two south Indian traditions, the Pāñcarātra and the Śrī Vidyā, for example, employ the *Śrī Sūktam* in a particularly Tantric way; to label that song Tantric, however, would be misleading. Therefore I feel it is important to reiterate that these categories are *broad;* the designations of Vedic, Purāṇic, and Tantric in this volume have as much to do with thematic considerations as they do with textual origins. Further, each of these categories is filled with its own complexities and resistance to categorization. It is for this reason that I have chosen to compose the introductory sections with a strong focus on the texts themselves. To discuss with accuracy the ways in which various schools have employed these texts in their worship or textual traditions could well require several large volumes. In addition, it would detract from our immediate purpose—to present a collection of poetry invoking the goddess, allowing that poetry to occupy a space of its own in all of its variegations and complexities.

The three broad categories will help us to understand the general themes and perhaps the origins of these texts, but we would be somewhat remiss in stating that any of these texts "belongs" solely to a specific tradition. This helps us to keep in mind the original audiences for whom the worship manuals were compiled. This also helps us to see that categories of "Hindu worship" are indeed quite fluid, that worshipers of the goddess may move freely within the vastly rich layers of these textual traditions as they seek words to express the deepest concerns of the heart.

Our focus, then, is not so much on who owns these texts, but on the goddess within them. How is she portrayed? How is she addressed? What do her devotees ask of her, and what do they expect to receive? As mentioned earlier, no other source in English presents such an abundant body of poetry to the goddess Lakṣmī. I have found that the sheer volume of these verses, taken together, evokes a sense of the goddess's abundant presence that cannot be experienced when we encounter such works piecemeal. I would therefore invite the reader to discover the goddess section by section, moving at will between the introductory chapters and the texts, perhaps reaching a point where the texts alone become a cherished place to return again and again. As for filling in the blanks where we have not provided precise details of school or origin, I invite future generations of scholars to use these translations as a guide into aspects of the goddess that are just beginning to come to light. The Hindu goddess of prosperity first expresses herself in this world in the form of a lotus. With that in mind, let us behold the petals of her divine personalities as they unfold, one layer at a time.

PART ONE

The Divine Personalities of Lakṣmī

The goddess of wealth expresses herself in infinite forms. Here we explore the development of the goddess's divine personalities as reflected in the songs offered by her worshipers, for the manner in which she is approached in song tells us much about how she avails herself for perception in the three worlds.

CHAPTER 1

The Awesome Power of Auspiciousness

Lakṣmī of the Vedic Traditions

The Primordial Lotus Goddess

In the spiritual imagination of her earliest worshipers, the goddess of prosperity revealed herself through the abundant riches that sweeten the experience of life. She existed in the exuberant life-force of plants and animals and in the prosperous well-being of individuals, families, and communities. The majesty of the day and night and the changing of seasons exhibited her splendor. The ways in which she manifested herself were infinite. And yet, who or what was the essence behind these manifestations? Who was this goddess? By what name could she be invoked?

The personification of this goddess took shape gently, tenderly, in the space between reality and surreality, where the as-yet undifferentiated divine essence blossomed into various categories of embodiment at once. In particular, her early worshipers recognized the earthly form of the goddess as something very much of the natural realm and yet not quite of this world, a hybrid apparition of a radiantly beautiful woman embodied in all living things, but most especially in the sacred lotus. Like all forms of life, the form of the goddess begins in the waters.

Long before the songs praising Lakṣmī were written down, ancient Indian visual art was replete with lovely and graceful motifs of lotuses rising from pools of water and of nymph-like figures curling lithely around tree trunks. Other images depict a female figure seated on a lotus, bearing in her hands blossoming lotuses and tender shafts of freshly sprouted grain. This same figure is sometimes flanked by plump elephants who shower her with water from belly-round urns. These images depict the primordial lotus goddess, earliest form of the Indian mother goddess, beneficent deity of life-force, fertility, and glorious abundance. The earliest of these images were created some four to five thousand years ago by the artists of the Harappa civilization.[1] The iconographic records from ages past have no written indications of her name, but when the sacred texts begin to recognize this deity in song, she is called upon with a variety of names that reiterate her images, among them Kamalā, Ambujā, Padmā, and Padmiṇī, all of which mean "lotus." Thus it is that in the opening verse of one of her earliest songs, Lakṣmī is addressed and identified as the lotus goddess Padmiṇī:

> Most lovely goddess Padmiṇī
> With lotus face
> And lovely lotus-petal eyes,
> O you who cherish the lotus,
> O you who cherish the world,
> O goddess whose heart pervades the universe,
> To your lotus feet I bow.[2]

As the hymn continues, each part of the goddess's body—her eyes, lips, limbs, and so forth—is said to consist of lotus petals. As well, she sits on a lotus, dwells within the lotus, bears lotuses in her lotus-hands, and indeed is the inner essence of the lotus. This is a hyperreality; the parts do not add up to make "ordinary" sense—nor are they expected to. As such, this is a more potent form of the goddess, less specifically manifest, yet containing every possibility, for as the unfolding petals expand outward, they express the goddess's essence in form, replicating the entire multilayered universe, which itself is the very body of the primordial lotus goddess. Her divine essence is understood to dwell in that form, and her worshipers see the lotus not only as a symbol but as an actual embodiment of the goddess. This having been said, it should be with informed interest that we can appreciate a vignette reported in an 1808 edition of *Curtis's Botanical Magazine*, in which horticulturist W. J. Hooker notes that "a native of Nepal, who entered Sir William Jones' study, made prostrations before a lotus, the flowers of which happened to be there for examination."[3] One can only wonder how the renowned philologist interpreted this gesture.[4]

The *Nelumbo necifora*, or sacred Indian lotus, has long captured the religious imagination in South Asia. To contemplate the serene and easeful characteristics of this aquatic plant is to be invited into an almost surrealistic realm of symbol. The lotus is considered to evoke the full range of existence in all of its elemental variegations, with its roots deeply embedded in the muddy soil of the pond-bed, its stalk holding steadfastly through the waters, and its flower rising gloriously in the air, untouched by the other elements. Some varieties of lotus may take two or more years to produce a bloom, which may then unfurl slowly and steadily over the course of three days, finally revealing the fullness of its exquisite flower, complete with its intoxicating fragrance. It then takes another three days to fold back in upon itself, perpetuating its cycle of incubation, unfolding, opening in full majesty, and then closing inward again. The luxuriant fertility of the waterborne lotus as it moves through these cycles replicates the process of the goddess as the one who gives birth to the world, nourishes it, and oversees its eventual dissolution. As well, the lotus flower in full bloom is seen as an expression of the abundance, beauty, purity, gracefulness, mystery, and revelation of this goddess.

In her laudatory songs, the goddess of creation, the goddess of prosperity, and the lotus goddess are recognized as one and the same. Just as her many epithets address this goddess as the foundation of the entire world, so too has the lotus persisted as a pan-Indian image that represents the very wellspring and support of the creation. In particular, her name as Padmā, meaning "lotus," also literally denotes a foothold: *pad* refers to *foot* and *mā* refers to a measured expansion across a spacial dimension. The lotus seat serves as the foundation upon which the gods rest in their embodied forms when they become manifest upon the earth, thereby serving as an intricate link between the earth and the realms of heaven. It is an image that extends beyond Hindu iconography to that of Jainism and Buddhism as well, for the lotus seat that supports the images of the Buddha has been taken far beyond the motherland to become established in the sacred arts of virtually all of the Buddhist countries.

In addition to representing the divine mother and her expression as the graceful yet steadfast support of the world, so too does the lotus come to be recognized in the interior, subtle body of the human being, itself a reflection of the divine consciousness of the goddess. As we shall see, aligning with the internal presence of the lotus goddess becomes an essential feature of the esoteric paths to spiritual liberation.

Other recognized forms of Lakṣmī—cows, gold coins, precious gems, sprouts of grain or green plants, for example—have traditionally also elicited devout response in her worshipers. It is the image of Lakṣmī as the lotus, however, that recurs most prevalently throughout our collection of sacred poetry, appearing in the selections from the Vedas, Purāṇas, and Tantras even as her personality and imagery develop with different emphases in each of these literary traditions.

The Goddess of Auspiciousness: Śrī's Essence, Lakṣmī's Form

The Vedas, or "wisdom books," are the earliest scriptures of the Hindu tradition.[5] When we turn to the tradition of the earliest Vedic texts, we encounter invocations for the presence of *śrī*, which translates as splendor, glory, majesty, brilliance, and the divine power of auspiciousness. *Śrī* is the power of life and vitality, and that which is touched by *śrī* becomes radiant with health, wealth, well-being, abundance, and bounteous prosperity. The radiant force of *śrī* can dispel the darkness of misfortune, decay, and poverty. *Śrī* is an abstract quality, and although as a feminine noun the term carries the connotation of a divine feminine force, it is not yet associated with any particular form or personification of divinity. Rather, there is a magnificent ambiguity in the term, for "splendor" is recognized as taking the form of wherever it manifests, as in the blossoming abundance of the earth, the life-giving waters, bounteous grains, and fatted cattle. *Śrī* is identified also in the auspicious workings of society: in the peaceful and prosperous realm of a righteous king; in the abundant circulation of gold and commercial exchange; and in harmonious relationships: happy, strong families, and loyal friends, colleagues, and attendants. In the Vedic consciousness, the stability of the universe (*ṛta*) depends upon the attraction and maintenance of the elusive *śrī*. Indeed, all that is auspicious—the luxuriant bounty of the earth, the resonant chanting of sacred songs, the virtuous actions of regents, the fullness of a contented heart, for example—is inextricably linked as *śrī* is propitiated to become graciously manifest on earth and in the affairs of society.

By the late Vedic period, when the scintillating and auspicious qualities known as *śrī* come to be recognized as manifesting in a particular form, they are also called *lakṣmī*, literally an imprint, a sign, a display, an embodied expression, that is, a specifically recognizable manifestation of *śrī*. No longer only an abstract quality, this divine force now takes form as a deity and, in particular, as a goddess, a personification of the abundance, prosperity, splendor, and beauty that have long been recognized as desirable qualities in life. The songs of the Vedas now sing of *śrī* (Śrī) and *lakṣmī* (Lakṣmī), sometimes as two independent goddesses, and at other times as one and the same goddess.[6] In all of her attributes of abundance and splendor, it is not surprising that the goddess of prosperity comes to be known by an abundant array of names, all of which lend further dimensions to the human perception of her identity.

Challenges of Translation: How English Constricts Sanskrit Expression

In appreciating these songs and the many designations of Lakṣmī, it is helpful to conceptualize softened edges between one form and the next, to categorize them not by differences but to perceive the fluidity of forms, as we have considered with that of the lotus-woman form of the goddess. Contributing to the ambiguity of the goddess's names and identities is the fact that *devanāgarī*, the script most often employed for writing in Sanskrit, does not distinguish between lowercase and uppercase ligatures, rendering common nouns and personal names interchangeable. Although such ambiguity is particularly challenging for the translator, it allows for a luxuriant complexity and multiple layering of nuance—the perfect expression for Śrī-Lakṣmī-Padmiṇī. She is, at once, the essence of the goddess as well as her only-partially revealed form, part sacred lotus, part lovely woman, never to be held captive in the world of names and forms (*nāma-rūpa*), or to be grasped entirely by the limitations of human consciousness.

Another difference between Sanskrit and English is that Sanskrit grammar does not employ definite and indefinite articles; whereas in English we may delineate an entire theology hinging on the difference between "God" and "a god" or "the Goddess" and "a goddess," for example, no such linguistic distinction exists in Sanskrit. Even a comparison between "God" and "the Goddess" becomes forced and uneven in English; we can't, for example, switch the language to compare "the God" with "Goddess" without many unnecessary permutations. Freedom from the terms *the* and *a* in Sanskrit is important to keep in mind as we consider the complexities of Lakṣmī or indeed of any of the Hindu deities. English compels us to choose: Are we discussing *one* goddess, is she the *only* goddess, is she *one of many* goddesses? Are they peers or is there an implicit hierarchy? Again, the ambiguity of Sanskrit reflects quite wonderfully the overlapping of these categories. In fact, the English language imposes categories of relationship that do not necessarily exist in the Indic consciousness. The Sanskrit word for *goddess*, as noted earlier, is *devī*. When speaking of her in an Indic language, one does not have to identify "the goddess" or "a goddess" in relationship to others of her kind. She is simply *goddess*.[7]

Alakṣmī, the Inauspicious

Splendor and well-being are not without a dark side. Just as the auspicious presence of the Vedic Śrī-Lakṣmī serves to uphold *ṛta*, the orderly working of the universe, so is inauspicious disarray associated with the personification of Lakṣmī's opposite, appropriately called by the names Nirṛtī, Alakṣmī, and Pāpī-lakṣmī. (The prefixes *nir* and *a* indicate a negation or absence.) Developing the concept of the dual aspects of Śrī even further, late Vedic literature frequently highlights the opposition between the concept of *śrī* with that of *pāpman*, or evil, misfortune, misery, disease, and death.[8] The auspicious presence of *śrī* is also referred to as *su-lakṣmī*, the prefix *su* meaning "good" or "positive." In contrast, the palpable lack of such qualities is known as *pāpī-lakṣmī*, the prefix *pāpī* meaning "bad" or "negative." However, the prefix *su* is usually not appended at all. Just as in English, where "luck" usually indicates "good luck," so too does *lakṣmī*—the manifestation of auspiciousness—indicate the normative quality of auspiciousness itself.

If the auspicious Lakṣmī is to be invited into one's presence, it is often deemed necessary first to take strong action to dislodge the presence of Alakṣmī or at least to take precautions against her arrival. Before the *yajña*, or Vedic fire sacrifice, is performed, the forces of inauspiciousness are invoked outside of the sacred precincts and specifically admonished to stay far from them. The elaborate ritual of the *rājasūya* (royal coronation), for example, includes the conscious expulsion of Nirṛtī by attracting her with sacrifices offered at a desolate area, facing south, the direction of death, keeping her far from the auspicious abode of the king and the sacred precincts where Lakṣmī is worshiped.[9] The inauspicious Pāpī-lakṣmī is identified and summoned so as to be kept away from the home and the palace, opening the way for the presence of the auspicious Lakṣmī to arrive. The two are understood never to exist in the same space.

How are we to conceptualize the relationship between these two entities, Lakṣmī and Alakṣmī? They are identified as exact opposites, each bearing the kernel of the other's name—and identity. Auspiciousness and inauspiciousness cannot inhabit the same space, but they can be very close and, seemingly without warning, Alakṣmī may appear where Lakṣmī once stood. In part, this has to do with what is known as Lakṣmī's *cañcalā* nature: she can be "fickle," "restless," "unsteady," "wavering." The invocatory verses therefore beseech her not only to arrive but to stay, to be "steadfast." If "Lady Luck" is fickle, the message in the imagery of Lakṣmī is that the acquisition of wealth, of Lakṣmī herself, is the recognition that all of this is part of a continuous movement of energy, an evocation of the fluid qualities of the goddess.

Essentially, to receive the blessings of this goddess one must be able to step into her effervescent energy field. Therefore, in a seeming paradox, the "steadfastness" of Lakṣmī must be invoked and generated continuously. Lakṣmī flees when her devotees succumb to laziness, apathy, fear, hoarding, circumstances of decay—when one's actions and thoughts, whether through neglect or default, become aligned with and hide behind the opaque and stagnant energy of Alakṣmī.

CHAPTER 2

Living the Good Life

Lakṣmī of the Purāṇic Traditions

The Burgeoning World of the Purāṇas

When we move from the Vedic hymns into the literature of the Purāṇas, we discover a world that has exploded into myriad expressions of form. The Purāṇas are a group of texts composed from approximately 200 BCE to 1000 CE, a period that also produced the two great epics of India, the *Rāmāyaṇa* and the *Mahābhārata*.[1] The expansive, elaborate cosmology of the Purāṇas extends through eons of time and vast stretches of space, describing cycle upon cycle of world-creation, world-preservation, and world-dissolution. The "three worlds" (*triloka*) of heaven-earth-netherworld are displayed as a multileveled expanse of realms stretching above, through, and below the earth. Here we find narratives about the gods and goddesses and their encounters with beings of all kinds. The inhabitants of the various realms move rather freely from place to place in this vast universe. All three realms constitute *saṃsāra*, that is, the world of birth and rebirth, and as such an embodied "living being" (*jīva*) does not necessarily inhabit any of these forever.

The motif by which gods and goddesses change shape—shifting into versions of each other, or being created from the essence of one another—highlights the concept that ultimately these forms and personalities are simply external expressions, guises adopted for mere *līlā*, or play. Divine activity, of course, is distinct from human activity, which is usually less play (*līlā*) and more work (*karma*). But the underlying substratum shared by both humans and gods is their essence, their "own true form" (*svarūpa*), which consists of consciousness. This helps to explain the often-quoted pronouncement that there is one God and yet 330 million gods[2]—both attest to the infinitude of the divine and its presence at all times, in all places. The gods may appear and reappear in subsequent world cycles, sometimes in forms similar to their previous existence, and sometimes in forms seemingly unrelated. Once embodied, all manner of beings may change from one form and situation to another, moving from divine to human to animal or to hybrid human-animal, or yet to plant or even to a part of the earth itself, as a mountain or a stream, and then back again. Even demons are included in this great shifting of modes, as they may undergo spiritual transformation to such an extent that they evolve into a higher category of being. Sometimes the circumstances motivating these changes *may appear* as mere caprice, and at other times they *may appear* to be warranted by the fruits of one's "good deeds." Ultimately, one never knows fully what lies in store; after all, such is the illusory quality that characterizes *saṃsāra*. If this all seems like the a game of Chutes and Ladders—riding high one day and sliding down the next—it should come as no surprise that a similar boardgame, intended to teach about patterns of karma, was played in India centuries ago.

Nothing embodied, then, is entirely fixed or stable in the realm of qualified existence, which goes a long way in explaining the high level of concern for stability, security, and the wisdom to perceive life behind its appearances. So it is that those struggling to stay afloat in the turbulent ocean of *saṃsāra* would understandably seek refuge in a deity who generates and embodies the qualities of cosmic order, social harmony, and a joyous existence on earth, as well as success in achieving eventual liberation from this existence.

Lakṣmī and the Lords of the Three Realms: Indra, Viṣṇu, and Bali

As the goddess who sustains the entire creation, Lakṣmī benevolently embodies herself in time and space, ever pervading each realm to maintain harmony, fullness, and equanimity. When the creation is in danger of losing its balance and falling into irreparable decay, she descends into the world, manifesting in a specifically recognizable form. All prosperity, all that nourishes the earth and its inhabitants, all that ensures benevolent increase—all of this is the expression of the auspicious goddess Lakṣmī. Through her pervasive auspiciousness she reveals herself in myriad ways, expressive of her luxuriant bounty and beneficence. Here, the abstract concept of *śrī* becomes personified more specifically in the form of the goddess Lakṣmī.

In the Purāṇic literature, Lakṣmī is most closely affiliated with Viṣṇu, lord of world preservation. In the Vaiṣṇava[3] understanding of her descent into the world, Lakṣmī accompanies Viṣṇu whenever he intercedes to uphold the creation. Together they infuse the universe with the energy of bounteous life to be lived on the hospitable earth. Just as her heavenly form dwells with Viṣṇu in Vaikuṇṭha and in other celestial realms, so also is Lakṣmī's domain the natural environment of the earth. In the Purāṇas we find details about Lakṣmī and the circumstances of her "descents" (*avatāras*) into the earthly realm: her parents, her birth, her physical characteristics, her deeds, her marriage, her offspring. We should note here too that the Vaiṣṇava themes and personalities of Lakṣmī carry over into other categories of literature, and some of the songs share two or more textual or worship traditions.

The "earthly" realm is but one part of the *triloka*, the "triple world," or the "three realms," which, as we have seen, consist of a series of heavens, the earth, and netherworlds. In addition to her affiliation with Viṣṇu, with whom she infuses harmony throughout the earthly realm, Lakṣmī's presence is sought by Indra, lord of heaven, as well as Bali, lord of the underworld. Each of these kings requires the splendor of Lakṣmī to animate his realm. Many of the Purāṇic stories illustrate the loss and restoration of sovereignty in terms of who can best attract and maintain this goddess, for she is the embodiment of every type of well-being. Both Indra and Bali exemplify male force and regency, yet recognize that when they lose their allegiance with goddess, so too do they lose their potency.

Because these texts contain stories that span many *kalpas*, or world-epochs, we find that the circumstances of Lakṣmī's manifestations move through many dimensions of time and space. In one story, she incarnates as the daughter of the sage Bhṛgu and the nymph Khyāti; in others, she takes the form of a sacred plant, such as the basil (*tulasī*) or, as we have previously considered, the lotus. Yet again, Lakṣmī emerges in her form as splendid, radiantly beautiful goddess, one of the "fourteen gems" to emerge from the churning of the Ocean of Milk.[4] In this lengthy and complex story, the gods (*devas*) of heaven and the demigods (*asuras*) of the underworld join forces to regain the *amṛta*, or elixir of immortality,[5] which has been cast into the ocean. Holding onto the divine serpent Vāsuki, who offers himself as a churning rope, both sides engage in a massive tug-of-war, churning the vast milk-ocean to force its contents to the surface. Some of these are deadly and others auspicious. Finally, fourteen treasures emerge, and first among them is Śrī-Lakṣmī bearing the golden urn of immortal nectar. The goddess's appearance is cause for jubilant rejoicing in the three worlds, expressed as some of the laudatory songs included in our collection.

All Women Are Embodiments of Lakṣmī

Whether exhibiting steadfastness or restlessness, nurturing, independence, or any other embodiment or mode of expression, Lakṣmī always retains her core essence as the divine feminine. Every one of her forms is specifically female. She incarnates as other goddesses—most distinctly as Rādhā, Sītā, and Rukmiṇī, who are consorts of various forms of Viṣṇu. She is Pṛthvī, the divine feminine embodied as Mother Earth, and nearly every river is recognized as a form of her. When she manifests as the lotus, she is Padmā, and when she manifests as the sacred basil plant, she is Tulasī. So too does she embody other fragrant flowers and is known by such names and identities as Ketakī and Mālatī.[6]

In the earthly realm, Lakṣmī expresses herself as every girl and woman. In the *Song for the Glorious Lotus Goddess* (*Śrī Kamalā Stotram*), Lord Indra lauds the goddess:

> [E]very woman is an embodiment of you[7]

In *The Heavenly Gods' Praise-Song for Lakṣmī* (*Śrī Daivakṛta Lakṣmī Stotram*), the assembly of gods sing:

> Every woman is an emanation of you[8]

And in the *Praise-Song for the Lotus Goddess* (*Kamalā Stotram*), the gods proclaim:

> You exist as little girls in their childhood,
> As young women in their youth,
> And as elderly women in their old age . . .[9]

From the gods' point of view, all women are recognized as embodiments of Lakṣmī, even if there may be difficulty remembering this in the human realm. However, certain roles and rituals may reiterate awareness of this expression of the goddess. This last point is important to keep in mind as we consider two of her most significant expressions, as Rājya ("royal") Lakṣmī, and Gṛhya ("household") Lakṣmī:

> O goddess, you are Royal Lakṣmī
> In the palaces of kings,
> And Lakṣmī of the Home
> In ordinary households.[10]

In both cases, the identities of the goddess and of human women merge as women step into specific roles that give form to their goddess-essence.

Lakṣmī of the Royal Palace

In traditional India, Lakṣmī played a central role in the king's court and in this capacity the goddess was known as Rājya (royal) Lakṣmī. Ideally, the king was an embodiment of virtue (*dharma*), itself a form of Viṣṇu, upholder of the universe. A kingdom could not prosper without the active presence of Lakṣmī at its center, in the royal court; many ritual activities, therefore, were performed to this end.[11] The queens were embodiments of majesty (*aiśvarya*), an expression of Lakṣmī most specifically aligned with the virtuous conduct (*dharma*) of the regent. Together they embodied virtue, stability, sovereignty, and prosperity.

Lakṣmī's presence at the court also took form as *devadāsīs*, literally,"servants of the gods," sacred royal courtesans who, as living embodiments of the goddess, would ceremonially invoke and awaken the goddess within their own bodies.[12] Their presence in the court upheld the prosperity of the kingdom, most specifically as expressions of the goddess's beautiful display of abundance in pleasure (*kāma*) and material wealth (*artha*). As we shall consider, pleasure (*kāma*), wealth (*artha*), and virtue (*dharma*) are all specifically expressions of Lakṣmī's prosperous essence.

Lakṣmī of the Home

Although the royal court and the home of an ordinary person may seem to be distant and distinct arenas, they are actually two versions of the same model, for the king, whose duty it is to ensure the well-being of the entire kingdom, is the quintessential householder.

Similarly, just as the palace provides the central foundation for the prosperity of the kingdom, so does one's home operate as the foundational center from which all of life's endeavors originate. The goddess of the household is known as Lakṣmī, and, like Rājya Lakṣmī, she is recognized not only as a celestial deity but in the form of a woman as householder:

> In homes, you are Gṛhya Lakṣmī, goddess of the
> household,
> Manifest as the woman of the house.[13]

Just as the king and queen represent Viṣṇu and Lakṣmī on earth, so do a husband and wife emulate the roles established by this divine couple. Drawing upon Viṣṇu and Lakṣmī as the divine source of all prosperity and well-being, the Hindu wedding ceremony casts the bride and groom as living representatives of the divine couple, roles that are to continue onward into married life. A married woman becomes a Lakṣmī in her household, for like the queen as well as the *devadāsī* in the royal palace, she is viewed as a living embodiment of Lakṣmī. This is in fulfillment of a woman's *strī-dharma*, or the inherent powers and responsibilities entailed in living a woman's life. Many of these responsibilities involve integrity in relationships—with her spouse, children, extended family, and with the gods—as well as attention to overseeing the acquisition, storage, and preparation of food, the upkeep of the home-space, and the management of finances.

Invoking Lakṣmī of the Home also entails performing obligatory domestic ceremonies. Here, women are responsible for preparing ritual offerings in the home, which range from simple daily offerings to complex vows and fasts at certain times throughout the year.[14] All of these draw upon the inherent energies of a woman to generate and sustain well-being in her home and family. It is women who sweep the threshold clean each morning in order to drive away Alakṣmī, and it is women who create *raṅgoli* or *colam*, decorative patterns on floors and walls to attract the goddess of wealth into their homes. In attending to these responsibilities a woman is transforming the family home into a temple of Lakṣmī.

By virtue of her being female, a woman is said to be a form of the goddess and thus an extension and repository of the goddess's power. Although the Vaiṣṇava paradigm tends to highlight Lakṣmī in her state of marriage to Viṣṇu, it is important to remember the goddess's primary identification as an independent force and entity. Women, as embodiments of her energy, are understood first as embodiments of the goddess's essence as *śrī*—splendor—and, from there, the specific personifications may be formulated. All females are recognized as forms of the goddess, regardless of age, station, or marital status. This helps us to understand that Gṛhya Lakṣmī, although a specific and localized form, also carries the full majesty of the comprehensive identity and power of the goddess.

As Lakṣmī embodies beauty in form as well as essence, conscious attention to this therefore begins with the proper attention to and nourishment of one's body as the body of the goddess. Ornamenting the body with cosmetic coloring around the eyes, on the parting of the hair, or on the hands and feet, and adorning it with jewelry is an act of honoring and invoking the goddess, for ornamentation itself is a display of auspiciousness.

Nearly every one of the songs in our collection beseeches the goddess specifically to dwell in one's home. The types of gifts that Lakṣmī provides continue to be the foundation of a harmonious life for those in the householder stage of life.[15] The way in which a woman relates to her home environment takes on special significance, for the home is the temple of Gṛhya Lakṣmī. Heightened attention to the home-space, then, clearly becomes a kind of ritual in and of itself. When infused with the consciousness that the world we inhabit is the body of the goddess, preparing a hospitable space for her to reside becomes sacred action. With the consciousness of that sacred, ritualized action, a woman generates the *śakti*—the creative cosmic power of the goddess—that is part of her own essential being. By stepping into the paradigm by which she is both an attendant of the goddess as well as her living embodiment, a woman may ensure that her home also becomes an abode of Lakṣmī.

We are well aware that the very idea of a Lakṣmī of the Home, or Household Lakṣmī, may suggest a sense of enslavement or drudgery. Is this really what Gṛhya Lakṣmī intends for women? It is useful, first of all, to remember that Household Lakṣmī and Royal Lakṣmī are the same goddess, merely dwelling, we might say, in different abodes. Both are embodiments of the goddess as majesty (*aiśvarya*). Therefore, when a woman is enjoined to imagine herself as the goddess of the home, it is intended as an act of empowerment, not enslavement. Even the *devadāsī*, whose name means "servant" of the gods, was never intended to be servile, but ideally to dwell in the elevated dignity of her sacred status. The kind of service and dedication to be cultivated here is not the same as a servile enslavement that would dessicate the spirit. A woman who is enslaved to her family and home, who has lost her own center, and whose home has lost its center, is not acting in accord with that divine mantle that the goddess has sanctioned with this particular form of embodiment. Such a woman has, for whatever reason, forgotten her *aiśvarya,* her innate majesty.

Our discussion here may be furthered by envisioning Gṛhya Lakṣmī in light of her ancient Greek counterpart, Hestia, goddess of the hearth. The essence of Hestia, like that of Lakṣmī of the Home, was recognized in the sacred flame of the hearth; without this fire, there could be no warmth, no light, no cooked food—essentially there might be the shell of a house, but no home. In order to recognize the continuance of Lakṣmī's radiant and empowering presence in *all* of her forms, it is useful to consider that for more and more contemporary women, the home has become a place to escape *from;* women are going elsewhere in order to feel and express their natural, personal power. However, such movement beyond the home is simply an expression of the goddess's sovereign essence already having left, for where she is not honored, Lakṣmī will not stay. Reimagining Hestia in contemporary terms, feminist philosopher Ginette Paris posits that a reevaluation of our contemporary understandings of the hearth goddess may empower women outside of the home, even as they draw strength from experiencing the home as a vital foundation of being.[16]

In a similar vein, Vodun priestess Luisah Teish speaks of the importance of the consecration of ordinary work: "Washing your dishes," she says, "can turn into an exquisite ritual" when you accompany the activity with the right music and add to the sink of dishwater "an ounce of river water, an ounce of ocean water, an ounce of rain water, and some lemon oil." Further, she concludes: "Woman's work has been degraded and it never should have been. It's what preserves life. When you start to make your everyday work a ritual, you become re-empowered as queen of the manor."[17] When a woman experiences herself not as a servant but as a sovereign in her domain, then she—and those around her—may experience Household Lakṣmī and Royal Lakṣmī as two aspects of the same goddess whose favor is essential to a majestic, fulfilling life.

Lakṣmī, Embodiment of the "Four Wealths" (*Caturartha*)

The Purāṇic songs to Lakṣmī highlight the themes of wealth, abundance, prosperity, harmony, and well-being in the natural world and in the lives of all beings as they experience the various aspects of moving their way through *saṃsāra,* or life in this world. And so it is that these songs extol the goddess of prosperity as embodied in the *caturārtha,* that is, four components that, when addressed together, contribute to a life of balance and harmony. The term *caturartha* is often translated as the four (*catur*) "goals" or "aims" (*artha*) of life. It is helpful to remember that the term *artha* has multiple shades of meaning, as it may also be translated with such terms as "purpose," "meaning," "component," "aspect," "wealth," and even "opulence." If we think of these four "goals" with all of those connotations in mind, we get a more holistic sense of Lakṣmī's attributes in each of them and how they operate collectively. In English, the term *goal* carries a resonance of diligent striving toward a single end, with little appreciation of the process along the way; I find it more useful therefore to consider these as "four wealths" or "four meanings" of life, for they address a process and quality of living as much as they do an end result. It might also be useful to vary our translation of the term each time we consider it, in order to keep its resonance fluid and closer to its original multivalence. That being said, let us consider the four categories to be addressed in living a balanced life: (1) *kāma,* or pleasure and enjoyment; (2) *artha,* or material prosperity: (3) *dharma,* or virtuous conduct and harmonious relationships; and (4) *mokṣa,* or spiritual liberation. Our songs remind us that these four aspects of living well are forms of the goddess herself:

> You are the supreme mother of all,
> And every woman is an embodiment of you.
> So too do you express yourself in the forms
> Of *dharma, artha, kāma,* and *mokṣa.*[18]

Through these songs, we come to view the four "purposes" as a fluid continuum, for a well-balanced life enjoys the blessing of Lakṣmī in many aspects of existence.[19] In this sense, the four are not separated by impenetrable walls of difference, but rather they exist as a spectrum, with shades that merge at the borders as one moves into different "frequencies" of experiencing life on earth. The first three goals, specifically world-affirming, are most readily apparent in their associations with Lakṣmī as the goddess of prosperity, yet the wealth of Lakṣmī is the full and harmonious infusion of Lakṣmī's abundance, culminating in liberation from attachment. In the worship of the goddess, one must first embrace the world, glorifying it as a manifestation of divine essence. Before liberation can be attained, one must live well in the world and yet grasp its hidden meaning, having evolved to the awareness by which Mahāmāyā—the goddess as

Great Illusion—is recognized as both the one who veils and the one who reveals the truth of existence.

Lakṣmī as Kāma*: The Wealth of Pleasure, the World's Delight*

Kāma is pleasure, delight, sensuality, sexuality. It is the passion that incites idea toward form. It is the pulse and the impulse of nature, deeper than thought or intention, that ignites the spark of procreation, ensuring the continuance of life from one generation to the next. Like the Greek Aphrodite, Lakṣmī is golden-skinned and scintillating, the exciter of passion, arousing the first stirrings of the sexual energy necessary to propagate life and expansion. Just as Aphrodite is the mother of Eros, so too is Lakṣmī extolled in the songs as Pradyumnajananī, "mother of the god of love."[20]

Kāma ranges from eroticism to the pleasurable appreciation of beauty in all of its aesthetic subtleties. Lakṣmī is manifest in every perceivable aspect of the material world, in its variegated fragrances and pungencies, in its array of *rasa*s (savors or flavors), and in all that expresses the pulse of divine energy as it ripples through the world. When the senses are enlivened, they heighten one's experience of the goddess's presence, for one's capacity for sensual receptivity is the very same that allows for the reception of Lakṣmī's grace.

As do the Vedic hymns, the Purāṇic songs recognize Lakṣmī in various forms that are part flower and part woman. They also glorify her as dwelling in the sensual, magical realms inhabited by Kṛṣṇa. Her essence is recognized in lush green vegetation sprouting from the moist earth, in the brilliant colors and intoxicatingly sweet fragrance of blossoming flowers, and in the languid waywardness of vines as they grow entangled with luxuriant abandon. The *kāma* aspect of Lakṣmī is abundantly lovely, graceful, fragrant, moist, and sensuous, and she expresses herself as much in the flowering vegetation of the forest as in the intertwined bodies and souls of lovers.

Through her expression of *kāma*, Lakṣmī becomes Rādhā, the beloved of Kṛṣṇa, whom she meets for secret love-play in the enchanted Vṛṇda forest. In *The Heavenly Gods' Praise-Song for Lakṣmī* (*Śrī Daivakṛta Lakṣmī Stotram*), the celestial ones celebrate Lakṣmī in her glorious display of such forms:

> In Goloka,
> You are the goddess more dear to Kṛṣṇa
> Than life itself,
> His own Rādhikā.

Deep in the forest,
Deep in the Vṛṇda forest,
You are mistress of the mesmerizing *rasa* dance.

In the boughs of the sacred *bhandira* tree,
You are Kṛṣṇa's desire.
In the sandalwood forest you are Candrā,
In the grove of sweet yellow jasmine you are Virajā,
And on the hundred-peaked mountain you are the lovely
Sundarī.[21]

Ecstatic in their union of hearts, bodies, and souls, and mournfully depressed when forced into separation, Rādhā and Kṛṣṇa (that is, embodiments of Lakṣmī and Viṣṇu) represent that which Vaiṣṇava theologians interpret as a perfect paradigm for the soul's longing for and blissful union with the divine. Passion, drama, exasperation, delight: All of these are expressions of the soul's journey in *saṃsāra*.

Lakṣmī as Artha*: Material Wealth and Prosperity Consciousness*

More than any of her other aspects, Lakṣmī is most widely identified and worshiped as the goddess of material prosperity. She is the quintessential embodiment of *artha*, or material wealth. Her qualities of fluidity and expansiveness take form as money and its circulation in society. It is no surprise that merchants are among her most ardent devotees, and many business establishments in India grace their premises with private shrines to the goddess. Lakṣmī's most important festival, Dīvālī (festival of lights), is also the occasion for closing out financial books and beginning a new fiscal year. This is also the only time that gambling is encouraged—as if to test one's faith in the blessings of Lady Luck.

There is a luxuriant gracefulness about Lakṣmī's wealth. As an expression of her own nature, it springs from the source of her being and pours forth bounteously. Thus is Lakṣmī lauded for her generosity, and her sacred images display her with open hands from which pour forth unending streams of gold coins. The easeful, life-giving currents of gold, of water, of fructifying rains, and indeed of any form of energy are all variations on the same image of Lakṣmī's bestowal of prosperity. In some images, elephants lustrate the goddess with streams of water, increasing the magnitude of bounty and also illustrating an important point—that the goddess of plenty herself enjoys replenishment. Thus does the cycle continue propitiously.

The Purāṇic songs address Lakṣmī with a variety of epithets, among them, Dhanadā, meaning "bestower" (*dā*) of "wealth" (*dhana*). The term *dhana* incorporates an expansive definition of prosperity: abundance, luxury, comfort, happiness, good health, well-being, material wealth, harmonious relationships with friends, family, and community, and a meaningful spiritual life.

Lakṣmī is also called Vasudhā, "yielder of wealth," referring to the goddess as the bounteous earth. *Vasu* is the wealth of the land and the abundant life that it yields. It is also the material wealth of the earth's hidden treasures—the precious metals, minerals, crystals, and gemstones that lie beneath its surface—as well as the mysterious treasures of the forests and in the depths of the sea. With this in mind, we may understand the context by which Lakṣmī is beloved by the elemental spirits of the woods and by the forces that dwell in caverns and deep into the earth's many layers. We may also further appreciate the expansive arena of the triple world (*triloka*) that is her domain. Heavenly, earthly, and subterranean beings alike all seek the wealth that Lakṣmī embodies. This allows us better to understand the place of the *asuras*, or "anti-gods" who inhabit the subterranean realms and the watery, dark netherworlds. In the Purāṇic literature, the *asuras* are cast as debilitating forces who continuously antagonize the gods, in large part because of their attitude toward Lakṣmī's wealth: The problem with the *asuras* is that they insist upon hoarding. As Devdutt Pattanaik points out:

> The *asuras* of Hinduism are not evil creatures like the demons of the biblical tradition. They are children of Brahma who live under the earth and who pull the earth's wealth downward. The gods who live above the earth pull wealth upwards. . . . In the language of modern economics, one might say that *devas* are distributors of wealth while *asuras* are creators of wealth. The former spend wealth, the latter hoard it. Both play vital roles in the cycle of wealth.[22]

When we consider the nuances of Lakṣmī's wealth, we may say, then, that *dhana* is prosperity, and *vasu* is the raw material behind that prosperity. *Artha* is the currency of value as it is recognized in a particular culture; it is the wealth that may be counted or demonstrated or used in the currency of exchange—as property, valuables, treasures, possessions, money, and the like. When one has received the blessing of *artha*, it is considered appropriate to display and enjoy it visibly. On the importance of the display of wealth in early Indic culture, Jan Gonda points out, "[T]he very manifestation of prosperity and liberality means esteem and satisfaction. A prosperous man is an honored man, because he gives evidence of possessing uncommon abilities."[23] To take this a step further, the goddess is the source of those uncommon abilities and of the material wealth itself, and to hide her gifts is considered to disrespect their divine source.

Just as Lakṣmī is a visible expression of *śrī*, so too is *artha* a material expression of the goddess's energy as money or material wealth. Attracting and maintaining wealth—however one interprets it—entails an attitude, a state of mind, quite literally a state of consciousness that aligns with the consciousness of the goddess. The poet of the *Song for Lakṣmī, Gracious Bestower of Blessings* (*Prasannavaradā Śrī Lakṣmī Stotram*), for example, seeks the ability to attract wealth as well as to discover the state of consciousness that produces it:

> Consumed by dire poverty,
> I am breathless with anxiety and fear.
> In this impossibly painful state,
> I am drawn to your side.
> O Lakṣmī, Ocean of Compassion,
> Bestow wealth,
> And guide me to a state of prosperity.[24]

The prayers to Lakṣmī ask for material abundance and at the same time for the conscious awareness to dwell in that state of prosperity, which is a state of consciousness, a state of engagement with the wealth-energy of the goddess. The energy of this goddess is the energy of prosperity itself, and to dwell in this is what truly empowers the supplicant.

It is interesting to note how modern writers on the metaphysics of prosperity speak in similar terms. Consider, for example, the words of Catherine Ponder, an American Christian minister writing in the middle of the twentieth century: "Money is filled with the desire for life, movement, expansion and activity. It does not like to be grasped, clutched or restrained in idleness. Indeed, it is the active circulation of money that brings prosperity, whereas depressions and recessions are caused by the miserly hoarding of money."[25] Centuries later and a world apart, Ponder's words read like a meditation on Lakṣmī herself.

As we have observed, most especially with our focus on Lakṣmī of the Home, women inherently contain the divine power of prosperity. This is best realized when a woman invokes the goddess by *becoming* the goddess: A woman becomes Lakṣmī when she models her attitudes, behavior, and *consciousness* on qualities that are recognized as embodiments of Lakṣmī. Prosperity begins with prosperity consciousness, to which can be applied the specifics of successful money management and financial planning. The Hindu goddess of wealth plays a key role in the work of yet another American writer on prosperity. Coming from a perspective that is generally more practical than metaphysical, popular financial writer Suze Orman has engaged millions in turning their financial lives around by offering systematic, nuts-and-bolts advice. Yet even this practical advice is grounded upon higher principles. In a work written specifically for women, Orman exhorts her readers to tackle feelings of powerlessness in matters of money by focusing on "the 8 qualities of a wealthy woman": "It is my wish that you will carry these eight qualities within you wherever you go and that they will serve as your guideposts to make sure you are always walking toward wealth rather than walking away from it."[26] By carrying these qualities, one imbibes them and becomes empowered by them. What are these eight qualities? Harmony, balance, courage, generosity, happiness, wisdom, cleanliness, and beauty.[27] As we shall see throughout the texts of our devotional songs, these eight qualities have long been lauded as specific expressions of Lakṣmī herself.

The Wealth of *Artha* and the Wealth of *Dhana*

The material prosperity denoted by the term *artha* does not necessarily resonate with the wider aspects of abundance that the term *dhana* carries. While Lakṣmī is most certainly the source of *artha* , or material prosperity, it is significant that she is never addressed as *artha-dā* ("bestower of money"), and only rarely is she supplicated to grant *artha* by itself. Rather, she is often addressed as *dhana-dā* ("bestower of wealth"), and she is consistently invoked for the more expansive designations of material wealth as an expression of the goddess's limitless abundance, of which *artha* is only a finite part. Material wealth is one thing; the energy that creates and sustains material wealth is quite another. It is this that the wise seek of the goddess; they request that the goddess bestow not only the material expression of wealth, but that she draw them into alignment with the limitless source of all prosperity. In fact, without alignment to this source, one may be incapable of receiving her blessings, much less of sustaining them should they arrive.

Failure to recognize the subtle yet essential differences between *dhana* and *artha* may contribute to misinterpreting Lakṣmī's prosperity as it pertains to money in the context of spiritual growth. Money—and its acquisition or its denial—quite obviously has been a highly charged issue throughout the ages and across cultures. The Purāṇic narratives highlight the emotional upheaval created among gods, humans, and demons as they gain, lose, and seek to regain Lakṣmī's wealth and favor. So too do they stress that the goddess listens to requests, and if she is pleased, she grants them. One may pursue and succeed in the acquisition of *artha*—material wealth—to the exclusion of other concerns, just as one may single-mindedly pursue pleasure or communal obligations or spiritual liberation. On the other hand, one may engage in a vigorous avoidance or denigration of material prosperity, deeming it as antithetical to "spirituality." In either case, the goddess is misperceived through a limited understanding of her expansive nature, and both extremes may be seen as a form of "poverty consciousness." This calls to mind an intriguing misunderstanding of Lakṣmī that I observed at a festival of Indian culture held in the United States. An American attendee was sifting through a stack of large lithographed "god-posters," indicating to the proprietor that she was looking for an image of Lakṣmī. He presented her with a popular image of the goddess standing on a lotus, with a stream of gold coins emitting from her hand. The woman shuddered and exclaimed, "Not that one! It's ruined by all of that money. I'm looking for a *spiritual* picture of Lakṣmī."[28]

The woman had missed the point that Lakṣmī's effulgent spirit streams into the world *as* palpable, "worldly" blessings. We are reminded that the name Śrī-Lakṣmī means "display of glory." So too does Lakṣmī's abundance resonate with elegance and harmony, manifest through the multifaceted aspects of life on earth. Those who seek her favor are reminded that an overly zealous attention to any one of the four aims of life to the exclusion of the others may create an imbalance that may actually send Lakṣmī fleeing. It is interesting to note that one of the manifestations of Alakṣmī in the Purāṇas is called Atulā, "Unbalanced": An unbalanced pursuit of Lakṣmī may inadvertently result in attracting her inauspicious sister instead.[29]

What, then, is a "balanced" propitiation of the goddess of wealth? How does one achieve an appropriate attitude toward *artha*? The successful engagement with Lakṣmī's abundance entails adapting the consciousness of the goddess of wealth, which is literally "prosperity consciousness." The abundant quality of Lakṣmī's wealth is also referred to as *vṛddhi*, which means expansiveness, opening outward, and reaching for a state of graceful equipoise. Therefore, Lakṣmī's divine benevolence manifests as a luxuriant, comfortable fullness in the human realm. This is achieved by maintaining an awareness that admits neither greedy and frantic excess nor the neglect that would either dishonor it or allow it to diminish and decay; such could be seen as motivated by either excessive *rajas* (the quality of intense energy) or excessive *tamas* (the quality of lassitude). Indeed, neither the excessive indulgence in, nor the excessive denial of material prosperity is in accordance with the essence of Lakṣmī's wealth and how she bestows it upon her worshipers. One must be open to the consciousness of wealth in order to receive it. And yet, how does one invoke both expansiveness and discipline at the same time? This becomes evident when we consider Lakṣmī's association with *dharma*.

Lakṣmī as Dharma*: The Wealth of Virtue and Harmonious Relationships*

There are many ways to translate the term *dharma*—"virtue," "virtuous conduct," "harmonious relationship," "religion," "etiquette," "religious duty," "communal obligation," "social consciousness," "balanced way of life," "living in right relationship," and even "doing the right thing." Because its meanings are so variously nuanced, it is often left untranslated, or it is translated with different terms according to context. The root of the term *dharma* is *dhṛ*, which means foundation or support. In general, we may consider *dharma* to be the energy governing harmonious relationships—with oneself, with one's spouse, children, and family, with one's community, with one's natural environment, and with the gods. *Dharma* may sometimes be described in terms of obligatory actions, as the scriptures designate codes of etiquette that range from good manners to religious canons and ritual observances. More than merely following rules, however, *dharma* is a way to cultivate wisdom. On a cosmic level, *dharma* is the harmony of interconnectedness that upholds society and supports the creation; it is Lakṣmī and Viṣṇu who reign over that auspicious function, and for this reason Lakṣmī is lauded in her poetry as "upholder of *dharma*."[30]

The auspicious preservation of the entire creation, of course, entails harmony on the personal level as well. Lakṣmī's association with *dharma*, therefore, informs one's appropriate and successful interconnections with others. This is why Lakṣmī is so often approached by those seeking a spouse, good home, steady income, and other such aspects of life:

> O Most Fortunate One!
> It is always through your propitious glances
> That men obtain wives and children,

As well as homes,
Loyal friends,
Bountiful harvests,
And every type of prosperity.[31]

In the Purāṇas, Lakṣmī is identified most strongly as the consort of Viṣṇu, and together they serve as sustainers of the universe. In world-cycle after world-cycle, they appear together as embodiments of *dharma*, restoring harmony among the various elements that constitute the realms of existence. Together they constitute the quintessential divine couple, existing as a singular energy that expresses itself in the complementary aspects of divine male and divine female. As we have previously considered, the unified image of Lakṣmī and Viṣṇu also sets the paradigm for the bride and groom in the Hindu wedding ceremony.

Dharma is an important enough feature of Hindu society to constitute a type of wealth in its own right. Even the earliest Vedic songs to Lakṣmī emphasized the importance of happiness in the home and communal well-being. In the Purāṇic songs too, we may see how attention to *dharma* is linked with other aspects of Lakṣmī's wealth. Both *kāma* (pleasure) and *artha* (material wealth) may be generated without attention to *dharma*. However, *dharma* governs the karmic aspects of thoughts and actions. Lakṣmī as an embodiment of *dharma* ensures the graceful balance of the continued flow of her energy, for it also reminds her devotees of the karmic results of benevolent as well as maleficent behavior. *Kāma*, or pleasure, may be enhanced by its appropriate application and attention to relationships. Similarly, the attraction of *artha*, or material wealth, may be more successfully sustained when generated within the context of appropriate types of exchange, for this ensures the healthy sending and receiving of the wealth-energy. In either case, *dharma* provides a richer context in which to express the fulfillment of excitement and good fortune. Once again, we are reminded that the root of this term is *dhṛ*, meaning foundation or support. It is through *dharma* that many of the aspects of Lakṣmī's wealth may be enjoyed and sustained in a palpable form, for the relationships that link one person to the next provide the conduits for the sustained flow of the goddess's energy.

As Lakṣmī upholds *dharma*, so then does the worshiper seeking her blessings invoke her by emulating her and adhering to dharmic behavior. From this perspective, the fluid nature of Lakṣmī's beneficence moves in a propitious cycle, pouring forth as divine grace to an individual, extending outward from the individual to the family, from there to the community, and from there, through ritual offerings, back to the divine source.

When material blessings are received, graciously enjoyed, and sent forth again, they expand even moreso; such circulation actively stirs up the goddess's energy, infusing the creation with the manifestation of her golden presence. *Dharma* entails a joyful awareness and gratitude for the source of that wealth, its generous use, and its bounteous circulation; *dharma* provides the human context for the flow of material wealth and can contribute to the happiness of meaningful relationships that Lakṣmī's devotees seek. As such, the act of receiving Lakṣmī's blessings entails becoming an active participant in her prosperity. The Purāṇic songs propitiate Lakṣmī for material well-being and for the easeful, trusting attitude that fosters such well-being.

Lakṣmī as Mokṣa: *The Wealth of Spiritual Liberation*

As we have seen, Lakṣmī is extolled as the goddess whose bright auspiciousness infuses the creation with *kāma, artha,* and *dharma,* or pleasure, prosperity, and living in right relationship. Together these three constitute a unit and are qualified as *bhukti,* the "enjoyment" or "relishing" of the world. The fourth and final component is *mokṣa* or *mukti,* release from worldy attachment. As well as providing the foundation for its delights, Lakṣmī is said to be the final refuge, the transport to liberation from attachment to the world. Devotees of the goddess are not forced to choose between "spirituality" and "materiality," and in fact to do so would be to disregard the magnificent arena of the goddess's essence. The goddess is invoked for both spiritual and material blessings, for she is the material and spiritual substratum, the platform upon which everything rests and moves; she is the experience of life and she is the wisdom to see past life's vicissitudes. Indeed, one her best-known epithets in this regard is *bhukti-mukti-pradāyinī,* that is, "bestower of worldly enjoyment and spiritual liberation."[32]

In this more expansive aspect, Lakṣmī is also known as Mahālakṣmī, or "Great Lakṣmī." The name Mahālakṣmī often refers to the goddess as the creator-preserver-destroyer. However, this more expansive definition does not automatically indicate a switch from the name Lakṣmī to Mahālakṣmī. (At this point in our understanding of this amazingly variegated goddess, would we really expect to find something so limited and predictable?) Some of the songs in our collection quite easefully interchange the names "Mahālakṣmī" and "Lakṣmī'—both within the texts themselves and between the texts and their colophons.

The Purāṇic songs also glorify Mahālakṣmī as Mahāmāyā, or "Great Illusion," speaking from a vision of the entirety of the creation and the engagement of living in it, through it, and beyond it. So too is she addressed as the origin and essence of all space and time, Mahākālā, as well as Great Goddess, Mahādevī. It is she who oversees the movement and measuring (*mātra*) of time and circumstance, who constitutes it entirely and is yet beyond it, expressing herself not only as Great Illusion, but also as Resplendent Wisdom, Śrī Vidyā, who fosters liberation. Just as she is the veil of illusion that keeps one from recognizing the truth behind appearances, so too is she the means to liberation. The release from cyclical existence in *saṃsāra*, then, comes from the same goddess who sanctions the world and embellishes it, even mesmerizing one to enjoy attachment to it for lifetime after lifetime. To the one who views *kāma, artha, dharma,* and *mokṣa* as disparate endeavors, the illusion of Māyā can be tormenting. To the wise, all of this is the majesty of the goddess's creation, unveiled:

> O Auspicious One,
> You are sacrificial knowledge,
> Supreme knowledge,
> And secret, mystical knowledge.
> You are knowledge of the higher Self,
> O Goddess,
> And you are the one who confers liberation.
>
> You are metaphysics,
> You are the three Vedas,
> You are the arts and sciences,
> And you are the purveyor of justice.
> O Goddess, the entire world,
> With all of its pleasing and displeasing forms,
> Consists of your essence.[33]

The protection and upliftment of the world sometimes necessitate that the benign goddess appear in a terrifying form, with the creator and sustainer expressing herself also as destroyer. The terrifying aspects of the goddess become manifest in separate forms as independent identities, such as that of the raging and bloodthirsty Kālī, whose auspicious nature takes ferocious expression as she vanquishes debilitating forces. Whether expressing herself as the gracious, benign, and bright (*gaurī*) Lakṣmī, or as the frenzied, destructive, "red," or "fiery-dark" (*raudri*) Kālī, the goddess is the embodiment of auspiciousness. That is, whether the goddess is smiling with favor or contorted with rage, these two aspects are equally auspicious and they both enhance the continuity of life and supreme wisdom.

In addition to these two extremes—the bright, merciful goddess of expansiveness, and the dark, fearsome goddess of contraction and destruction—there is a multifaceted form of Lakṣmī who is the gracious goddess of prosperity and well-being and yet wields destructive weapons, surrounds herself with poisonous snakes, and accepts blood sacrifice. The seeming disparity of these elements will be brought together when we consider Lakṣmī as a Tantric goddess, in the following chapter.

Before we do so, however, we must consider a different sort of paradigmatic dichotomy that exists in the Lakṣmī literature, also manifesting as opposing personalities. Here it is not a matter of pacific as opposed to ferocious qualities of auspiciousness but rather it is the auspicious as against the inauspicious. Here we refer to Alakṣmī, the opposing counterpart to Lakṣmī and the embodiment of inauspiciousness.

The Absence of Lakṣmī: Is Lady Luck a Fickle Goddess?

Most of the Purāṇic songs that we present in our collection express gratitude to the goddess for restoring something that had been lost: wealth, rank, sovereignty, well-being. The words of the songs are said to be those used by the gods themselves as they communicate with the goddess, and these same words are transmitted to her devotees so that they in turn may attract her attention. Indra, lord of heaven, speaks not only for himself but for all inhabitants of the three worlds when he sings to the goddess. Touched by Indra's performance, Śrī replies:

> . . . Never shall I turn my face
> From that person
> Who offers morning recitations
> Of the song you have sung to me.[34]

Lakṣmī the Cañcalā*: The Mystery of Lakṣmī's Capricious Nature*

Never shall she turn her face from that person . . . and yet if Lakṣmī brings balance, harmony, abundance, wealth, and a sense of security, she is nonetheless, as we have considered in the Vedic songs, also known as Cañcalā, the "fickle" or "restless" or "capricious" one. The sense of security can be just that—a sense, perhaps an illusion—when its true nature is not understood and approached properly. Even Indra, lord of the gods and regent of heaven, learns the hard way that disrespecting the goddess of wealth—even if unconsciously—results in the loss of her favor. Indeed, one of the events leading to the previously mentioned Churning of the Ocean story entails disregard for this goddess: The sage Durvāsa bestows a fragrant wreath of flowers upon Indra's elephant, Airāvata, who casts it off and stomps it under foot. The irascible Durvāsa flies into rage at the affront shown not only to his generosity but to the inhabitant and true essence of the flower garland, Śrī-Lakṣmī herself. The sage thereupon curses Indra, and Lakṣmī flees his side, leaving the lord of the gods and his kingdom, which comprises the entire three worlds, with nothing but chaos, poverty, and misery.

How, then, can Lakṣmī be sought for security when she herself may leave without a moment's notice? At least one text has stated that Śrī is so fickle that she moves even in her pictures, and that she is attracted to Viṣṇu only because, with his many *avatāras* ("descents," or incarnations) he himself is restless and always changing form.[35] Certainly, Lakṣmī is beseeched to be steadfast and to leave behind the restless aspect of her nature as the capricious Lady Luck.

The seeming paradox of steadfastness and movement may be explained through Lakṣmī's quality of *sattva*, or dynamic equipoise. This is the ebullience, not frozen stagnancy, that comes from the harmonious balancing of pleasure, wealth, and sacred ceremony. The word *sattva* literally means to be in a state of *truth* or *beingness*. This is Lakṣmī's fullness and life-energy, and it expresses what the Greek philosophers put forth: *truth is beauty* and *beauty is truth*. Lakṣmī dwells in expansion and reception: in the fullness of giving and receiving of gifts, nourishment, and pleasure; in the commercial exchange of goods and services; and in the ritual exchange of offerings and boons. Therefore, when Lakṣmī is called Cañcalā, this also refers to the sparkling and bright quality of her presence; that which is scintillating may be difficult to capture, but it is exquisitely enticing. It is in resplendence that the true nature of Lakṣmī expresses itself, ever pulsating with the essence of life. One attracts Lakṣmī by engaging in that exquisitely beautiful essence. And one sustains Lakṣmī by engaging in the conscious awareness, appreciation, and invocation of her presence.

The Purāṇic Alakṣmī

We have already been introduced to the inauspicious Alakṣmī in the Vedic literature, where she is also called Nirṛti. In the Purāṇic literature,

Alakṣmī also manifests as Daridrā (Poverty)[36] as well as Akīrti (Ill Repute), Atulā (Unbalanced), and Jyeṣṭhā (Elder or Eldest). The latter name refers to her as Lakṣmī's "elder sister," for when the world is re-created from the churning of the ocean, all that is inauspicious is born together in a group (which includes Jyeṣṭhā), followed later by the birth of the auspicious, the first of whom is Padmā (Lakṣmī).[37] Just as the identity of Lakṣmī expands in the Purāṇas, so too does Alakṣmī develop from a conceptualization to an entity in her own right, with identifiable physical characteristics, life-episodes, and even marriage.[38] Her detailed personification brings the qualities of Lakṣmī even more sharply into focus, articulating the contrast between what the two represent.

Lakṣmī and Alakṣmī never reside in the same place, for that which attracts one repels the other. For example, Alakṣmī is said to be frightened away by the sound of sacred chanting[39] and the sweet smell of incense. She is said to be drawn instead to homes "where the family members argue constantly with one another," where "neither Śiva nor Viṣṇu is honored ceremonially," where the inhabitants are "deluded," "lethargic," "gluttonous," and "neglectful of the home," where "guests are not cared for appropriately," and where "adults partake of food in the presence of children without feeding them as well."[40] The extensive exemplification of Alakṣmī's whereabouts demonstrates the ways in which the inauspicious may pervade worldly existence, manifesting in all four of the "wealths," or purposes of life discussed earlier. In her aspect as Atulā, or Unbalanced, she manifests as either the extreme denial of or the obsessive indulgence in pleasure.[41] As Daridrā, or Poverty, she embodies not only the lack of material goods but the greed that springs from miserliness, hoarding, and fear that there is never enough; she is poverty of the spirit and poverty of the creative imagination. Akīrti, or Ill Repute, entails the neglect of *dharma,* the observance of which fosters respect, and she attaches herself to one who shuns responsibilities toward the home, family, ancestors, community, and the gods.

The continued invocation of Śrī-Lakṣmī, especially through the chanting of sacred songs, is said to keep away the inauspicious Alakṣmī in any of her forms:

Those who hear or recite
This birth story of Lakṣmī
Attract the presence of Śrī in their homes
For three generations.

Alakṣmī, repository of penury and strife,
Never gains entrance into those homes
Whose inhabitants offer songs to Śrī.[42]

CHAPTER 3

Living the Powerful Life

Lakṣmī of the Tantric Traditions

We have reserved the most complex, multilayered, and in many ways most fascinating selections for our final section of songs invoking Lakṣmī. Here, we see a culmination of the personality of the goddess and, at the same time, a culmination in the how the worshiper may access her presence. We shall see that the goddess expresses herself in powerful forms that the worshiper may access and draw into alignment with his or her own being. All of the concerns about prosperity expressed by the poets of the Vedic and Purāṇic songs are here taken a step further. Concerns for abundant food, wealth, and happiness continue to occupy the petitioners, but the source of generating and maintaining their successful acquisition through the blessings of the goddess may now be located in the body and consciousness of the worshiper himself. The arena for worship, we could say, has expanded. So too has the identity of the goddess.

The Tantric personality of Lakṣmī continues to express itself as the lovely, sweetly smiling lady of the lotus, bestower of all auspiciousness, bounty, and prosperity in the world. However, this same Lakṣmī also dons the accoutrements of the fierce goddesses. She may bear a lotus, discus, and conch, and also a sword and a necklace of severed heads. She may be attended not only by smiling, sweet-natured, plump young elephants who shower her with life-giving rains, but also by poisonous cobras whose hoods sway menacingly as they stand poised by her side. So too we shall see that, from some perspectives, the goddess pervades one's consciousness and indeed all that exists, even beyond the time-space continuum. In this regard, we shall see that the Tantric Lakṣmī expresses herself as Kuṇḍalinī Śakti—the divine power that exists within our own bodies.

Every form of Lakṣmī—whether Vedic, Purāṇic, or Tantric—is worshiped for abundance and prosperity in the world. We have already considered an epithet of Mahālakṣmī extolled in the Purāṇas: She is "bestower of worldly success and spiritual liberation" (*bhukti-mukti-pradāyinī*). In this, we recognize attention to the material world and the freedom to disengage from it. In the Purāṇic consciousness, spiritual liberation is a goal that may remain distinct from that of pleasure-wealth-virtue. The Tantric Lakṣmī, however, instead of focusing directly on liberation, applies her awesome powers to destroy whatever stands in the way of a successful, fulfilling existence on earth, right here, right now. Instead of *mukti* (spiritual liberation), she grants *siddhi* (spiritual power). The *Song for the Lakṣmī of Spiritual Power* (*Siddhalakṣmī Stotram*) reiterates this in its closing verses:

> This song was composed by the gods
> For the benefit of all living beings. . . .
>
> For Lakṣmī is the destroyer of every affliction
> And the bestower of every success.[1]

The World According to Tantra

The nature of worldly embodiment is such that the mind perceives a duality between the human and divine. Spiritual quests are undertaken to mend that rift. Many of the esoteric traditions of India maintain that the so-called duality of the world is a misconception, though a misconception that may work well enough until one seeks to awaken from it. Part of the mystery unveiled in these esoteric traditions is that the misconception (or illusion) has been created by the divine source itself—Mahālakṣmī in her form as Māyā (Illusion) or Mahāmāyā (Great Illusion). Some are drawn to move beyond the web that Māyā has spun, in search of the source from which all has arisen. In the monistic esoteric traditions, all is understood to come from one source—the joy, the horror, the illusion, the revelation, the human, the divine, in short, everything imaginable and everything beyond our imagination. This is why adherents of these traditions seek spiritual liberation by means of that which creates bondage. The world is only an obstacle to those who would not understand its divine origin and essence.

Tantra is a means of uniting the disparate elements of a person's entire being. *Tantra* means "weaving," and the Tantrika, or Tantric practitioner, seeks to weave together what are usually experienced as irreconcilable opposites: the "worldly" and the "spiritual." The physical body, like the material world, is not to be ignored or necessarily transcended, but rather is to be engaged as the ground for spiritual realization. Further, the "hybrid" aspects of Lakṣmī's Tantric personalities are in accordance with this understanding of wisdom through the weaving together of seemingly disparate forms.

The Tantric traditions refer to themselves as the most expedient and necessarily the most intense route to the goddess and to her magnificent blessings, both mundane and spiritual. Initiation into a Tantric path and proceeding under the guidance of a perfected master are said to be essential for the efficacious awakening of such powers and for the beneficial manifestation and application of their results. Within the heightened awareness that comes with such tutelage or simply with such intentionality, the recitation of *mantra*s (sacred syllables and formulas) and *stotra*s (sacred songs of praise) is acknowledged in the Tantric traditions to be a potent practice for awakening one's consciousness to the presence of Lakṣmī and her blessings.

Chanting, singing, or listening to these songs provides a way to activate the goddess's energy, for, according to Tantric understanding, she dwells inside of their very syllables, and her divine power is released with their utterance. So too may the *mantra*s of these songs be inscribed directly on one's body. From the highest level of understanding, the same divine energy that exists inside the syllables exists deep within each person. The chanting or recitation awakens that which is already present, though dormant, within the seeker. The existence of the goddess within the body of the practitioner is, according to certain Tantric teachings, a fundamental aspect of her cosmic personality. Some schools of Tantra are dualistic, maintaining that the goddess exists outside of the individual, and she must be drawn from afar. Even so, the goddess's energy exists in her *mantra*s, and when they are applied ritually to the body (as will be explained further in Chapter 6), they envelop the practitioner in the goddess's sacred mantle of sound.

Lakṣmī as Kuṇḍalinī

As we further appreciate the complexities of Lakṣmī's identity, we are reminded of her ever-present manifestation as the lotus goddess. In the Vedic materials we find the first literary expressions to laud the primordial goddess of beauty and fecundity, embodied in the lotus. The Purāṇic materials develop the symbolism of the exquisite flower whose roots in the mud and blossom in the air remind the worshiper that even when entangled in the mire of worldly existence, one may transcend to the pristine realms of the liberation of the spirit. In the Tantric imagery of the lotus, we encounter the fulfillment of Tantric wisdom. The Tantric perspective allows us to stand back and view the entire situation holistically, beholding the roots, the stalk, and the flower as the integral organism that it is. The roots stretch deep into the mysterious, subterranean realms that are the essential foundation of all life in this world. Often it is the very darkness, turbulence, and messiness of life that fuels the most successful of Tantric spiritual endeavors. The Tantric practitioner does not attempt to transcend or to escape the earthly situation but to engage with the energy of life in the fullness of its expression—to ride *with* that energy as it moves through the entirety of our beings. Success in this endeavor constitutes its own kind of liberation from the shackles of the world.

In the symbolism of the lotus lies the image of the human born into the earthly realm of *saṃsāra*; the ocean of existence is the venue for an individual's karmic struggles and triumphs. The Tantric understanding of the lotus goddess as the goddess of supreme wisdom may be seen again in this imagery. Of significance, however, is not so much that one ascends from the lower or baser or "muddier" centers upward to attain the highest space in the rarefied element of air or the ethers, but rather, Lakṣmī's message in the Tantras is one of integration. One attains *siddhi*—spiritual or magical success, attainment, accomplishment, perfection, or power—*while remaining consciously and intentionally rooted* in the moist, life-engendering soil of the earth. One need not relinquish materiality for spirituality, sexuality for asceticism. Instead of a separation of categories, there is a marriage of complementary segments, a conscious integration of what only appear to be disparate elements to create a harmonious, differentially patterned, vibrant whole. Again, we are reminded that the root of the term *tantra* is "to weave." The Tantrika does not seek to relinquish the "base" station in exchange for the "transcendent," but rather to enliven and integrate all aspects of being.

Just as the lotus epitomizes the essence and form of Lakṣmī's nature, encompassing the myriad dimensions of "spirituality" and "materiality," so too does the subtle body of a human contain the form of a lotus within itself. Yogis and intuitives from many esoteric traditions have witnessed in meditation the internal structure of these subtle bodies, in which the central stalk or channel, like the lotus stalk, reaches down to the energies of the earth and upward toward the etheric realms.[2] This central channel is called the *suṣumnā nāḍī*, and it is located along the physical spinal column. Along this stalk are seven[3] centers of energy, envisioned as round spinning vortexes, variously labeled as *cakras* (wheels) or *padmās* (lotuses),[4] each with specific numbers of petals in specific positions and of specific hue. Along the vertical axis, the first *cakra*, called the "root support" (*mulādhāra*), is located at the base of the torso, roughly at the spot of the perineum, and is connected energetically with the earth. Here is where the Kuṇḍalinī Śakti resides, envisioned as a coiled snake, lying dormant until her arousal. Kuṇḍalinī Śakti, the great serpentine power of transformation, is recognized as a manifestation of Lakṣmī herself.[5]

Each subsequent *cakra*, moving higher up the axis, resonates with aspects of an individual's consciousness; the highest is the "thousand-petalled" (*sahasrāra*) lotus on the crown of the head, abode of Lord Śiva. When the awakened goddess rises to the crown *cakra*, she merges there with Śiva, and the bliss of their union creates the full opening of the thousand-petalled lotus, experienced as both the exquisite collapsing of limited consciousness and the blissful expansiveness of divine consciousness. The fullness of this experience resonates outward around the crown, relaxing back downward like a waterfall over the body, toward the earth, and cycling back up again into the first—the earth-based—root *cakra*, the place from which the cycle may continue again. Without that full circuit and effulgence, the wisdom of integrative consciousness may become lost in the "transcendent," and the practitioner may remain literally ungrounded, unsettled, and unfulfilled (as well as feeling "spacy"). The experience is not complete unless it is integrated throughout the entire being, for it is with integration that authentic spiritual transformation occurs.

It is the goddess herself who initiates the process of transformation, for her energy in the form of Kuṇḍalinī moves throughout the centers, causing each of the lotuses to open, allowing the divine transformative energy to activate that center, purify it of blockages, and move farther upward, enlivening the consciousness. *The Secret Heart of Lakṣmī* (*Śrī Mahālakṣmī Hṛdayam*) speaks of the holistic transformation that occurs in this process; it reminds us that the awakening is not only at the crown of the head, but in one's entire being as it scintillates with the integrative consciousness that results from that awakening and merging. One may experience something like "heaven on earth," with the focus on both the heavenly and the earthly. More specifically, the poet of this text speaks of experiencing one's body as Vaikuṇṭha, the heavenly realm where Lakṣmī dwells with Lord Viṣṇu. So too are all of the faculties of an individual's perception transmuted into the magnificent awareness enjoyed by the gods:

At the moment of awakening,
Let my body become Vaikuṇṭha,
From the seat to the forehead and in the crown of my head.
Grant that my eyes become the abode of Śrī.
Grant that my speech become anchored in the Realm of Truth.
O Lakṣmī, grant that by experiencing
A mere portion of your essence within me,
I may inhabit that glorious White Island
Illumined by its own splendor.[6]

Lakṣmī, Śiva, and the "Ten Great Wisdom Goddesses" (*Daśamahāvidyās*)

A number of the works in our collection are addressed to Lakṣmī specifically as Kamalā ("Lotus") or Kamalātmikā ("Soul-essence of the Lotus"). Although she has many designations, Kamalā is often identified as a Tantric goddess. The Tantric traditions include a group of deities known as the *daśamahāvidyās*, that is, the "Ten Great Wisdom Goddesses." We may understand these as Supreme Wisdom expressed through ten paths or sacred personalities of the goddess. Together they express the totality of existence. The exact identities of these goddesses vary somewhat from region to region, and indeed some lists include more than ten. Each list, however, begins with Kālī, the fierce, dark (*raudrī*) goddess of death and dissolution, and ends with Kamalā, the beneficent, bright (*gaurī*) goddess of life, prosperity, beauty, and well-being. Kamalā, the charming essence of the lotus blossom, foundation upon which the entire creation rests, is none other than Lakṣmī herself. As such, the inclusion of Kamalā-Lakṣmī into the established category of the Ten Great Wisdom Goddesses offers further opportunity to appreciate the variegations with which her personality expresses itself.

Lakṣmī as Kamalā, Tantric Lotus Goddess

The identity of the ancient lotus goddess Kamalā, like that of the ancient Śrī, developed in various directions throughout time and geographical region. Most traditions view Kamalā and Lakṣmī as the same goddess, although some differentiate the two.[7] The songs in our collection address the lotus goddess in ways that point both to the gracious goddess of prosperity who is associated with Viṣṇu, as well as to a group of multifaceted wisdom goddesses, all of whom are associated with Śiva. The *Song-Amulet of the Lotus Goddess* (*Kamalātmikā Kavacam*), for example, invokes Kamalā by addressing her with names that clearly identify her as the Vaiṣṇava Lakṣmī, such as Jayā, Vijayā, Kameśī, Viṣṇumāyā, and, indeed, as Lakṣmī. Yet in the same song she is also extolled as Śaṅkarī, Pārvatī, and Śivadūtī, thus linking her with Śiva, and most particularly with Sadāśiva (the "everlasting" Śiva), an association shared by all of the *mahāvidyā* goddesses.[8]

If such various names and identities are invoked within the corpus of one particular song, does this indicate that all are aspects of one all-encompassing goddess, or do they constitute an array of individual goddesses? The answer lies somewhere in between: All of these individual goddesses are aspects that lie within the goddess in potential form; as one of the *mahāvidyā* goddesses, Kamalā shares a common substratum that constitutes her nature as Supreme Wisdom. When called to the fore, such ferocity takes on independent form and identity, all the while maintaining the underlying transformative power of that supreme wisdom. With a shift in frequency, as it were, the tenor of the particular expression of that wise force may be expressed as anything from the obsidian darkness of Kālī at one end of the *mahāvidyā* spectrum, to the golden brilliance of Kamalā-Lakṣmī at the other.

It is generally understood that Kālī, being the most conspicuously terrifying of the group, is the most potent form of the Tantric goddesses available to the householder as she presides over severing the ties that bound one to the world and worldly consciousness.[9] In contrast, the beneficent Kamalā presides over the attainment of worldly comfort and prosperity.[10] In a very basic sense, it is necessary to come to terms with the world before one can leave it behind. Maintaining her modest position at the end of the list of Great Wisdom goddesses, Kamalā represents the turning point, the point of departure from complete immersion in worldly consciousness and onto the path of spiritual transformation. Yet when the Tantric practitioner undergoes an intense *sādhana* (spiritual practice) in which ordinary worldly consciousness is collapsed and burned in the fiery destructive energy of a Kālī or a Chinnamastā, it is through Kamalā that his presence in the world can be reintegrated.

Kamalā's Secret

The divine essence of the goddess that motivates the Tantric path is by nature ever moving, never entirely known, and certainly not to be contained entirely in any category. Its fullest truth always remains a mystery, a mystery that expresses itself in *līlā,* the playfulness of the goddess as she moves through the worlds. The Tantric goddess of transformation who can be easily identified *solely* as world-destroying is perhaps not, after all, the fullest expression of the Tantric goddess of transformation. Some of the most powerful Tantric masters have chosen not to relinquish their ordinary clothing and "day jobs" for a mantle of sacred ash, wandering from place to place, but remain as householders and perform their Tantric practice (*sādhana*) while conducting a life of relative normalcy. The old Tantric adage applies well here: To worship Viṣṇu in the world, Śiva at home, and the goddess in one's heart. Might not, then, the supreme divine expression of worldly transcendence abide in the image of a perfectly benign and worldly goddess?

The deepest Tantric mysteries are actually right before our eyes; experiencing this truth is a matter of rending the veil of illusory expectations and of ultimately changing perspective. Part of what makes Tantra heterodox is that it recognizes and highlights the divinity that exists everywhere, even as it is embedded in the mundane. One penetrates its mysteries in order to awaken and gather its inherent spiritual power. The vehicle for transformation is not necessarily that which is far and away, abstracted and devoid of color, but rather that which is embodied, located in space and time, filled with color and scintillating movement. As well, we should remember that these ten goddesses operate together, on a continuum, each sharing the essence of divine wisdom as it plays out through various "goddess personalities."

Integrated awareness of the material and physical world and the role of the human body—with its thoughts, emotions, capacity for sensuality, and so forth—lies at the core of Tantric spiritual transformation. And so it is that the force of the most complete transformation—so complete and seamless that it escapes all but the most discerning Tantric eye—may indeed be embodied in the most seemingly ordinary, the least "threatening" embodiment of the Ten Great Paths of Wisdom, the lovely and delicately smiling Kamalā.

From this perspective, the list categorizing divine vehicles of wisdom may begin with ferocious destruction, but it ends in the serene attainment of the goal. We might consider that last in line, Kamalā embodies the integrated consciousness, the successful culmination of the Tantric path. The perfection of *sādhana* is not just severing the bonds of the world, but reentering the world and living within it, mastering it instead of being mastered by it. The lotus goddess invites the worshiper to be in the world, of the world, and beyond the world, all at once. This is the Tantric vision, a vision of integration, harmony, and continuous, on-the-edge, awareness. This is the secret of Lakṣmī as the Tantric lotus goddess, spiritual perfection clothed in the exquisite, variegated, and challenging beauty of the world. It is for this reason that the Tantrika who achieves this mastery is recognized as *siddha*—one who has "perfected" this integration. Such a person is also called *vīra*—"hero"—for to achieve mastery of life's physical, emotional, intellectual, and spiritual challenges requires consummate courage.

The full integration of a happy life, an awakened heart, and magnificent wisdom are the blessings bestowed by this goddess. The *Song for the Lotus Goddess* (*Kamalā Stotram*) extols her with these words:

> Through your power of illusion,
> A person can become disconnected
> From his Higher Self,
> Wandering about from place to place,
> Bereft of clear thought,
> Lost in destructive behavior.
>
> It matters not how much truth
> May shine forth in the world,
> Illuminating the entire creation,
> For one cannot acquire wisdom
> Unless it is experienced
> Through the opening of the heart.
>
> A person immersed in the depths of your wisdom
> Enjoys the fullness of a happy life
> Blessed with a spouse, home, family, good friends,
> And the banishment of debilitating sorrow.[11]

The Tantric Alakṣmī

The glorious embodiment of auspiciousness is not, as we have seen in the Vedic and Purāṇic materials, without its opposite. Just as Alakṣmī, the inauspicious, appears as the Vedic Nirṛti and the Purāṇic Jyeṣṭhā, so also does she appear among the Ten Great Wisdom Goddesses as Dhūmāvatī, the "smoky one." Withered and frightening, described as "crow-like" in appearance, Dhūmāvatī is the embodiment of inauspiciousness. She is identified as a widow, severed from all that is bright, colorful, sensual, and life-engendering. Seated in a chariot disconnected from anything to pull it, she represents fragmented, unsatsifying existence. In contrast to the ever-moving Kamalā-Lakṣmī, Dhūmāvatī is literally stuck in one place.

Dhūmāvatī's presence represents the absence of the auspicious life-force. And yet, as with Nirṛti and Jyeṣṭhā, we should not misconstrue her as an "evil" entity, for in a dark and uncomfortable way, the smokiness of Dhūmāvatī, much like that of Śiva, represents the smoldering ashes of the world destroyed; it is such distaste for the world—or at least disappointment with it—that may inspire one to take the first steps on the spiritual path of transformation. Hers is not the rampant, colorful, dramatic destructiveness of Kālī in her auspicious rage. Rather, we might say that the disquietude and stagnancy of Dhūmāvatī provide the subtle, initial, necessary inspiration to contemplate life behind its appearances. They also remind one to recognize with conscious gratitude the blessings of Lakṣmī once they arrive.

In an even deeper sense, Dhūmāvatī is the smoky haze that is the goddess in her aspect of cosmic obscuration. Just as Kamalā, the full-blown lotus, embodies life at its most effulgent and abundant, so does Dhūmāvatī, her opposite, embody the complete absence of being. She is the embodiment of the cosmic *pralaya*, or the fallow period between cycles of the universe, where time, space, and being collapse into absolute nothingness. Just as the universe expands and contracts cyclically, so does one's walk through this life. During the course of the spiritual quest, one may expand one's consciousness and move forward, only to encounter fallow periods where one may feel stuck, uninspired, depressed. This is where Dhūmāvatī manifests as the absence of life and hope, but in this she holds the space for the next leap forward. Dhūmāvatī is an embodiment of the silence and stillness of nonbeing. Here, one may remain stagnant, or, once that abandoned chariot can be reconnected to a horse (auspicious and regal symbol, of course, of Lakṣmī), then Dhūmāvatī may be understood as not only the stillness that follows death but the gestation that precedes life.

The Grace-Bestowing Mother

As we have noted, the worship of the goddess (Śakti) as the supreme reality is known as Śāktism, and in many ways the Śākta principles overlap with those of Tantra. According to the teachings of Śāktism, the goddess expresses herself in five eternal functions (*pañcakṛtya*s): In addition to her functions of creation (*sṛṣṭi*), maintenance (*sthiti*), and dissolution or destruction of the universe (*samhāra*), she also expresses herself through obscuration (*tirodhāna*) and, as the glorious complement to obscuration, she then reveals herself through her bestowal of grace (*anugraha*).

From the monistic perspective of Lakṣmī's five aspects, everything that exists, everything that occurs in one's life and in the cycles of the universe is an aspect of the goddess. When life is experienced as bleak and fraught with pain, when Lakṣmī seems not to be present, the Śākta scriptures would articulate such poverty and constriction as the expression of the goddess's quality of obscuration. Whether due to karmic propensities or simply to the lack of appropriate ritual and devotional actions, the worshiper has not sufficiently moved through the darkness of Lakṣmī's obscuration into the light of recognizing her and receiving her blessings. Whether misfortune is conceptualized as the presence of an independent entity such as Dhūmāvatī or Alakṣmī, or whether it is attributed to the goddess's expression as obscuration, the transformation that occurs as an antidote is *anugraha*, the goddess's bestowal of grace.

If the Tantric Lakṣmī may be identified as Kamalā, the lotus goddess, force of life and regeneration, and source of magnificent wisdom, she is, as we have considered, the Great Goddess as well. Like the lotus flower that embodies the message of Lakṣmī's gifts, wisdom may be transcendent, but its roots are deeply anchored in an earthly, even subterranean, abode. The goddess of supreme wisdom is ever approachable, a generous mother whose worshipers, while standing in awe of her magnificence, nonetheless feel secure in a warm and intimate relationship with her. Just as the Tantric songs convey philosophical wisdom teachings, they also contain verses of spontaneous, heartfelt emotion. The Tantric worshiper, like the worshiper in the Vedic and Purāṇic traditions, expresses concerns with life in the world, and turns to the beneficent goddess of prosperity for relief when the world presses down too hard:

> Homage to you,
> Destroyer of crushing poverty and woes.
> Homage! Homage to you,
> Pacifier of all fears,
> Bestower of abundance,
> Abiding on the chest of Lord Viṣṇu.[12]

The Tantric worshiper recognizes a correlation between the goddess's influence in external affairs and the awakening of divine consciousness within his or her own inner being. The true prosperity of Lakṣmī is qualified by an abundant state of mind, expansive and courageous as one moves through life. Even as she bestows these qualities of ferocious strength, the goddess's devotees clearly approach her as a gentle mother of infinite compassion:

> *"Give me. . . ."*
> *"There isn't any. . . ."*
> In an anxious state
> I intrude with these words,
> Casting myself down before you for refuge.
> Even as I fall before you,
> I beg you to dwell securely within me
> And bestow never-ending fearlessness.[13]

Lakṣmī as *Siddhi*: Magical Attainment, Spiritual Power

Siddhi is one of those Sanskrit words with a wide resonance of meanings, all of them operative at once. It denotes perfection, accomplishment, mastery, prosperity, success, spiritual power, magical power, magical attainment, and more. An integral feature of the Tantric paths is the acquisition of *siddhi,* which may be applied to whatever the practitioner is focused upon. The fullness of *siddhi* leaves no remainder, no further longing. We could therefore translate "the *siddhi* of wealth" as "the attainment of wealth," but it means more than that. To beseech the goddess for the *siddhi* of wealth means not only to be blessed with material prosperity, but to have full and complete mastery of the inherent power that generates and sustains such wealth. The *siddhi* of wealth means mastery of the state of prosperity consciousness.

We include in our collection a song dedicated to an aspect of the goddess known as Siddhalakṣmī (also called Siddhilakṣmī or simply Siddhi).[14] Like Kamalā of the Ten Great Wisdom Goddesses (*daśamahāvdyās*), Siddhalakṣmī is an exquisitely complex form of Lakṣmī. She is lauded as the bright (*gaurī*) and beneficent goddess of beauty and prosperity who bears a lotus, discus, and royal mace, and who is associated with Viṣṇu and the bounty of the world's creation. At the same time, she is extolled as the dark (*raudrī*), ferocious goddess of destruction and transformation who wields a sword and trident, and who is associated with the destructive god Śiva. The *Song for the*

Lakṣmī of Spiritual Power (*Siddhalakṣmī Stotram*) lauds the goddess who exhibits both beneficent and terrifying characteristics; in this hymn, the lovely "embodiment of the unfathomable bliss of Viṣṇu" is also the "demon-destroying Śakti,/ Garlanded with enemies she has slain."[15] Her devotees appreciate her alluring beauty even as she wields the weapons to protect them from harm. Note the description in the verse for her visualization:

> That goddess
> Who is the feminine aspect of Brahmā, Viṣṇu, and Śiva,
> Who has six arms, four faces, and three eyes,
> Wielder of sword and trident,
> Bearer of lotus, discus, and mace,
> Revealing herself as an alluring young woman
> Dressed in bright yellow garments
> And adorned with a dazzling array of jewels—
> Upon that resplendent goddess
> Let us meditate.[16]

In his illuminating study of Siddhalakṣmī's worship in Kashmir and Nepal, Sthaneshwar Timalsina demonstrates how this goddess exhibits an exquisite synthesis of qualities from two extremely different traditions:

> Whether Siddhilakṣmī properly falls within the Śaivite or Vaiṣṇavite tradition highlights the rich paradoxes of this deity. She contains within herself the Purāṇic Lakṣmī—a gentle, loving figure linked with the beneficent Nārāyaṇa—while also embodying a Tantric nature that demands the consumption of wine, blood offerings, and other left-handed elements clearly linking her with the Śaiva Tantra and specifically the Kāpālika tradition . . . Placement of Siddhilakṣmī within the deities of the northern transmission further suggests that Siddhilakṣmī, like other deities in the Śaiva family, emanates from Lord Śiva and specifically falls within the family of Kālī. The difference between the Purāṇic and Tantric texts that deal with deities of the same name lies in the way the respective ritual visualizations are executed.[17]

This form of the goddess is certainly a departure from the Purāṇic Lakṣmī who accepts only fruits, flowers, and other sweet, vegetative offerings. Yet it demonstrates once again how her expansive essence need not be contained within a singular definition of who she is. Just as she provides material blessings of food, wealth, and material well-being, so too does Siddhalakṣmī infuse her devotees with the insight to penetrate the meaning of the world from beyond the ordinary human perspective, and into the goddess's unlimited consciousness. In addition, she grants the courage to live life from this wider perspective, so that one may boldly engage the angers, jealousies, insecurities, and other debilitating aspects of one's life and direct them to become fuel for the path toward spiritual perfection.

The Tantric songs to Lakṣmī continue to seek the goddess's blessings in all aspects of life, but their focus is more clearly directed toward the internalized identification with the goddess's *siddhi*. This spiritual and magical power is what motivates the seeker, for it brings one's consciousness into direct contact with the source of all prosperity, courage, mastery, sovereignty, and freedom. The Tantric songs to Lakṣmī demonstrate that the magnificent power of *siddhi* is but another expression of *śrī*, the auspiciousness of the goddess. Is not the ferocious beauty of the Tantric Lakṣmī but another expression of the Vedic Śrī-Lakṣmī? We might say that the difference lies in her devotees' understanding of where she exists and where one must go to meet her. In the Vedic *Hymn to Śrī* (*Śri Sūktam*), the poet beseeches the sacred fire to bring the goddess into his presence: "Draw unto me . . . the goddess Lakṣmī." In the Tantric hymns, the poet speaks directly to the goddess and asks that she establish her auspicious essence not only around him, but *within*:

O Mother,
Deeply embedded
Is my fear, my insecurity.
Have mercy, O Mother, on my wretched state.
Uproot it
With the joy that arises
From your sweet and compassionate glance.
O Mother of the Universe,
Infuse your children with fearlessness!
Plant in us the seed of auspiciousness
As we make our way in this world.[18]

PART TWO

The Power of Poetry to Summon the Goddess

Sound is a form of the goddess's powerful essence. The *mantras* that constitute the songs to the goddess carry her sacred energy, for their syllables are understood to constitute her sonic body. In this section we explore how the various genres of sacred songs operate as vehicles for calling forth her presence.

CHAPTER 4

The Power of Vedic Hymns

Generating Auspiciousness

Reciting the Hymns (*Sūkta*s)

We open our collection with the two earliest known songs to Lakṣmī, the *Hymn to Śrī* (*Śrī Sūktam*) and the *Hymn to Lakṣmī* (*Lakṣmī Sūktam*). Their recitation continues to be an important part of Hindu worship to this day. Literally meaning "well said" (*su* = well; *ukta* = said), or "eloquently stated," a *sūkta* is a verse format employed in the Vedas for songs of praise.

The *Hymn to Śrī* is a well-known hymn that has been appended to the fifth *khila* (song-cycle) of the *Ṛg Veda*. The structure and vocabulary of the Sanskrit indicate that all but a few of its verses were composed somewhat later than the *Ṛg Veda*. The verses of the *Hymn to Lakṣmī* appear to be even more recent, for in addition to linguistic indications, the imagery of Lakṣmī as a goddess with specifically recognizable characteristics is further developed than in the earlier verses. The text of the *Hymn to Śrī* exists in several, slightly varying, versions. As well, it is sometimes blended with the *Hymn to Lakṣmī* and recited as one continuous hymn. However, this blending slightly compromises the structural integrity of the *Hymn to Śrī*, which has its own story to tell.

The *Hymn to Śrī* is chanted to accompany the ancient Vedic fire sacrifice (*yajña*). The opening three verses and closing three verses provide a framework describing a majestic procession in which the goddess, riding a splendid chariot attended by horses and elephants, enters into the human realm. The sacred fire is the avenue upon which the goddess and her entourage arrive from the heavens. The poet is the spectator, waiting eagerly, eyes trained on the fire. Most of the hymn is addressed to Agni Jātavedas, fire god and sacred fire itself, to impel the movement of that procession. Excitement grows as the goddess comes closer, for her presence infuses this world with vitality, prosperity, and abundant good fortune, transforming and enlivening everything in its path. The *Hymn to Śrī* begins:

> Draw unto me, O sacred fire, the goddess Lakṣmī,
> The resplendent, the golden,
> Doe-like, moon-lustrous,
> Garlanded in silver and in gold.[1]

The goddess of the *Hymn to Śrī* is an apparition of splendid luminosity; her visage is that of the sun, or of the moon, or of rain on a petal. Her most identifiable physical characteristic is her radiance; she manifests as golden light.[2] So too is she "doe-like," indicating a gentle, tender nature that is also fleeting, glimpsed in a moment's flash like the swift and graceful bounding of a deer. As yet, the poet is not close enough to be able to discern a form other than that of shimmering light. He can barely look at her, much less address her directly in speech. In only one verse does the poet employ the vocative voice.[3] Rather, a certain distance remains between the worshipers and the presence referred to as "that goddess Śrī"[4] or "that goddess Lakṣmī."[5]

The images in the second hymn, the *Hymn to Lakṣmī* (*Lakṣmī Sūktam*), demonstrate a slight shift toward the personification of a beloved goddess. Here we encounter glimpses of a personality whose attributes continue to be the magnificent forces of abundance and prosperity that fill the earth with splendor, but here too are indications that the goddess is developing a personality with aspects recognizable in the human realm, and she is therefore approached on a more personal level. Some of the verses address her directly, lauding her not only for her radiant splendor but for her beauty, tenderness, and generous capacity for showing favor.

Here, as in the earlier hymn, are invocations of Kubera (god of wealth), along with Kardama, Ciklīta, and Ānanda. Kardama ("mud") and Ciklīta ("moisture") are sons of Śrī who take form both as Vedic seers as well as the rich, moist, primordial wetlands of creation. Ānanda, whose name means "bliss," is also known as a sage and a son of Śrī, and his presence introduces the rapturous sensation of experiencing divine consciousness. If Kardama and Ciklīta remind us of the lotus's subterranean origins, Ānanda reflects its highest effulgence in the full-blown lotus. It is here, too, that Lakṣmī's association with Viṣṇu begins to develop, for together they represent the flourishing of the creation and of human affairs by means of unity and integration, with its focus on harmony, the sacred union of male and female, and the experience of the heart as a vehicle for personal transformation.

Ritual Application of the Vedic Hymns

Perhaps the earliest known form of Lakṣmī's worship specifically linking ritual with the recitation of the *Hymn to Śrī* is the Śrīkalpa ceremony, described in the *Baudhāyana Gṛhya Śeśa Sūtra*.[6] In the Śrīkalpa, the goddess is invited, sprinkled with water, given a ritual bath, and offered sandalwood, camphor, flowers, incense (*dūpa*), light (*dīpa*), and food. Each of these ritual attendances is to be accompanied by a specified verse of the *Hymn to Śrī*. In addition, the worshiper is instructed to repel the inauspicious Alakṣmī by brushing a lotus flower over his body while reciting the mantra *"kṣutpipāsāmalā jyeṣṭhā."*[7]

Other ritual uses of the *Hymn to Śrī* also prevailed, for each verse constitutes an independent mantra and energy of its own. As such, any of its verses may be chanted independently to a specific end, whether as the sole mantra or as joined with another series of mantras. In various worship traditions throughout India, the verses of the *Hymn to Śrī* continue to accompany particularized ritual actions in specified formats.

Especially noteworthy is a verse known as the *Lakṣmī Gāyatrī* (verse 10 of the *Hymn to Lakṣmī*). Like the *gāyatrī mantra*s to other deities, this is a compact, concentrated verse, revered as a potent collection of syllables for invoking the deity, and employed more for its incantatory powers than for lyrical expressiveness. Like the *gāyatrī*s to other deities, the *Lakṣmī Gāyatrī* is often chanted independently. The *Lakṣmī Gāyatrī* is as follows:

oṃ mahālakṣmī ca vidmahe
viṣṇu patni ca dhīmahi
tanno lakṣmī prachodayāt
Oṃ. Let me meditate on the great goddess Lakṣmī, consort of Viṣṇu.
Let Lakṣmī inspire that meditation and illumine my mind.[8]

Ritual advice from Saunaka's *Ṛg Vidhāna* singles out other individual verses of the *Hymn to Śrī* to be chanted on specific occasions to generate prosperity and auspiciousness, whether for an individual or for the entire kingdom. Thus, according to Saunaka, verse 11 of the *Hymn to Śrī* is to be chanted by or for one seeking to have children. Verse 6 is to be chanted for generating all types of prosperity; we should notice that this is the only verse in the hymn that speaks to the goddess directly. Verse 7 is to be chanted by the king on the auspicious occasion of his royal consecration.[9] Indeed, in traditional India, the king had to be Śrī-Lakṣmī's most ardent devotee, for he was responsible for attracting and maintaining her presence in the royal court. If the king failed to attract Śrī, the entire kingdom would suffer. It would appear, then, that the *Hymn to Śrī* was compiled specifically in behalf of the king, for he required the presence of Śrī-Lakṣmī to bestow prosperity on the entire kingdom, which was an extension of his royal person.

In the Vedic context, the recitation of the hymn is closely aligned with ritual action. Śaunaka therefore advises:

> For one desirous of *Śrī*, sacrifices should be performed where the fuel of the fire should consist of Bilva, and the number of oblations differ according to the desire of the sacrificer. The possession of *Śrī* for eternity (*śāśvatī śrī*) which can be possible only by offering oblation for hundred thousand times, can be very easily accomplished just by the *japa* (muttering) of *Śrī-Sūkta* for ten thousand times.[10]

Such "easy accomplishment"—after just ten thousand recitations—explains why Vedic worship engages ritual specialists—full-time priests whose family's sole occupation and lineage is to carry forth such rituals and recitations with absolute precision and accuracy. The Vedic tradition continues to this day, and its priests still to invoke the goddess's presence through *mantra*s offered at the flames of the sacred fire.

CHAPTER 5

The Power of Purāṇic Songs

Drawing Down the Goddess

Reciting the Songs of Praise (*Stotras*)

To a great extent, the fortune in one's life is believed to be dictated by *karma*, which serves to explain why Lakṣmī's blessings may seem to be more readily apparent with some than with others. However, the Purāṇic narratives indicate that individuals may exert a certain influence over their fortunes and misfortunes, the latter being exacerbated by the neglect of Lakṣmī and a perhaps inadvertent invitation to Alakṣmī either by inappropriate indulgence or simply through lassitude. The texts urge worshipers to take action against misfortune—whatever its cause—and the chanting of *stotras*, or sacred praise-songs, is said to have tremendous power in remedying and possibly even reversing the effects of *karma*.

The extent to which the goddess dissolves one's karmic residues and alters the situation of one's worldly circumstances is a matter of one's own *karma* as it is intercepted by the bestowal of Lakṣmī's grace, both of which remain, ultimately, a mystery. At the very least, one's attitude and capacity for acceptance are strengthened by the power generated through the recitations. In addition, such a shift in perception informs the choices one makes in the creation of new *karma*. By no longer adhering to the thought and behavioral patterns dictated by previous *saṃskāras* (residual karmic patterns), one allows those effects of debilitating actions to wear away and lose their hold. The teachings within these songs suggest that by chanting them, it is indeed possible to alter *karma* and thus the circumstances of one's life.

The *stotra* is a genre of sacred poetry used in the Purāṇic and Tantric sources. Its Sanskrit root is *stu*, "to praise in song." Related terms for songs of praise are *stava* and *stuti*. A *stotra* may be sung, chanted, recited, read aloud, read silently, or simply listened to attentively. In yogic terms, the power of the Sanskrit verses may generate enough psychic heat (*tapas*) in the subtle body to begin to burn karmic residues and transmute karmic propensities. However, on a very basic level, the chanting of the songs is simply a way to call forth the goddess, to get her attention and compel her to shift from her undifferentiated state to a localized state or place—to come before the petitioner.

The goddess is imagined as inhabiting both a limitless "state" of consciousness as well as a heavenly realm, most often the heavenly locale known as Vaikuṇṭha, where she dwells with Lord Viṣṇu. By singing these invocations, the petitioner is literally drawing down the goddess from that place or state. When she comes to this world, the goddess appears in a form that resonates with worldly consciousness; she meets the inhabitants of the three worlds in forms that they can recognize. As previously discussed, gods in heaven, humans on earth, and demigods in the underworld all seek Lakṣmī. When they call upon her, they remain in their own locales and in their own state of consciousness. In her abundant mercy, the goddess accommodates her infinite Self to match the needs and the capacities of her devotees.

The Propitious Glance of the Goddess

Many of the songs ask that the goddess "be pleased" (*prasannā*), for the goddess's happiness generates the flow of her radiance, which constitutes the essence of all abundance, prosperity, and auspiciousness. So too do the petitioners ask for a boon (*vara*), a specified gift from the deity, often granted in return for a sacrifice or offering. As these songs indicate, the offering of a song may be enough to please the goddess and compel her to bestow boons and blessings. In some cases the goddess has fashioned the very words of the songs and presented them to her devotees as a means for calling her back into their presence; she promises that when she hears these words, she will respond to the call. It is believed that the *stotra*s to Lakṣmī should be recited in a way that resonates with the essence of this gentle and beautiful goddess. One does best to deliver them in a soft, tender, and unhurried manner.

The Purāṇic songs most clearly portray Lakṣmī as the goddess of wealth, the deity who oversees concerns of pleasure, virtue, wealth, and spiritual liberation. Most of these verses are said to have been uttered by the gods themselves—whether as petitions for the goddess to restore lost wealth, or to thank her for having restored it once again. These songs have been extracted from (or inserted into) longer narratives that explain the details of a cosmic drama that ends happily when the goddess arrives. The goddess arrives through the force of song, and it is said that the goddess will return whenever she is called with these verses, thus re-creating that original cosmic moment enjoyed by the gods, right here on earth. The songs are *tīrthas*—sacred crossing points—that connect the local and limited with the cosmic and infinite.

By their very nature, the Purāṇic songs of praise contain many more references to cosmic events and personages than the Vedic or Tantric songs. Although these songs may play a greater role in the Vaiṣṇava traditions, their recitation is not limited to Vaiṣṇavas alone. Of all the songs of praise in this book, perhaps the most widely recited remains the *Eight Verses Praising Mahālakṣmī* (*Mahālakṣmyaṣṭakam Stotram*). Devotees from many different backgrounds recite this brief hymn daily as a powerful way to invoke the essence of the goddess of prosperity.

The chanting itself, then, may be enacted as a spiritual discipline to evoke a feeling of closeness with the goddess. It is an active way to call her forth and a receptive way to prepare for receiving her blessings. How, exactly, is her arrival envisioned? In the Purāṇic songs, devotees seek the goddess's gracious and propitious *glance*. She is drawn from heaven to embrace the worshiper with her look. The power of this glance is what ignites the changes in the life of the devotee.

Fruits of the Recitations (*Phala*)

Many Sanskrit devotional songs—whether Vedic, Purāṇic, or Tantric—conclude with stanzas known as *phala* verses. Thematically separate from the potent core of the actual song of praise, they are appended as closing verses. These additional verses enumerate the *phalas*—the "fruits" or "results" that one may obtain by reciting or listening to a recitation of the song. The *phala* verses are sometimes quite specific, but more often they indicate that the song's purpose is to attract *prasannā*, the "favor" or the "pleasing" of the goddess.

Such is the beneficent nature of Lakṣmī that when she is pleased, she reveals herself in one's life by altering one's material circumstances; she reveals herself in one's consciousness by replacing nescience and obscuration with the wisdom of awareness. The songs are believed to provide a vehicle by which one can uplift and actually transform the experience of earthly existence. As the *phala* verses indicate, there are often particular prescriptions for the recitation of these songs of praise, with certain expected results. In this sense, the worshiper can exercise a certain amount of will in how his or her life unfolds. The recitation of the sacred songs constitutes a honing and discipline of one's faculties that develop one's consciousness so that when the favor of the goddess is indeed attracted, it may be recognized, received, and sustained.

Both the Vedas and the Tantras assume the potency of their verses on a vibratory level. It is not always entirely clear, however, whether the potency of the Purāṇic songs is believed to exist in the intrinsic, sonic power of the Sanskrit words as *mantra*s or in the devotee's discursive understanding of the words as prayers and expressions of devotion. These texts do not always make a clear distinction between reciting the song and listening intently to another recite it; what seems to be important is the sincerity of devotional mood as the sacred sound is released into the atmosphere. Such songs may be recited by priests or other professional readers who have been engaged by a pious householder. Nowadays, live professional readers are frequently replaced by electronic recordings. The instructions for recitation that occur in the *phala* verses as well as in the body of the songs suggest that their efficacy in invoking the goddess requires both attention to perfect enunciation of the sonic forms—in Sanskrit—as well as to giving oneself over to a mood of devotion, contemplating the meanings of the words. This would occur in whatever language the devotee requires to understand them.[1] Such a harmonious combination engages a vigorous mental concentration attended by the emotional softening of the heart. The space one creates by sending forth petitions and releasing one's emotions may then become filled with the blessings conferred by the goddess. The songs to the goddess serve as the vehicle for such communion. As the verses in our collection note, Lakṣmī promises to respond when she hears the words of particular songs, offered to her with verbal precision, but, moreover, with complete devotion.[2] She promises to bestow every type of prosperity, culminating in the boon of liberation, so pleased is she with songs of praise.

CHAPTER 6

The Power of Tantric Songs

Waking Up the Goddess

Alchemy of the Goddess: The Magic of Transformation

According to the Tantric traditions, the way to achieve true prosperity is by focusing not so much on its forms as on its essence, going behind the specific expressions to the source from which they spring. In this way, the worshiper participates with the goddess in the manifestation of prosperity. Because their verses constitute the body and essence of the goddess, recitation of the Tantric songs is believed to unite the worshiper with the source of all life, all abundance, all prosperity.

As we further consider the Tantric songs invoking Lakṣmī, it becomes even more apparent that the identity of this goddess is not limited to her various physically recognizable forms and personalities, but that it is closely aligned with the *mantra*s that constitute the songs. Tantric philosophy holds that *mantras* are vehicles to the deity because they are actual embodiments of her being. Among all of the goddess's infinite forms, the most subtle—and therefore most potent—is her form as a vibration of sound. The songs in this section not only glorify the goddess, they are constructed as vehicles for preparing the worshiper to meet the goddess as she rises to the surface of his consciousness.

Awakening the Goddess Within

Tantric *sādhana*, or spiritual practice, is a continuing process of enlivening and strengthening the awareness of the goddess's presence within; the worshiper recognizes a correlation between the goddess's influence in external affairs and the establishment of awakened divine consciousness within his or her own inner being. Worshipers of Lakṣmī seek health, wealth, abundance, beauty, peace, and prosperity in every aspect of life; they may beseech her for success with very specific situations in life—passing an exam, securing employment, finding a suitable mate, giving birth to and raising healthy children, business success, a comfortable place to live—as well as more general states of being, such as mental clarity, emotional stability, and spiritual contentment. The lists are as varied and yet as stable as human concerns have been through the ages. The prosperity of Lakṣmī may be expressed in any of those particular forms, and many more, and yet in its fullest sense, the true prosperity of Lakṣmī is an abundant state of consciousness, fostering an expansive and courageous way of being as one moves through life. The wise seeker asks not only for the external manifestations of wealth, but for conscious union with the essence of true wealth at its source.

Spiritual transformation along a Tantric path entails a change of heart, of vision, and of consciousness, so that ultimately one's entire being comes into perfect alignment with the source of all. If one is to become perfected on the path of the goddess, if the divine consciousness of Lakṣmī is to be discovered within—and made manifest in every aspect of life—then one's perception must be continuously purified and expanded so as to move beyond viewing the world from the perspective of the limited self, ultimately becoming integrated with the Highest Self, the consciousness of the goddess. The Tantrika seeks to recognize the presence of the goddess that has always been there, to enliven it, and to rid the mind of obstacles in perceiving it. The esoteric path assists the worshiper in moving from an external awareness of the transformation of consciousness to a complete and steadfast interior transformation, so that one lives each moment perceiving the world through the eyes of the deity. Seeing the world through the goddess's eyes, integrating that vision into the depths of one's being, one may come to experience life as infused with the power, fearlessness, and supreme consciousness of the goddess.

Invoking Lakṣmī is, for the Tantrika, another way of asking the goddess to manifest in one's awareness so that one may perceive and experience the world not only from a limited, ego-based perspective, but through the perspective of the goddess. The one who has mastered the Tantric perspective (*dṛṣṭi*), who has become perfected (*siddha*) in the Tantric path (*sādhana*), is understood to have gained the capacity for perceiving the holistic vision. In order to obtain that vision, one seeks alignment with the supreme inner being that is the goddess. It is important to note that the Tantric practitioner does not seek to eradicate the ego, but to infuse it with divine vision. Tantra is a means to resonate more fully and securely with the world, not to lose touch with it.

Integrating the Awakened Energy

Spiritual transformation on the Tantric path entails the integration of the supreme consciousness of Mahālakṣmī into, or with, the consciousness of the devotee. The smaller self is fraught with debilitating tendencies—such as fear and limitation—that may be transmuted by the goddess, thereby allowing the worshiper to live a harmonious worldly life characterized by spiritual bravery and freedom. Although they express an esoteric understanding of the world, these texts are specifically for the use of householders, and they address ordinary obstacles to the householder's peace of mind. These may manifest as concerns about illness, disharmony in relationships, material loss—in short, anything that disrupts an easeful, abundant experience of life. The Tantric songs are actively engaged with the intent of receiving material blessings from the goddess as well as the spiritual blessing of guidance to the source of all prosperity. This achievement (*siddhi*) is recognized in the forms of material and spiritual wealth simultaneously.

In the Purāṇic songs, invoking the presence of the goddess of wealth and prosperity entails addressing a divine presence who dwells in a heavenly realm. The worshiper beseeches her to manifest in the earthly realm and tend to her supplicants, which of course she may do instantaneously, for time and space are but constructs that impose limitations on humans, not on the gods. The Tantric traditions hold that since the divine dwells within each individual, the successful supplication of the goddess is not only a matter of drawing her "down" from a heavenly realm to earth, but of waking her "up" from within the depths of one's own being.

As we have seen in the Purāṇic songs, the levels of the created universe are understood to exist on a vast continuum, often referred to as the triple world, or the three realms of heaven, earth, and the netherworlds. And again, each of these is further subdivided, with many subtle levels existing in each stratum. According to the Tantras, the entire macrocosmic universe also exists in microcosmic form within the subtle bodies of the human being. Thus the entire creation stretches outward in many levels of space and time to comprise the realms of the gods, and it stretches inward in many levels of subtle space and transcendent time to comprise the interior universe of the human being. Because divine consciousness pervades all that exists, the deities also dwell within each individual.

Within the vast comprehensiveness of Purāṇic cosmology, Lakṣmī incarnates in various subsequent world-ages. Lakṣmī abides, for example, in the heavenly realm of Vaikuṇṭha as well as in a heavenly locale within the cosmic Ocean of Milk known as the White Island. On earth, she is born in Ayodhyā as Sītā, the queen and wife of Rāma, in order to support *dharma*. For the Tantrika, all of these times and spaces exist both within and beyond human time and space. Therefore, when the goddess is addressed in the Tantric songs as dwelling in a particular heavenly location, it is understood that such a realm exists in the exterior universe as well as within the consciousness of the worshiper. A "state" is as much a level of consciousness as it is a location. A devotee of Lakṣmī petitions the goddess to remain steadfast in his home, and the Tantric devotee seeks to achieve this by anchoring awareness of the goddess steadfastly in his consciousness, as well, for just as "home" is the external abode that houses the physical body, it is the physical body that houses the subtle bodies—deep into one's consciousness and in one's very Self.

The Secret Heart of Lakṣmī *and the Goddess's Marvelous Elixir*

Just as Tantra recognizes an interior map of the body, so does Indian alchemy (*rasāyana*) consider such changes as eminently tangible within the physical and subtle bodies. This aspect of goddess worship is still relatively unexplored, and its texts and traditions remain obscure. The lengthiest, most passionate, and in many ways most intriguing song in our collection is *The Secret Heart of Lakṣmī* (*Śrī Mahālakṣmī Hṛdayam*). It consists of 108 verses plus another dozen or so introductory verses that guide the worshiper in the process of applying the text in its ritual and experiential context, moving from pure devotional lyricism to the urgent evocation of the goddess's energy to arise within the worshiper. Its verses seek to awaken the goddess and generate her mysterious elixir that effects an alchemical transformation within the body and the consciousness of the devotee.

This text comes to us without written commentary. Its colophon, that is, its scriptural signature, states only that it is contained within the *Atharvana Rahasya* (*Secrets of the Atharva Veda*). This designation refers in name, at least, to the lineage of the *Atharva Veda*, that limb of the ancient Veda containing some of the earliest recorded expressions of magical religiosity. Sometimes called the "fifth Veda," the *Atharva Veda* is a compendium of sacred formulas concerned with inner knowledge as well as spiritual communication with and influences upon the physical and material worlds, addressing such concerns as the appeasement of illnesses, rivalries, or debilitating conditions of nature and the elements. The *Atharva Veda* also contains more goddess worship than any of the other Vedas combined. The "secret" (*rahasya*) traditions of the *Atharva Veda* developed independently of the Vedas, and in a much later time period, although they were consciously aligned with the spirit of the original sacred songs and *mantra*s specifically focusing on mystic knowledge, personal transformation, and worship of the goddess.

The Secret Heart of Lakṣmī (Śrī Mahālakṣmī Hṛdayam) describes an alchemical process of transformation with the "magical elixir" of the goddess operating as the philosopher's stone, that is, the agent of change:

> O Śrī, in addition to the Wish-fulfilling Jewel
> And the Tree of Paradise,
> There exists a delightful, magic elixir
> Formed from just a portion of you.
> As this nectar moves through me,
> Touching all of my parts from head to toe,
> *Hak!* It transmutes them into a body of gold.[1]

This golden, invincible body is the one that may be attained by the Tantric worshiper who is devoted to Lakṣmī and has received even the smallest amount of her favor. The recitation enlivens the verses, and the "nectar" is an etheric manifestation of the goddess's essence. Just as the goddess takes form as the Kuṇḍalinī Śakti, or energy within the subtle body, so too does she manifest as the exquisite nectar tasted by yogis who have achieved a certain level of spiritual mastery.

The poets of the esoteric songs acknowledge that a mere glance from the goddess is enough to set the transformative process into motion. In fact, a mere glance initiates spiritual perfection (*siddhi*); however, it is a matter of the mind's catching up with the bestowal of grace that slows down the realization of that perfection. The poet thus asks for continuity in the flow of blessings so that the alchemical process of transmutation—or spiritual transformation—may become realized completely:

> O Indirā, lady of the blue lotus,
> Just a glance from you—
> And my desires

Are satisfied here in this world,
For you are the Wish-fulfilling Jewel,
The celestial tree of the gods,
And the nine eternal treasures.
And yet, a marvelous elixir there is,
Distilled from the nectar of your compassion.
Secreted from just a portion of you,
It fulfills desires beyond imagination.
May this your nectar flow with steady ease.

O Kamalā, lady of the lotus,
Just as the touch of magic elixir
Transmutes iron into gold,
So, O Mother, does the touch of your gracious glance
Transform even the most inauspicious
Into a blessing of splendid good fortune.[2]

While beholding this amazing journey into the interior realms of alchemical transformation, it is important to remember that these practices are intended to enhance the lives of the goddess's devotees—here in this world. An esoteric text specifically for householders, *The Secret Heart of Lakṣmī* therefore eloquently concludes:

O Goddess, it is you who protect
This most secret of teachings,
A scripture brought into existence
For the benefit of householders.
Let its power flourish within me.
Let me ever abide in your bounteous grace.[3]

Vibratory Essence: Engaging the Sound-Forms of Lakṣmī

Popular images often portray Lakṣmī with the lotus and urn, as these are central features of her descriptions in much of her literature. Although the golden vessel that she holds is usually understood to contain the cosmic *amṛta* (immortal nectar), *The Secret Heart of Lakṣmī* (*Śrī Mahālakṣmī Hṛdayam*) describes its contents as seeds:

O Śrī, grant me fearlessness in every moment.
Let steadfastness ever be mine.
Let me always remain joined with the resplendent one

Who bears the lotus
And the brilliant golden vessel filled with seeds.[4]

The "seeds" in the golden vessel are the sacred *bīja mantras*, the "seed-syllables" that are produced from the body of the goddess as vibratory patterns of sacred sound. These seeds are the *ova* that the goddess bears within her womb, which is represented by the beautiful golden vessel, and they hold the potentialities of all of creation.

The seed-*mantras* are the most potent names with which devotees may invoke the goddess, for they resonate with the highest essence that can be expressed in any perceptible form. Embedded within these names of Lakṣmī—these sonic extensions of the goddess—lie the essential powers of prosperity, auspiciousness, and abundant well-being. The advanced *sādhaka*, or aspirant, is able to recognize and resonate with the goddess in her most highly abstracted sound-forms, and to unlock their potency. In this sense, less is more: the less discursively understandable the words of the *mantras*, the closer they are to their undifferentiated source. The *bīja mantras* are the most potent of all, for they resonate as a core of discursive meaning but do not fit into grammatical categories for use in ordinary speech. Instead, they are expressions of divine power and essence through pure sound. Reciting the mantras invokes and releases the energy of the goddess; reciting the mantras brings one into powerful alignment with creation at its very source.

Mātṛkā Śakti *and Surfing the Cosmic Ocean*

The universe begins with sound, and Lakṣmī exists as the *mātṛkā śakti* (matrix of cosmic energy), unfurling herself into the universe, as the universe, through her sound-forms, which are expressed as the fifty-two letters of the Sanskrit alphabet. These sound-forms of the goddess are also explained as the constituents that comprise the entire universe. *Mātṛkā* refers to the goddess as the mother of the universe. The term *mātṛkā* is cognate with the Latin word *matrix* and the English words *mother* and *maternal*: the mother of the universe is the matrix or web of all existence as well as the energetic source from which it has been woven. The goddess moves in ordered expression from vowels to consonants, all of these aligned in the six linguistic categories of the Sanskrit alphabet called *varga*s. As the substance of all sound is the sonic body of the goddess, each of these categories represents a specific vibratory expression of the *mātṛkā śakti,* flowing from one level into the next like a spectrum of sound. If the goddess extends herself outward as waves of sound, it is by means of these waves that the worshiper may be conveyed back to their divine source.

This ocean of consciousness, divinity, and transformation is the very same ocean that is *saṃsāra,* which is experienced as turbulent and wearisome to those who cannot behold its divinity. The Tantrika recognizes the world's "poison" as life-renewing elixir. To the one who succeeds on the Tantric path, life is experienced as a playful dalliance between the goddess's grace and one's own actions.[5] We might say that such a person does not resist the waves of the cosmic ocean, but catches them and rides the *śakti* all the way to the far shore.

In order for the worshiper to meet the goddess and "ride the *śakti,*" there must be a place of union where the devotee and deity resonate with a similar consciousness, and it is not always possible to begin with the abstracted form that exists in the *bīja mantra*s. Various genres of Tantric *stotra*s take the worshiper closer to the goddess's level of consciousness by establishing a common ground of resonance. The *nāmastotra,* or recitation of the deity's names, for example, provides such a meeting place, for these names are *tīrtha*s, or sacred crosspoints that connect and are accessible from both realms—from the ordinary, discursive consciousness of the devotee, and from the name-sound-form of the deity. When reciting or chanting the name of the deity, the devotee has the benefit of discursive thought combined with lyrical poetry, along with the aesthetic components of rhythm (*tāla*), melody (*rāga*), and often instrumental accompaniment and dance as well. The body and heart soften and open to the power that is inherent in the names that not only describe the deity, but encapsulate her mantric essence. In our collection we have included several *nāmastotra*s to Lakṣmī.

Even before "meeting" the goddess in the recitation of her names and personalities, one may prepare for a merging of the entire consciousness by conducting *nyāsa,* a blessing in which the goddess's sound-forms are ritually placed onto the body of the worshiper. Forming a protective coating of the goddess's sacred *mantra*s upon the body inaugurates the process of worshiping her and becoming integrated with her cosmic essence. How *nyāsa* works will be explained further in a later section, on the internal structure of the Tantric songs.

"Twilight Language" and Word Play in Sanskrit

Tantric literature makes use of word play and the bending of language in particularized ways. This is known as *sāndhya bhāṣa,* or "twilight language," where meanings are scrambled and obscured, sometimes to confound the non-initiate. Some of the Tantric songs in our collection embed puzzles within the language of the text. Just as the goddess reveals herself in the world and then retreats behind her persona as Māyā (Illusion), here it is as if part of the goddess is manifest and part remains hidden in the verses. Deciphering the puzzles embedded in Tantric literature is but another motif representing one's existence on earth; part of Tantric *sādhana* consists of learning how to read to the signs, and some of the most potent signs are in the language-bodies of the goddess.

Let us consider some examples of how this works. The *Song-Formulary of the Glorious Mahālakṣmī* (*Śrī Mahālakṣmī Pañjara Stotram*) contains within it an intriguing little song, the *Six Verses on the Root Mantra* (*Mūlamantra Ṣaṭkam*). A *ṣaṭkam* is a song of praise in six (*ṣaṭ*) verses, and here, each of the verses extols an aspect of Mahālakṣmī as the *mātṛkā śakti*, following her expression as it unfolds across each of the six linguistic categories (*varga*s) of the Sanskrit alphabet. This brief yet finely constructed song invokes the goddess of prosperity in multiple layerings of her form, moving from her *bīja mantra*s, to her various names, to her unfolding as the *mātṛkā śakti*, that is, the source of all that exists and the matrix though which it expresses itself.

The malleable features of its verses, in which the linguistic components are deconstructed and recast in a new pattern, reflect the linguistic categories (*varga*s) constituting the matrix through which the fluid and mutable sonic energy of the goddess may flow. Such a song is a type of riddle to be unraveled as the various components may be extracted from one context and put together into another in order to discover yet another level of meaning. The *ṣaṭkam* begins:

> *Oṃ śrīṃ hrīṃ aiṃ klīṃ.*
> Homage to Viṣṇu's beloved, Mahāmāyā.
> *Kaṃ khaṃ gaṃ ghaṃ ṅaṃ.*
> Homage! Homage to you.
> Protect! Protect me.
> Shield! Shield my wealth, grains, and prosperity.
> Bestow! Bestow glorious success.
> Homage to Śrī. *Svāhā.*

And it concludes:

> *Oṃ śrīṃ hrīṃ aiṃ klīṃ.*
> O Kamalā, lady of the lotus,
> Be gracious! Be gracious to me.

O Mahālakṣmī, I offer you obeisance.
Homage to you, O support of the world.
Yaṃ raṃ laṃ vaṃ śaṃ ṣaṃ saṃ haṃ kṣaṃ.
Homage! Homage to you.
Protect me! Keep me in your care.
O most beguiling goddess,
Śakti of the one who surpasses all thought,
Grant me majestic power.
Grant me prosperity.
Homage to Śrī. *Svāhā.*[6]

In a manner similar to the mapping of the six verses of the *Mūlamantra Ṣaṭkam* across the Sanskrit linguistic categories (*varga*s), so too are certain words separated into their syllabic components and embedded within the texts. In the *Song-Amulet of the Bestower of Wealth* (*Dhanadā Kavacam*), the syllables of the goddess's *mantra*s are divided and placed among other words or syllables, thereby treating the individual monosyllables as if they were *bījā*s. This serves to disengage the discursive meaning from the sonic component of the words as well as to apply the power of all sound-forms onto the worshiper. For example:

Let the seed-syllable *dhaṃ* protect my head.
(Let) the seed-syllable *hrīṃ* (protect) my forehead.
Let the seed-syllable *śrīṃ* protect my face.
Let the syllable *a* protect my heart.

Let the syllable *ti* protect my abdomen.
Let the syllable *pri* protect my back.
(Let) the syllable *ye* (protect) both of my legs.
(Let) the syllable *svā* (protect) the soles of my feet.
Let the syllable *hā* cast a mantle of protection over my entire body.[7]

Here, the essence of Lakṣmī is invoked to cloak the petitioner with the goddess's powerful essence of wealth, delight, and prosperity, represented by the phonemes *dhaṃ*, *hrīṃ*, and *śrīṃ*, respectively. After this, six more syllables are invoked, and if these are extracted from the text and viewed together, they form the phrase *a-ti pri-ye svā-hā,* that is, "O dearly beloved! *Svāhā*," thus reinforcing the power of the song-amulet with the strength of the worshiper's adoration of the goddess.

The Potency of a Woman's Recitations

As in the epic and Purāṇic materials, the Tantric songs acknowledge women as living embodiments of the goddess. Because women are "extensions" (*kalā*) of the goddess's essence, they are closer to the full identification with the goddess that the Tantric songs generate. Just as the goddess is visualized carrying the round, golden urn filled with the seed-syllables that engender all life, so are women envisioned as nourishing the potent mantras within their bodies and giving birth to the fruits of their recitation. One of the *phala* ("results") verses of *The Secret Heart of Lakṣmī* (*Śrī Mahālakṣmī Hṛdayam*) offers the image of a woman literally pregnant with its verses:

> A woman impregnated
> With this scripture's sacred *mantra*s
> Gives birth to prosperity for her family,
> And her husband becomes equal
> To the lord of Śrī.
>
> Misfortune never destroys
> The lineage of a man
> Whose woman immerses herself
> In the sacred mantras of *The Secret Heart of Lakṣmī*.[8]

A woman's recitation of the *mantra*s, then, is particularly efficacious. Women by nature contain and nourish the *ova* of creation and new life. As we considered earlier, the belly-round urn containing the goddess's seed-mantras is yet another form of the female body. The most fertile environment for the seed-mantras of the goddess is the womb-essence of a woman. As she nourishes them within her own body and with the power of her recitations and intention, a woman, by virtue of her own feminine power, then may give birth to prosperity, a blessing enjoyed by the entire family and lineage.

The feature of a woman's magical nourishment of seed-syllables, and subsequently her magical power over *mantra*s and indeed of all speech, appears throughout the rich textual traditions of the Tantric goddess. In her brilliant study of Nīlasarasvatī (Blue Goddess of Speech), Loriliai Biernacki brings to light textual elucidations of such principles. In one passage that she translates from the *Bṛhannīla Tantra*, for example, we learn: "The restrictions which men contend with [in the practice of] *mantras* are not all there for women. Anything whatsoever, by whichever [means], and moreover in all ways [is attained], for women magical attainment [*siddhi*] occurs, without any doubt . . . for a woman, by merely contemplating [on the *mantra*] she in this way becomes a giver of boons. Therefore one should make every effort to initiate a woman in one's own family."[9]

If we read the Tantric texts in our collection closely, we find very clear indications that some of these texts are intended specifically for women to recite. Let us consider, for example, the *Song-Amulet of the Lotus Goddess* (*Kamalātmikā Kavacam*), a text whose *mantras* are literally applied to the body of the practitioner so as to create a mantle of power and protection, and further, to homologize the worshiper with the energies of the goddess. As with other song-amulets, the worshiper begins by systematically blessing each part of the body with the ritual placement of *mantra*s on each of its parts. Here, the worshiper is clearly female, for the prayers call for the placement of the *mantra*s "on my two breasts" (*stanadvandve*), "on my feminine private parts" (*guhye*, literally "secret" or "private"), and, reaching the head, "on the parting of my hair" (*sīmante*).[10] The latter is a "body part" that is specifically feminine and that signifies the shared essence of a woman, the goddess Lakṣmī, and auspiciousness itself. It is on the hair part that married women place red powder to signify their auspicious state of marriage.

Literary Genres of the Tantric Songs

All of the Purāṇic and Tantric songs in our collection may be designated as *stotra*s (songs of praise). The rich variety of Tantric *stotra*s, however, may be further categorized as follows.

The Hṛdayam *(Essence, Heart, "Secret Heart")*

Literally denoting "heart," the term *hṛdayam* refers to the precious, core essence of something. It lies deep at the very center, requiring a pilgrimage of sorts to approach and unravel its mysteries. When the term *hṛdayam* appears in the title of a work, it may be translated as "the heart of," or "the hidden mystery of," or "the essence of," for such a title announces the sanctity of the text and the suggestion that its contents are addressed to the initiate of an esoteric tradition. The contents of a *hṛdayam* are not always easily understood. However, as one progresses in spiritual practice, uncluttering the mind and infusing all of the faculties of perception with ever stronger currents of purifiying divine energy, the deeper meanings of such a work become increasingly clear. As well, these texts sometimes accompany esoteric traditions in which the transmission of the text, its application, and its interpretation are necessarily part of orally transmitted teachings from guru to initiated disciple.

The Kavacam *(Song-Amulet)*

Designating "armor," "amulet," or any kind of protective device, the song style known as the *kavacam*, or *kavaca stotra*, may be thought of as a verbal amulet or song-amulet. It is a song of protection. Its verses include instructions for placing (*nyās*) the *bīja mantra*s onto the body of the worshiper, constructing a mantle of protective sounds whose essence is that of the awakened deity.

The Pañjaram *(Formulary)*

The *pañjaram* is a formulary, or composite work of several different types of invocations, each of which may also stand on its own as an independent *stotra*.

The Nāmastotram *(Recitation of Names)*

As the essential energy of the deity exists within its name (*nāma*), the *nāmastotram*, or "recitation of the names," is a conduit for contemplating the deity and invoking her presence. The enunciation of the names activates the various aspects of the deity's vibratory essence. Usually a *nāmastotram* will be composed of 100, 108, 1000, or 1008 names. Sometimes the word *hundred* is used to indicate "many," so there need not be exactly one hundred epithets enumerated. However, the designation of a sacred number such as 108 or 1008 calls for an exact enumeration.

Structure of the Tantric Songs

The heart of the esoteric text is the *stotra* (song of praise). Preliminary verses serve as a preparation leading to the core text. Just as external worship entails purification of the ritual space, physical body, and interior spaces of the heart and mind before engaging in the performance of the ceremony, so does the recitation of the Tantric *stotra* engage preliminaries. These direct the worshiper's body, mind, and consciousness away from life's ordinary distractions and toward a deeper receptivity for encountering the goddess. The chanting or recitation of the *stotra* activates the syllables that are Lakṣmī's sound-body and releases their inherent power as auspicious blessings of abundance and prosperity. Many Tantric songs are prefaced by the following formulaic preliminaries that introduce the actual song of praise (*stotra*), as follows.

*Setting the Intention (*Viniyoga*)*

The *viniyoga* is the formal introduction to the work. As the literature of a tradition that is transmitted orally by those who are privileged to read and recite the sacred texts for others, such a prologue is not uncommon. The *viniyoga* is usually in prose, giving brief formulaic information about the seer of the text, its poetic meter, and, above all, its anticipated purpose and the circumstances under which it is to be recited. The following information for a Tantric song is usually included in its *viniyoga* section:

- Seer (*Ṛṣi*)

Authorship is not generally considered to be entirely human, but rather lies in a relationship between the poet, or seer, and a divine source, in which the poet perceives the verses of the text through mystic insight.

- Deity (*Devatā*)

Each of the songs is believed to have been sent to the human realm as a vehicle for communication with a particular aspect of the divine. The *devatā* is an independent, embodied aspect of the great cosmic consciousness of the deity who presides over the efficacious outcome of the song. Each of the songs in this collection is presided over by Lakṣmī, in one or in various particular formulations of her divine personality.

- Meter (*Cchanda*)

Specifically identifying the metrical pattern of the poetic verses is one way to categorize the songs for the benefit of the musicians and dancers whose performance, in some traditions, accompanies the chanting of the song. Each meter also replicates an aesthetic consideration in the variegation of the deity's sound-form as metrical rhythm (*tāla*). From this perspective, the meter is also recognized as a form or body of the deity.

- Seed-Syllable (*Bīja*)

The *bīja* is the most compact form of the deity's body in sonic form. It is literally the "seed" from which emerge all other forms of the deity's manifestation. The *bīja mantras* are grammatically untranslatable, yet they do hold discursive meanings. Just as Lakṣmī manifests in varying personalities or aspects as designated by the different names in the "deity" section of the *viniyoga,* so do these aspects manifest through specifically corresponding seed-syllables. The main seed-syllables expressing the essence of Lakṣmī are *śrīṃ* (indicating splendor and prosperity) and *hrīṃ* (indicating sustenance and delight).

- Animating Power (*Śakti*)

This is the force that launches the song into action. The specific power is that which is responsible for enlivening the particular *mantra*s of the sacred song and rendering the whole recitation efficacious. This too corresponds with the deity of the song. The animating power of the esoteric songs to Lakṣmī in our collection is either a *bīja* mantra or another component of a mantra, such as "*svāhā.*"

- Nail (*Kīlakam*)

To understand the role of a "nail" or "pin" within the context of a poetic composition, it is useful to remember that the Tantric song of praise is not only a lyrical composition, or an expression of devotional sentiment, or a philosophical missive, but, in addition, a means for generating spiritual power—for calling forth divine energy and directing it toward a specific goal in the human realm. The *kīlakam* is that which "pins down" and contains the goddess's energy so that it neither be released with dangerous abandon nor dissipate before producing auspicious results.

- Intention (*Viniyoga*)

The *viniyoga* at the conclusion of the introductory segment specifies the result expected from reciting the song. This creates a focal point in the verse-offering. Each of the songs in our collection is to invoke the prosperous nature of Lakṣmī herself: they are chanted to draw forth the goddess's blessings of health, wealth, harmonious relationships, and overall good fortune. The concluding *phala* verses reiterate the results in more specific terms, although one may address the goddess with any manner of personal concerns. Ultimately, however, it is believed that Lakṣmī's powerful boons are greater than anything a worshiper could articulate, and the intentionality of a particular song serves as but the starting point for one to establish a communicative bond with the goddess of prosperity.

Ritual Placement of Mantras *on the Body (Nyāsa)*

Literally a "placing down" or "placing onto," *nyāsa* refers to the implanting of the song's *mantras* onto the body of the worshiper. It is a blessing of the body with *mantras*. The purpose of this is to create an adamantine body, that is, to cover the physical body and thus the subtle bodies with a protective shield composed of the *bīja mantra*s of the goddess. By placing these *mantra*s onto the body and investing them with enlivening power, the adept receives the mantle of her vibratory essence upon and within his own being. Such placement may be done by forming ritual hand gestures (*mudrā*s) to touch the specified parts of the body, or by literally painting the mantras onto the body with specific substances, such as pastes of turmeric or sandalwood. By performing the preliminary *nyāsa*s, the practitioner begins the process of homologizing the "mundane" with the "divine," toward the goal of complete alignment of oneself with the consciousness of the goddess. These blessings help to activate, protect, and seal in the awakened energy on the cardinal points of the physical body that correspond with residences of deities within the subtle bodies. This highlights the use of the term *mudrā,* which literally means a *seal* and is used to designate the formation of the hands and fingers into ritualized gestures.[11]

The *nyāsa*s are presented in categories. Each of these provides an increasingly subtle way of aligning the divine *mantra*s of the song with the worshiper's body and state of consciousness.

- Ritual Placement of "The Seer, and So Forth" (*Ṛsyādi-nyāsa*)

The broadest category of preliminary *nyāsa* for reciting the songs, the ritual placement of "the seer, and so forth" entails the alignment of all of the preliminaries previously listed in the *viniyoga* section, coordinating each part of the song's introduction to a part of the worshiper's body.

The sacred song is the inner essence of the worship, and to protect its sanctity and to offer it a steadfast receptacle through which the devotee can approach the sound-form of the goddess and interact with her, the *mantras* are applied to the worshiper's body in order to construct a sanctuary where the goddess can manifest and also upon which the worshiper can focus to encounter the deity. Human, divine, aesthetic, and pragmatic forces come together to create a venue for engaging the divine presence. The seer (*ṛṣi*), the personality-form of the goddess (*devatā*), the metrical pattern (*cchanda*) with which her energy is expressed, and the other components are then homologized with parts of the worshiper's body. The first step is to align the worshiper's body with the external fabrications that will house the deity aesthetically, for these are the causes and conditions that have been woven together to generate the sacred presence. The next two rounds of *nyāsa* work on yet more subtle levels.

• *Mantra* Placement on the Hands (*Kara-Nyāsa*)

Here, the purification focuses on the energies residing in the hands, including specific locations on each of the fingers. The hands are important because they are the agents of ceremonial performance. The fingers and hands may be positioned in specific gestures (*mudrās*) to accompany the utterance of the *mantras* contained in this section of the song. By the purification and infusion of divine energy through the *mantras*, the hands become transformed and are thereafter no longer referred to as *kara* ("hands") but as *astra* ("weapons," "arrows," or "missiles"); they are transformed into vessels of concerted power to project the powerful mantras and intention of the recitation.

• *Mantra* Placement over the Entire Body (*Saṭaṅga-Nyāsa*)

One of the words for *physical body* is *ṣaṭaṅga,* meaning literally "six limbs." The "six limbs" that together constitute the physical body are: (1) the heart, (2) the head, (3) the top back of the head, (4) the "armor" [torso], (5) the "third eye" [located between the eyebrows], and (6) the "weapon" [hands]. Just as the hands become "weapons" (*astra*) when enlivened by the *mantras*, so does the torso become transformed into armor (*kavaca*) when coated with *mantras*.

We note here that the "top back of the head," which indicates a literal spot as well as the tuft of hair grown on that spot to designate ritual status, is a specifically male reference. In distinction, some verses refer instead to the "parting of the hair," which is a specifically female reference.[12]

The *ṣaṭaṅga-nyāsa* segments also specify a *bīja* ("seed") *mantra*, an instruction for placement on the body by paying homage to (or upon) that part, and a concluding verbal articulation such as *huṃ*, *vaṣaṭ*, *vauṣaṭ*, or *phaṭ*. These are strong, explosive sounds, like missiles themselves, the very ones that Vedic priests launch verbally to accompany ritual offerings. Such words, which mean something like "so be it," convey an additional volley of concentrated and steadfast sound-energy. *Phaṭ* is well known for its use in purification rituals, where its onomotopoetic, firecrackery sound is engaged to frighten away demons. Similarly, the thunderous sound of "*huṃ*" is the same ferocious roar made by the terrifying goddess Kālī as she roams the battlefield, vanquishing demonic armies.

Svāhā is another verbal form employed to seal the mantric expression. Equally powerful, though more graceful than explosive, *svāhā* is pronounced when offerings are poured into the sacred fire, an auspicious send-off to accompany those offerings to the realm of the gods. Like the previous terms, *svāhā* may, in a general sense, denote something like "so be it" or "amen." Most likely it derives from the verb *ah*, "to pervade," to which has been joined the prefix *su*, meaning "well" or "auspicious," therefore meaning "may it pervade well." In addition, *svāhā* is personified as a goddess, the consort and shared energy of Agni, the sacrificial flame. As well, the goddess Svāhā is recognized as a form of Lakṣmī.

*Meditation (*Dhyāna*)*

The *dhyāna* is a verse that describes the deity. It is both a song of praise and a means by which the worshiper may begin to focus concretely on the object of worship, to meditate upon her through visualization. It reminds the worshiper that supplications are communications with an actual presence. With the recitation and contemplation of the *dhyāna mantra*s, the worshiper may begin to experience a very real sense of the deity.

*Sacred Syllables (*Mantra*)*

Like the *dhyāna*, the presiding *mantra* helps the worshiper focus and draw forth the goddess. However, whereas the *dhyāna mantra*s evoke an image and form of the deity that is consonant with "ordinary" reality, the *mantras* here are the seed-syllables, the energetic resonances of the goddess's core being and as such elicit her cosmic essence more fully than her material expression.

Song of Praise (Stotra)

The previous four sections constitute a formal preparation of physical and subtle bodies leading to the recitation of the *stotra* itself. The worshiper's heart may have softened, and mind become calm. One may now enter a state to invoke the goddess and recognize her presence when it manifests. Within the pure space of the *stotra*, the worshiper may now offer the expressions of his or her needs, desires, and glorifications. Wishful thinking and frantic hopes give way to mature internalization of the goddess's blessings in a progressive transformation and ultimately an alignment between external circumstances and interior spiritual life.

PART THREE

Ceremony

INTRODUCTION

Invoking Lakṣmī in Ceremony

Lakṣmī Pūjā

Creating Space to Receive the Goddess

The ritual of *pūjā*, generally translated as "ceremonial worship," consists of specified actions for invoking and honoring the gods. It is performed in order to invite the deity into our space and to experience—on some level—her palpable presence. Sacred songs operate on the mantric level of sound; *pūjā* operates more tangibly in the physical, material world, working through the third dimension to draw the goddess even more fully into the earthly realm. Tradition holds that whether she is worshiped in homes, where laypeople make their offerings with varying degrees of formality, or in temples, where priests offer precise and elaborate ceremonies, the beneficent goddess Lakṣmī receives all offerings graciously. The words contained in the songs of our volume certainly attest to this; the gods themselves are recognized as worshipers of Lakṣmī, and the "fruits" (*phala*) verses enumerate the many types of blessings that gods and humans can expect to receive if the goddess is pleased.

Pūjā is conscious, even hyperconscious action. It consists of specific parts and sequences, which will be discussed next. Hindu *pūjā* engages the natural and physical world in its most splendid expression. The underlying purpose of performing a *pūjā* to any of the Hindu deities is to generate the sacred power of auspiciousness. The attitude of the *pūjā* for each deity corresponds with the essential qualities of that deity. The ceremony is in a sense an embodiment of the deity's divine personality traits and varying expressions of the fundamental essence that constitutes all things. The Lakṣmī *pūjā* is performed to arouse the power of *śrī*—a richness of being that enlivens health, wealth, beauty, prosperity, longevity, happiness, harmony, well-being, balance, glory, majesty, splendor, and luxurious bounty: As we have seen in this volume, the expressions of *śrī* are endless. The devotee consciously sends forth the offering of the ceremony with the subtle awareness that what is being offered is actually the essence of the deity herself. The performance of the ritual draws this quality from the transcendental, back into the realm of human experience. Having been immersed in the timeless essence of the sacred through performance of the ritual, one may then return to the realm of human experience refreshed and better able both to navigate its tumultuous challenges and to savor its beauty.

In performing the Lakṣmī *pūjā*, the worshiper participates in creating a sacred precinct that becomes infused with *śrī*'s essence. In contrast to the joyously piercing clamor of percussive instruments that characterize a Śiva *pūjā*, for example, the Lakṣmī *pūjā* is delivered with a sweet, tender attitude. In order to invite such qualities—or the goddess embodying those qualities—into one's presence, the worshiper must take the preparatory steps toward creating an auspicious environment, for Lakṣmī, like all of the deities, is attracted to that which is similar to herself. One summons the goddess by welcoming her into a ritual space that is replete with the abundance of Lakṣmī herself. In the preliminary rituals, even imitation is enough to inaugurate the process of drawing the goddess near. Without the conscious preparation for receiving such qualities, one essentially stalls the process before it has even begun.

To invoke auspiciousness, one must first consciously banish the inauspicious and engage in auspicious actions and ways of being. As we have previously considered, for example, Lakṣmī and her "sister" and antithetical counterpart, Alakṣmī, never dwell in the same place at the same time. Therefore, the worshiper who propitiates the deity of auspiciousness must consciously abandon any manifestations of the inauspicious. For example, as the time of the *pūjā* draws near, participants are enjoined to become conscious of their speech—to avoid gossip, abusive language, and upsetting conversations, and instead to speak gently, and of uplifting, lighthearted topics. This is both a yogic discipline and an initial engagement of Lakṣmī's energy. Sometimes, circumstances call for a separate *pūjā* beseeching the inauspicious Alakṣmī to absorb and remove negative influences before Lakṣmī can be invoked to bestow her auspicious blessings. Usually, however, the preliminary actions preceding the *pūjā* serve this purpose, and Gaṇeśa, remover of obstacles, is invoked to clear the way for the auspicious entrance of Lakṣmī.

The physical preparations for the ritual entail that the worshiper must first have bathed, dressed in clean clothing, and adorned himself or herself appropriately. The clothing need not be new, but it should be "untorn," just as, later, the offerings to the deity must not have been used or in any way "broken in" by humans; the first impressions set onto one's body and accoutrements should be instilled by the goddess herself. Similarly, the goddess must be the first to partake of the ritual offerings. This explains why the ceremonial rice grains will necessarily be "unbroken" (*akṣata*), or "unhusked," why the food offered will not have been tasted, and why the fragrance of the flowers and incense should not have been breathed in by the human participants until after the ceremony.

All *pūjās* generate a flow of cyclical interaction from the worshiper to the deity and back to the worshiper again. In the Lakṣmī *pūjā* the worshiper gathers together but a small portion of that which Lakṣmī gives to the world, and offers it back to the goddess. Lakṣmī *pūjā* features gold coins, ripe, sweet fruits, fresh flowers, sanctified water, fragrant substances, and delectable confections of honey, sugar, and milk-based ingredients—milk, of course, being the product of the sacred cow, long recognized as an embodiment of Lakṣmī. The atmosphere generated is sumptuous and sparkling, bright with the colors of red vermilion powder, golden turmeric, and fresh green leaves. These symbolize Lakṣmī's life-sustaining power as the flow of blood in the human body, the flow of monetary currency in society, and the flow of sap in all types of plants as they sustain the natural world with nourishment, medicine, shelter, refreshment, and beauty.

When the goddess receives the offerings into herself, ordinary substances such as foods and flowers are transformed into repositories of sacred potency. It is the goddess who alters one's state of consciousness, transforms one's material circumstances, and transmutes the essence of "ordinary" substances. As with other festive occasions, participants are given favors upon their departure. At the end of the ceremony the worshipers receive back the sanctified foods and flowers, which are known as *prasāda*, or "favor." What the goddess bestows upon the supplicant refers not only to the tangible goods at hand—partaking of the ritual foods, enjoying the fragrance of the flower offerings, receiving the purificatory blessing of the sacred flame by waving the right hand across the *āratī* lamp and drawing its essence across the top of one's own head, and so forth—but also receiving her blessings of health, prosperity, and the overall improvement in the circumstances of one's life. Above all, it is the deepest essence of an individual that is touched and expanded so as to receive these blessings and allow them to take root. In one's most profound experience of the Lakṣmī *pūjā*, the noise and vicissitudes of the world become absorbed back into their source; the world's dissonance collapses and leaves a resonance of the goddess's exquisite serenity. From that source, one's circumstances can unfold and begin anew, guided by the beneficent hand of the goddess of prosperity.

The Ancient Art of Hospitality

The performance of *pūjā* reflects ancient Indian customs of hospitality. The simple act of offering a comfortable haven to the traveler after a lengthy journey evolved, long ago, into an elaborate and aesthetically significant art of hospitality, in which both the host and the guest enacted specifically designated and complementary roles. Certain aspects of the ritual, such as the offering of the seat, have roots at least as old as Vedic times.[1] The motif is patterned upon receiving a guest of royal status. The complementary figure to the king would be the guru, or spiritual preceptor, in that whereas the king holds the highest worldly status, the guru is the regent of one's spiritual life. The king's throne and the guru's *gaddi*, or sacred seat, are easily transferable to a designated chair, usually the most comfortable or beautiful seat in the house. Any visitor from afar, as the stories constantly remind their listeners, is potentially a god in disguise.

By opening to accept these actions, the guest respects his designated position as gracious recipient of the host's hospitality. The guest therefore remains immobile while the host performs all of the actions. Such is the paradigm of hospitality that even were this a human guest, food and drink would be borne on trays and then presented to the one being honored; never should the guest even have to reach out and take them for himself. Related to this is the notion that the offerings have been prepared especially for the guest and none other. Further, the host does not dine *with* the guest, but watches attentively and affectionately while the guest partakes of the meal. The underlying principle is that one does everything and takes care of everything for the guest. The host enacts the role of the servant. The ancient Indian etiquette of hospitality maintains clearly designated boundaries between the one who humbles himself to serve and the one who humbles himself to receive.

Although the guest motifs were transferred to the ritualized hospitality toward the gods as a means of invoking them, honoring them, and seeking their blessings, it was understood that the gods do not actually require any of these attendances. As is well recognized in the literature, the gods neither thirst nor hunger, their feet never touch the ground, they do not perspire, they do not cast shadows, and no matter how dusty or dirty the environment might be, they remain unsullied. Devotees, however, participate in the details of the ceremony *as if* the gods needed these things. Certainly, the elaborate forms that *pūjā* may take—and again, elaborateness is not a requirement, especially in daily offerings—serve the supplicant as much as they do the deity being served. This is in part due to the aesthetic power inherent in the symmetry, discipline, and beauty of the ritual. The intense and abundant overtures with brilliant colors, aromatic fragrances, and chanting serve to awaken the senses and direct them toward a heightened experience of the deity. The effects of a *pūjā* are to compel the mind's chatter to be still and to move away from the distractions of mundane life, in order to allow the supplicant to encounter divine consciousness.

The purpose of *pūjā* is to call forth and receive the presence of the deity. Performed to its highest standards, *pūjā* culminates with the host and guest exchanging roles. The devoted worshiper now becomes the recipient of the abundant gifts and blessings of the deity. Here, though, there is a departure from exact symmetry, for that which the goddess confers always exceeds what the devotee has offered.

Structure of the Ceremony

The Lakṣmī *pūjā* that we present in this volume is an example of *smārta pūjā*, "*smārta*" indicating an orthodox tradition of worship based on the *smṛti*, that is, "remembered" or traditional literature of the Vedic tradition, which includes the voluminous lore on deity worship contained in the epics and Purāṇas. Although *smārta pūjā* is in its strictest sense performed by priests, this type of worship does not carry the exclusivity of the Vedic rituals. *Pūjā* indeed has deep roots in the Tantric traditions, and its present form may actually be more "Tantric" than "Vedic." *Smārta pūjā* therefore has always had a certain degree of malleability, and it is not uncommon for householders to perform these rituals themselves. The Lakṣmī *pūjā* that we present here was compiled by Pandit Rajesh Dixit and published in *Śrī Lakṣmī Upāsanā*, the same manual for Lakṣmī's worship that has provided the Sanskrit texts for most of the songs in our volume.

The structure of *pūjā* traditionally contains sixteen *upacāras*, which may be translated as ritual attendances, offerings, or reverent actions performed for the deity. Each ritual attendance is accompanied by the recitation of a verse, usually from the *smṛti* literature. The original paradigmatic structure of the *pūjā* contains sixteen *upacāras* to accompany the recitation of each of the sixteen verses of the *Puruṣa Sūktam* (Vedic *Hymn to the "Cosmic Man"*). Although modifications developed regarding the verses sung and in the details of some of the ritual substances, the general motifs covered by the sixteen ritual actions continue to adhere to the original structure of the *pūjā*. On the other hand, some traditions, such as the Śrī Vidyā and the Pāñcarātra, celebrate a version of Lakṣmī *pūjā* in which the sixteen *upacāra*s are accompanied by a verse of the *Śrī Sūktam* instead of the *Puruṣa Sūktam*.[2]

The entire ritual procedure as presented in the *Śrī Lakṣmī Upāsanā* consists of six preliminary actions, followed by twenty-seven ritual attendances. These adhere to the general format of the traditional sixteen-part *pūjā*, and they can easily be seen to follow the general guidelines of the sixteen ritual attendances (*upacāra*s); the main difference is that some of the actions are enumerated with subcategories.

We turn now to our text of a Lakṣmī *pūjā*. We introduce each ritual attendance with a brief explanation, which is followed by the translation of its offertory verse. At the end of the text is an outline articulating the correspondence between two enumeration systems of the ritual procedures.

Lakṣmī Pūjā Text

Preparation and Purification

Prayer for Well-being (Svasti-vācana)

In the opening mantras, the Vedic gods are invoked for overall well-being (*svasti*) and for the success of the ceremony. These are the ancient deities who are extolled in the earliest written scriptures of the Brahmanic tradition as presiding over the forces of nature. There is very little mention of them again in the rest of the *pūjā*, but their invocation here at the outset creates an important statement just in their inclusion; it lends the authenticity and the power of the *śruti*, the revelatory scriptures that were "heard" by the earliest sages and that have their origins in heaven itself. Calling upon the names of these deities constitutes the recitation of a powerful Vedic *mantra*, thus offering protection in the highest as well as undeniable continuity of a sacred tradition.

These deities are considered to be intensely potent entities whose identity hovers in the space between the undifferentiated cosmic essence of the universe and its expression as heavenly presences and the forces of earthly natural phenomena. These include, for example, the dawn, the day, the pole-star, rainstorms, and the waters. They dwell in the sound of their *mantra*s, and recitation of their names releases their power. Invoking them generates their thunderous presence, stirring up the requisite surge of primal energy to propel the *pūjā* into its first motions.

Prayer for well-being

Oṃ. May Indra, lord of expansive powers, grant well-being.

May Pūṣān grant well-being.
May Bṛhaspati grant well-being.
May the gods of the universe grant well-being.

Oṃ. May the vital powers of the earth rise up to greet us.
May the vital powers of the plants rise up to greet us.
May the vital powers of the sky rise up to greet us.
May the vital powers of the cardinal directions rise up to greet us.

Oṃ. Salutations to the spirit of fire,
To the spirit of the winds,
To the spirit of the sun,
To the spirit of the moon,
To the Vasus,
To the Rudras,
To the Ādityas,
To the Maruts,
To the gods of the universe,
To Lord Bṛhaspati,
To Lord Indra,
And to Lord Varuṇa.

Oṃ. May there be peace in the heavens,
Peace on the earth,
Peace in the waters,
Peace in the herbal kingdoms,
Peace in the forests,
Peace among the gods of the universe.
May the peace of *brahman* be unto all.
Peace. Peace. Peace.
Let there be peace, peace, peace.

Purification of the Worshiper (Pavitrīkaraṇa)

The purification of the worshiper actually begins when the devotee bathes and dresses in clean clothing in preparation for the ritual. At this point, however, there is a further purification in which the worshiper touches his head three times with water while reciting the "verse for the purification of the worshiper." This takes the preparation from the gross physical level of the body into the various levels of the subtle body.

Verse for the purification of the worshiper

Whether in a state of purity or impurity,
The one who remembers the lotus-eyed lord
Becomes ritually pure, within and without.

Clearing Away Disruptive Spirits (Bhūta-śuddhi)

Bhūta refers to a restless spirit, often the ghost of a person who has suffered a violent or untimely death, or simply a spirit that lingers restlessly on the earth, unwilling or unable to move beyond. A *bhūta* can also be a disembodied being that is maleficent by nature. Either type of entity can obstruct the success of the ritual. *Śuddhi* denotes cleansing or purification. The *bhūta-śuddhi*[1] mantras are recited in order to pacify and/or send away disruptive spiritual influences, clearing the sacred space to receive the auspicious presence of the deity.

The worshiper should clasp a bundle of sacred sweetgrass (*dūrvā*), unhusked rice, and flowers in the right hand, and dipping it into water, he should use it to sprinkle the area while reciting the "verse for clearing away disruptive spirits."[2] Some advise the worshiper also to kick the earth three times with the heel of the left foot during this purification.[3]

Verse for clearing away disruptive spirits

By the powerful authority of Śiva
Let the lingering earthbound spirits be gone
And the disruptive spirits hereby be destroyed.

Verses for Meditation on Lord Gaṇeśa (Śrī Gaṇeśa dhyāna mantra)

Widely venerated as the remover of obstacles and the lord of auspicious beginnings, Gaṇeśa is invoked at the outset of any important enterprise, whether secular or religious. No *pūjā* would be undertaken without first seeking the blessings of the elephant-headed god to ward off negative influences and to ensure a clear path between the worshiper and the deity invoked in the ceremony.

Verses for meditation on Lord Gaṇeśa

Oṃ. Salutations to the one with a beautiful face.
Salutations to the one with a single tusk.
Salutations to the red-hued one.
Salutations to the one with elephant ears.
Salutations to the pot-bellied one.

Salutations to the handsome one.
Salutations to the one who destroys blockages.
Salutations to the one who removes obstacles.
Salutations to the one with the grey banner.
Salutations to the lord of the spirit-troops.
Salutations to the one with the moon on his brow.
Salutations to the elephant-headed one.

There is no obstacle that cannot be overcome
By a person who recites or listens to these twelve names—
When beginning studies,
When getting married,
When entering or departing any place,
When meeting in assembly or on a battlefield,
Or when moving forward in any situation.

Let us meditate on the god
With the pleasing countenance,
Who has four arms,
Is dressed in moon-white garments,
And who pacifies all forces of disruption.

Statement of Intention (Saṅkalpa-vākya)

Although in its most general sense *pūjā* is performed to receive the blessings of the deity in whatever form the deity wishes to bestow them, a specific intention should be verbalized by the worshiper. The statement of intention draws the focal point to psychological reality and away from mere theoretical abstraction. It emphasizes the clarity and reality of the worshiper's expectation, and it compels the worshiper to reflect upon his human condition and his relationship with the deity. The statement of intention here does not have a designated mantra or verse, for these words are unique to each worshiper.

Verses for Meditation on the Goddess (Dhyāna Mantras)

Here the worshiper begins to focus on the deity to be invoked in the ceremony by reciting *mantras* for visualization. These describe her physical appearance, clothing and other accoutrements, her beneficent deeds, and so forth. The preparatory segment of the ritual guides the worshiper's consciousness to shift, ever so subtly, from ordinary consciousness to the relaxed, meditative state that is more conducive to reception of the deity. Physical and mental preparations have initiated the process; here, the focus hovers between mental imagery, which serves an intellectual purpose, and the resonance of the Sanskrit syllables as *mantras*, which serve to create awareness beyond intellectual perception; the *mantras* here have discursive meaning and yet they transcend that as well.

As has been noted with some of the other songs of praise in our collection, the extraction and inclusion of verses from one song to the next is a feature of this genre of devotional literature, especially where authorship remains anonymous. Five verses are presented here for meditation on the goddess. Four of these five also appear in the well-known *Eight Verses Praising Mahālakṣmī* (*Mahālakṣmyaṣṭakam Stotram*).[4]

Verses for meditation on Lakṣmī

Salutations to you, O Supreme Enchantress,
Abode of good fortune,
Adored by all of the gods,
Holding in your hands a conch, discus, and mace,
O Mahālakṣmī, salutations to you. 1

Salutations to you, O Rider of the Eagle.
O terror of the hostile spirit Kola,
O destroyer of all iniquities,
O Goddess,
O Mahālakṣmī, salutations to you. 2

O lotus-seated goddess,
Embodiment of Ultimate Reality,
O Supreme Lady, Mother of the Universe,
O Mahālakṣmī, salutations to you. 3

O Goddess clothed in white,
Adorned with a dazzling array of magnificent jewels,
You are the foundation of the world
And its divine mother.
O Mahālakṣmī, salutations to you. 4

May my home ever be blessed
With the presence of Śrī,
That wholly auspicious goddess

Who embodies herself as the divine Lakṣmī
Seated on a lotus,
With lotus in hand,
Bearing a golden urn inlaid with jewels,
Dressed in the most resplendent apparel,
Who has eyes like lotus petals,
A slender waist,
5 And rounded hips that curve like lotus leaves.

Heart of the Ceremony: Receiving the Goddess

Invocation (Āvāhana)

Here begins the *pūjā* proper. The devotee invokes the goddess with words of praise.

Verse of invocation

Oṃ.
O you of the lovely eyes
Who bear the lotus in your hand
And who bear all the gods within your majestic being,
O Goddess, mother of the entire creation,
1 I invoke you!

Seat (Āsana)

The goddess is invited to be seated. In addition to providing comfort to the divine guest, the seat serves to anchor the ritual in time and space with a solid foundation and focal point. It literally establishes the presence of the goddess.

Verse for offering the seat

Please accept this beautiful lotus seat of brilliant gold,
2 Resplendently ornamented with magnificent gems.

Water for Bathing the Feet (Pādya)

Bathing the feet is an ancient custom of hospitality whereby the host receives the honored guest in a physical display of graciously attentive pampering. An important feature of this aspect of hospitality is that the host performs the action for and upon the guest; the graceful pouring of water upon the feet is an intimate and humbling way for the host to receive the guest. Washing the feet provides cleansing and refreshment as well as the ritual purification to remove defilements that may have been collected on the journey or indeed anywhere that lies outside of the sanctified space. The soles of the feet are believed to be particularly susceptible to the absorption of impurity, whether physical, emotional, mental, or spiritual.

Verse for bathing the feet

The water for bathing your feet
Has been collected from sites of holy pilgrimage
And is mixed with sandal and other perfumes.
O Goddess,
O you who adore your devotees,
Accept my offering. 3

Fragrant Water (Arghya)

Arghya is water into which fragrant and aromatic substances, such as sandalwood paste, have been mixed, and it is offered for refreshing the face and mouth.

Verse for offering the fragrant water

Accept my gift of refreshing water
Mixed with eight fragrant substances,
And served to you in a vessel of gold.
O Mahālakṣmī, salutations to you. 4

Pure Water for Sipping (Ācamana)

The goddess is offered pure water to sip as refreshment after partaking of the flavored offerings.[5]

Verse for offering the water for sipping

To the *śakti* of the entire world,
Who is lauded by Brahmā, Viṣṇu, Śiva,
And the other gods,
I present water for sipping.
O Mahālakṣmī, accept this offering. 5

Bathing (Snāna)

The ritual bath consists of the pouring of sacred substances over the image of the deity. If the physical image could be damaged in some way by actual contact with the bathing materials, these may be poured over a betel nut or simply offered reverently and poured into a bowl before the image. The first of the bathing ingredients is holy water (ideally Ganges water, which may be substituted with any other holy water or water collected from a river on the day of the *pūjā*).

The other necessary ingredients are known collectively as *pañcāmṛta*, "the five nectars": milk, yogurt, ghee (clarified butter), honey, and jaggery (raw brown sugar made from palm sap). Some texts and worship manuals advise that these five nectars should be presented in order, so that the oilier substances (due to their milk or butter content) are followed by the more astringent ones, leaving the body fresh afterward and facilitating the final offering of pure water.[6] The milk products are especially significant because these are derived from the sacred cow, a form of the goddess Lakṣmī. Further, each of these five auspicious substances is said to represent a particular aspect of divine power as it manifests on earth. The *Aitareya Brāhmaṇa* notes that yogurt is "power in this world," ghee is "the brilliance of animals," sugar is the "distilled sweetness of plants," and honey is "the sap in plants and trees."[7] These substances are embodiments of Lakṣmī and therefore they represent not only the goddess's sweet and powerful sanctity that lies at the center of all things in nature, but the tenacity and purity of her vital energy in the world. With each new cycle of life, the goddess transmits her essence as fluid energy from one generation of living beings to the next.

The ceremonial worship of various other deities also includes the five auspicious substances. At every such *pūjā*, as they pay homage by offering these substances, the worshipers also pay honor *to* the substances, thereby also invoking Lakṣmī herself. How much more potent, then, is the worship of Lakṣmī when she is offered the very substances that she embodies; in this sense, Lakṣmī *pūjā* embraces the essence of every *pūjā*, and every other deity worshiped in this way can be seen as a manifestation of Lakṣmī, quintessential embodiment of auspiciousness.

Verse for the bathing

O Mother of the Universe!
O you who adore your devotees!
Accept for your bath

This auspicious Ganges water
Mixed with the five immortal nectars. 6

Clothing (Vastrayugma)

After being bathed and patted dry, the deity is dressed in fresh, new clothing of a pure material, ideally silk. Traditionally, images of Lakṣmī depict her wrapped in a red sari with gold borders.

Verse for clothing the image

O Mother of the World,
I present you with a stunning garment
Of fine woven fabric.
O Goddess, graciously accept these gorgeous new clothes. 7

Milk-and-Honey Drink (Madhuparka)

Madhuparka is a sweet milk-based drink whose most important ingredient is honey (*madhu*). It also usually contains yogurt and cardamom. Serving *madhuparka* is widely recognized as a way to express honor when receiving a guest.[8]

Verse for offering the milk-and-honey drink

O Goddess,
Accept the sweet contents
Of this golden vessel,
A gold-colored mixture of
Yogurt, milk, and honey. 8

Ornamentation (Ābharaṇa)

Adorning the body is regarded as a highly auspicious action, and the visual effect of embellishing the image of the goddess of wealth amplifies the quality of her abundance and luxurious splendor. Furthermore, the wearing of ornaments serves not only to enhance beauty but to form a protective coating over the wearer. Pure gold is believed to act as a reflector against inauspicious or debilitating forces. As attested to in the manuals on the sacred science of gems and minerals, each precious gem and metal is valued not only for its beauty but for its inherent potencies—whether as prophylaxis against negative forces, many of which are attributed to the interference of malevolently positioned planets and other astrological configurations—or as attractors and magnifiers of auspicious planets and other forces. Beauty can be disarming, and ornamentation enhances beauty.

Of course, as has been stated before, the goddess does not *need* any of this, but rather an image so adorned exudes the commanding and palpable presence of beauty, luxury, splendor, and invincible power.[9]

Let us add a word here concerning a difference in the *pūjās* for male and female deities. As noted above, the paradigm for *pūjā* is based upon worship of a male deity, and in the offertory sequences, the "clothing" (*vastra*) of the image is followed by "that which is placed after or upon the clothing" (*upavastra*). In the worship of a male deity, the "clothing" consists of an uncut cloth to be wrapped and folded onto the lower part of the body as well as a shawl to drape over the upper part. What follows is the placement of the sacred thread, which is conferred upon males of the upper castes to signify their religious status as "twice-born" (*dvija*).[10]

Where ceremony for male deities calls for investiture, the Lakṣmī *pūjā* instead calls for ornamention (*ābharaṇa*), and instead of the singular placement of the sacred thread there are five independent ritual attendances in which the goddess is adorned with various types of jewelry, perfumed ointments, and sacred powders, all emblematic of the auspicious state of the goddess.[11]

Verse for offering the ornaments

O Goddess,
Accept these jeweled bracelets.
Take delight in strings of pearls,
Cat's-eye gems,
9 And precious ornaments of every kind.

Sandalwood Paste (Candana)

Preparing sandalwood paste is a time-consuming endeavor that requires both patience and a fair amount of physical strength. The wood of the sandal tree is ground continuously in a circular motion, eventually producing a highly perfumed, gold-colored residue. This exquisitely fragrant paste may be blended with other aromatic unguents, as is indicated in the following verse.

Verse for offering the sandalwood paste

Please accept your anointment of sandalwood paste
Blended with camphor, aloe, and musk.
Salutations, O you who adore your devotees. 10

Red Sandal (Rakta candana)

A variety of sandalwood, red sandal is especially significant to the goddess because of its golden-red color. Certain rituals in the *Lakṣmī Tantra*, for example, specify the offering of "a million pieces of red sandal" in order to call forth the presence of Lakṣmī.[12]

Verse for offering the red sandal

Please accept my offering of red sandal
Blended with fragrant essential oils
Of coral tree and sandalwood. 11

Vermilion Powder (Sindūra)

Used widely to signify the auspicious life-force, *sindūra* is a bright red powder that is the quintessential emblem of the goddess. Red is the color of blood, the conduit of *śakti*, the power of the life-force. A mark of *sindūra* on a woman's forehead, or in the parting of her hair, indicates that she dwells in *saubhāgya*, that is, the auspicious state of good fortune, especially in the form of a happy marriage. As part of the *pūjā*, the auspiciousness generated in the ceremony is sealed into the forehead—seat of the "third eye" of mystical sight—with the application of the red powder. This seal, called a *tilakam*, is applied both to the image of the goddess and to the participants in the ceremony.

The qualities of transformation and life-energy are not necessarily merely symbolic, for *sindūra* is a powdered form of red mercuric oxide that features in the alchemical traditions of medieval India. In English, *sindūra* is known both as vermilion and red lead. Red lead is also a common name of *darada*, mercuric sulfide, or cinnabar, extolled in the alchemical traditions of India[13] and China[14] for promoting vitality, longevity, and even immortality. Perhaps because it bears similarities—both alchemical and symbolical—to mercuric sulfide, *sindūra* is also called synthetic cinnabar,[15] reinforcing its identification with unconquerable vital energy and the power of transformation.

Verse for offering the vermilion

O Goddess, with great devotion
I offer this vermilion.
O beloved Goddess,
Accept this auspicious marking
12 Of bright red vermilion.

Red Powder (Kumkuma)

Known in English by its Indic vernacular name, *kumkum* is another red powder that is used as a forehead adornment to symbolize the energizing power of the goddess and auspiciousness in general. As such it resembles *sindūra,* although it is constitutionally quite different, for *sindūra* is a metallic powder, whereas *kumkum* is ground from vegetable substances—either saffron or red turmeric.[16]

Verse for offering the kumkum

Kumkum is sacred.
It grants every desire.
Kumkum is the embodiment of earthly delight,
Exquisite happiness,
And the auspicious state of a happy marriage.
13 Kindly accept this *kumkum.*

Perfumed Oils and Unguents (Sugandhita taila)

Pleasant fragrances attract the goddess, for they are manifestations of her essence. Consider, for example, the *Hymn to Śrī* (*Śrī Sūktam*): "I invoke that goddess Śrī,/ Who reveals herself through scent."[17] According to *pūjā* instructions in the *Viṣṇudharmaśāstra,* "Unguents should be one or more out of sandalwood, pine tree paste, musk, camphor, saffron, [or] nutmeg."[18]

Verse for anointing with fragrant unguents and oils

O Supreme Lady,
Please accept my offering of anointment
With a wonderful mixture of essential oils
14 And fragrant perfumes.

Flowers (Puṣpa)

Ideally, flowers offered to Lakṣmī should be brightly colored and/or sweetly scented, although not so much as to be overpowering.[19] The particular flowers cited in the following verse are paradigmatic of any flower offering to the goddess. The devotee should refrain from inhaling their fragrance until after the *pūjā* has been completed, for just as with the other gifts to the goddess, they should be savored first by the one to whom they are offered. At the end of the *pūjā*, these offerings will be distributed back to the devotees as *prasāda*, or blessed favors.

Verse for the flower offering

Please accept these heavenly blossoms
From the trees of paradise—
Mandāra, pārijāta, pāṭala, and *ketakī.*
Salutations to you! 15

Sweetgrass (Dūrvā)

Dūrvā is a type of sweetgrass regarded as a sacred substance and sometimes venerated as a goddess.[20] It is considered to have nutritious and cooling properties. Its use in ceremony as one of the ritual attendances (*upacāra*) is unique to the Lakṣmī *pūjā.* This may be due to its role in the story of the Churning of the Ocean, where Lakṣmī brings forth the cherished golden urn of immortal nectar from its depths. When the anti-gods are about to steal the vessel, the eagle Garuḍa swoops down and grabs it in his talons, and, as he flies away, some of the nectar falls to earth, landing on a section of *dūrvā*, thereby charging the grass with sacred power for all time.[21]

Verse for offering the sweetgrass

O most lovely and beneficent Goddess
Who arose from the Ocean of Milk
To the joy of Viṣṇu and all of the gods,
Accept this sweetgrass,
Now and evermore. 16

Incense (Dhūpa)

Dhūpa is a soft, gummy, and extremely sweet-smelling tree resin that is set upon coals and burnt as incense. In more recent times, *agarbatti* ("stick incense"), formed by rolling and pressing the powdered aromatic essences onto a thin sliver of wood, is also burnt as a fragrant offering, although the traditional *dhūpa* is considered to be of greater purity and potency.

Verse for offering the incense

The lord of the forest
Yields this highly perfumed incense
Whose fragrance charms the hearts of all the gods.
17 O Goddess, accept this fragrant offering.[22]

Clay Lamp (Dīpaka)

This is the offering of a small bowl-shaped clay lamp (*dīpaka*) with a single flame, fueled with ghee to which camphor has been added. Also called *dīpa*, this is the derivation of the name of the festival of lights, Dīpāvalī, which refers to the "lamps" (*dīpa*) spread out in "rows" (*āvalī*) to attract Lakṣmī and lead her into one's home.[23]

Verse for offering the clay lamp

This lamp of camphor and ghee
Dispels darkness and delights the heart.
18 Please accept this light, O Supreme Queen.

Food (Naivedya)

The simplest food offerings consist of fruits, unrefined brown sugar, and puffed rice. The verses here indicate attention to aesthetic sophistication as well, with a meal containing the "six savors" (*ṣaḍrasa*), which are sweet (*madhura*), sour (*amla*), salty (*lavaṇa*), pungent (*kaṭuka*), bitter (*tikta*), and astringent (*kaṣāya*).

Verse to accompany the food offering

O Goddess,
Accept for your enjoyment
This delectable meal
Prepared with the six exquisite savors.
19 O Goddess Lakṣmī, salutations to you!

Refreshing Water for Sipping (Ācamanīya)

As in "pure water for sipping" (*ācamana*), the goddess is offered water to sip. This time, a small amount of cooling camphor has been added, appropriately astringent for clearing the palate after a meal.

Verse to accompany the water for sipping

I offer water, cool and clear,
Enhanced with refreshing camphor perfume.
Accept this water for sipping, O Great Queen. 20

Betel-nut Confection, or Paan (Tāmbūla)

Tāmbūla is a confection in which the astringent nut of the betel palm (*Areca catechu*) is mixed with other ingredients such as cardamom, camphor, nutmeg, clove, saffron, almond, and coconut, and folded in a fresh, green betel leaf upon which has been spread a thin layer of *cuunam* (a white paste of lime, or calcium hydroxide). This delicious mixture is chewed after a meal to refresh the palate, aid digestion, and sweeten the breath.[24] It is widely known by its Indic vernacular name, *paan*.

Verse for offering the paan

Graciously accept this confection of *paan*—
Areca nut, cardamom, camphor, and clove
Mixed in an aromatic blend
And folded together with betel-nut leaves. 21

Fruit (Phala)

Here we may detect a subtle change in the *pūjā*'s focus. With the offering of fruit (*phala*), the attention begins to shift slightly away from the deity and toward the results (*phala*) to be obtained by the devotee as a result of the ritual actions. This is a pattern that we have recognized in the songs of praise, where glorification of the deity is followed by the verses articulating the fulfillment of the devotee's desires.

Fruits that are round in shape, sweet, succulent, and of bright color are best suited as offerings to Lakṣmī. The coconut is often called *śrīphalam*, meaning "Śrī's fruit," or "auspicious fruit." It may be adorned with red powder (*kumkuma*) and sacred ash (*bhasma*), and set with banana leaves upon an urn (*kalaśa*) filled with water as a representation of the goddess; the waters in the belly-shaped pot (as the coconut itself) are reminiscent of the amniotic fluids of a pregnant woman or of the wide, round earth containing the life-yielding seas.

Verse for the fruit offering

Through the offering of fruit
Everything comes to fruition,
Even the three worlds,
Complete with the animate and inanimate.
By offering this fruit,
22 Let me obtain my heart's desires.

Gold Coin or Money (Dakṣiṇā)

As with all the other offerings in the *pūjā*, the devotee presents the goddess with a gift that she has already actually provided, so that it may be blessed by her and returned back multifold. The offering of gold typifies the invocation of the goddess of wealth. As the songs elsewhere in this volume attest, Lakṣmī is recognized as manifesting in the form of gold coins and in the precious element of gold itself, for the purity of its constitution, the beauty of its dazzling radiance, and the timelessness of its monetary value. In modern times *dakṣiṇā* may also take form as any type of money or currency, although gold, with all of its resonant meanings, is still considered the ideal *pūjā* offering.

Verse for the gold coin offering

Gold is the very seed of fire.
Born from within the depths of Lord Brahmā,
It therefore bestows the fruit of endless merit.
23 O Goddess, grant me peace.

Waving of Lights (Nīrājana)

Somewhat more elaborate than the clay lamp (*dīpaka*) previously offered, the lamp used here is usually made of brass and contains five small cup-shaped indentations into which are placed hand-rolled cotton wicks soaked in ghee. The worshiper grasps the handle of this lamp in his or her right hand and waves it before the deity in a circular, sweeping motion, creating brilliant streams of light. When ghee fuels a fire, it casts a flame of penetrating luminescence and exquisite beauty.

As in the Vedic sacrifice (*yajña*), fire is a form of the deity and constitutes a conduit between the heavens and the earth. Like the auspicious flame of the Vedic fire, the flame offered in *pūjā* is regarded as an embodiment of Lakṣmī. So too does Lakṣmī inhabit the fuel for this flame, as ghee is a perfectly distilled product of the sacred cow, herself a form of Lakṣmī.

As has been discussed, the multiple components of the *pūjā* may be modified according to individual circumstances. Waving the lights, however, is the one indispensable segment of any *pūjā*. In the vernacular languages the waving of lights is called *āratī*, and so central is this ritual segment that *āratī* may constitute a ceremony unto itself. In this case, a small ghee lamp is placed on a silver tray adorned with flowers, *kumkum*, uncooked white rice, and turmeric, and the entire tray is waved in a circular motion before the image of the deity.

Verse for the waving of lights

This lamp has been prepared with loving devotion.
O Supreme Lady, please accept its light
And allow it to pervade the four directions,
Dispelling the darkness of all the worlds. 24

Circumambulation (Pradakṣiṇā)

Pradakṣiṇā means literally "toward the right." Here the devotee circumambulates the sacred image by positioning the right (i.e., auspicious) side of his own body toward the image while walking around it in a clockwise direction.

Verse for the circumambulation

Whatever evils may have been committed—
Even the taking of a brahman's life—
The residues of these actions shall be destroyed
With every step around the sacred center.[25] 25

Handful of Flowers (Puṣpāñjali)

In distinction to the previous offering of flowers, here flowers (*puṣpa*) are cradled within the worshiper's folded palms (*añjali*), itself an honorific gesture of greeting and hospitality. The cupped hands containing the petals are held upward and open, and then the palms slowly move apart to release a graceful shower of petals before the image.

Verse for offering the handful of flowers

Tenderly I offer this handful of flowers—
Ketakī, citrus, jasmine, and more.
Accept these sweetly scented blossoms.
26 O Goddess, praises to you.

Farewell (Namaskāra)

In a complementary action to the opening invocation, the devotee now brings the formal part of the *pūjā* to a close by bidding farewell to the honored guest. Just as the guest was invited to enter and fill the space within the sacred boundaries, so too are those boundaries acknowledged and dissolved at the conclusion of the ceremony as the goddess is given leave to return "home." For this reason, some texts refer to the final part of the *pūjā* as *visarjana*, or the "sending forth."

Although her entire essence is never fully contained by the *pūjā* or by any human ceremony or activity, the goddess allows a part of herself to manifest within the confines of human space and time. In so doing she transforms the realm of the *pūjā* into a sacred space in which time stands still and ordinary human activity is suspended. The *pūjā* is performed as much to experience the goddess's presence within that timeless framework as it is to savor her lingering resonance throughout the ordinary activities that are to resume.

Verse for the farewell

Salutations to you, O Beloved of Viṣṇu,
O you who bestow boons on all of the gods.
If you have been pleased with these offerings,
27 Then please grant us your favor, again and again.

Outline of the *Lakṣmī Pūjā*

Following is a list of the ritual attendances (*upacāras*) for the heart of the Lakṣmī *pūjā* as presented in *Śrī Lakṣmī Upāsanā*, edited by Pandit Rajesh Dixit. As previously discussed, the format of *pūjā* often enumerates sixteen ritual attendances to correspond with the sixteen standard verses of the *Hymn to Śrī* (*Śrī Sūktam*). Because our text follows a *smārta* format using selections from other sacred texts to accompany its attendances, it actually incorporates twenty-seven separate steps. The following outline demonstrates that, regardless of these variations, the sixteen-part format remains as the underlying structure, allowing diversity of expression without compromising the integrity of the ritual. For the sake of comparison, I have numbered and categorized the attendances of our text in order to illustrate how its components reflect the paradigmatic sixteen-*upacāra* pattern.[26]

1. Invocation (*Āvāhana*)
2. Offering the seat (*Āsana*)
3. Water for bathing the feet (*Pādya*)
4. Fragrant water for refreshing the face (*Arghya*)
5. Pure water for sipping (*Ācamana*)
6. Bathing (*Snāna*)
7. Clothing (*Vastrayugma*)
8. Milk-and-honey drink (*Madhuparka*)
9. Adornment
   a. Ornamentation (*Ābharaṇa*)
   b. Sandalwood paste (*Candana*)
   c. Red sandal (*Rakta candana*)
   d. Vermilion powder (*Sindūra*)
   e. Red powder (*Kumkuma*)
10. Perfumed oils and unguents (*Sugandhita taila*)
11. Vegetative offerings
   a. Flowers (*Puṣpa*)
   b. Sweetgrass (*Dūrvā*)
   c. Incense (*Dhūpa*)
12. Clay lamp (*Dīpaka*)
13. Food
   a. Food (*Naivedya*)
   b. Refreshing water for sipping (*Ācamanīya*)
   c. Betel-nut confection, or *paan* (*Tāmbūla*)
   d. Fruit (*Phala*)
14. Gold coin or money (*Dakṣiṇā*)
15. Waving of lights (*Nīrājana*)
16. Farewell[27]
   a. Circumambulation (*Pradakṣiṇā*)
   b. Handful of flowers (*Puṣpāñjali*)
   c. Farewell (*Namaskāra*)

PART FOUR

Song

Vedic Hymns to Lakṣmī

Hymn to Śrī
(*Śrī Sūktam*)

Draw unto me, O sacred fire, the goddess Lakṣmī,
The resplendent, the golden,
Doe-like, moon-lustrous,
Garlanded in silver and in gold. 1

Draw unto me, O sacred fire, that goddess Lakṣmī,
The constant one
In whose presence I shall be blessed
With gold, horses, and loyal friends. 2

The procession of the goddess draws near,
With horses, chariots, and
Trumpeting elephants who announce her arrival.
Let the goddess Śrī approach me. 3

I invoke that goddess Śrī,
Who manifests as golden light.
She blazes with the effulgence of fire
Yet glistens like soothing, cool waters.
Seated on a lotus,
The lotus-hued one
Smiles benevolently.
Contented, she bestows contentment. 4

I seek refuge in Śrī,
Who manifests as the world's abundance.
I seek refuge in the one garlanded with lotuses,

The one who manifests as the moon's beautiful luminosity,
The one celebrated by all of the gods.
5 O Śrī, send misfortune afar!

O sun-brilliant goddess!
Through the force of austerities
Did your *bilva* tree spring up.
Through the power of its fruits
6 Let Alakṣmī be dispelled.

Let Kubera,
Together with Fame
And the [wish-fulfilling] Jewel,
Approach me.
As I have been born into this world,
7 Let me be granted renown and prosperity.[1]

I banish Alakṣmī, the elder sister,
Squalid with hunger,
Shrunken in thirst.
All poverty and misery
8 Be gone from my home![2]

I invoke that goddess Śrī,
Who reveals herself through scent
And through the inexhaustible blessings of cattle.
Exceeded by none,
9 She is the majestic sovereign of all creatures.

Let me obtain the pleasures
Of a good mind,
Fulfilled wishes,
And truthfulness in speech.
Let the abundance of cattle,
Food,
Prosperity,
10 And renown abide with me.

O Kardama, moist earth of primordial creation,
The goddess gave birth to you.
Dwell in me, Kardama.
Let your mother, the lotus-garlanded Śrī,
11 Establish herself in my home.

Let the waters pour forth,
Spreading love and affection.
O Ciklīta, fertile wetlands of primordial creation,
Persuade your mother, goddess of prosperity,
To inhabit my home.[3] 12

Draw unto me, O sacred fire, the goddess Lakṣmī,
The moist, the glistening,
The honey-colored one
Who delights at the trumpeting of elephants.
Garlanded with lotus blossoms,
She is the gentle luminescence of the moon. 13

Draw unto me, O sacred fire, the goddess Lakṣmī,
The moist, the glistening,
The golden one
Who wields the mace of sovereignty.
Garlanded with necklaces of gold,
She is the brilliant splendor of the sun. 14

Draw unto me, O sacred fire, that goddess Lakṣmī,
The constant one
Upon whose arrival I shall be blessed
With abundant gold, cattle, attendants, horses,
And loyal friends. 15

Hymn to Lakṣmī
(Lakṣmī Sūktam)

Most lovely goddess Padmiṇī
With lotus face
And lovely lotus-petal eyes,
O you who cherish the lotus,
O you who cherish the world,
O goddess whose heart pervades the universe,
1 To your lotus feet I bow.

O lotus-born,
With lovely lotus-petal thighs,
O goddess whose face is a lotus in bloom,
With eyelids shaped like lotus leaves,
Cast upon me your lotus-eyes,
2 For your glance bestows every prosperity.

Bestower of horses,
Bestower of cows,
Bestower of wealth,
Bestower of prosperity,
O goddess, bless me with abundant wealth.
3 Grant my every desire.

You are the mother of beginnings
And of continuity.
Bless me, O goddess,
With children and grandchildren,
Stores of grain,
Elephants, horses, cows, and chariots,
4 Good health, and longevity.

You are the wealth of Fire,
The wealth of the Wind,
The wealth of the Sun,
The wealth of the Earth.
You are the wealth of Indra,
The wealth of Bṛhaspati,
The wealth of Varuṇa,
5 And the wealth of the Aśvins.

Partake, O Garuḍa, of *soma.*
Let the slayer of Vṛtra drink *soma.*

By imbibing *soma,* I absorb into myself
The wealth of *soma.* 6

Those who recite this auspicious hymn
With reverence and devotion
Accrue the spiritual merit
To become free of anger, jealousy, greed,
And a dissatisfied mind. 7

O lovely one who dwells in the lotus,
Clothed in shimmering white,
With lotus in hand
And adorned with a garland of fragrant white flowers,
O goddess,
O charming one, beloved of Hari,
Mother of the three worlds,
Show me your favor. 8

I bow to the patient goddess,
Wife of Viṣṇu,
Beloved of Viṣṇu,
Wife of Mādhava,
Deeply cherished by Mādhava,
Dearest friend,
Precious beloved of the imperishable lord.[4] 9

Oṃ. Let me meditate on the great goddess Lakṣmī,
consort of Viṣṇu.
Let Lakṣmī inspire that meditation and illumine my mind.[5] 10

Ānanda, who is bliss,
Śrīda, bestower of wealth,
And Kardama and Ciklīta, the moist, primordial
Wetlands of creation,
Are renowned sages and sons of Śrī.
Let the glorious goddess, along with these radiant ones,
Dwell with me. 11

Let illness, debt, poverty, evil,
Cowardice, sorrow, untimely death,
And the mental anguish that burns the mind
Forever be destroyed. 12

The recitation of this sacred song
Confers the greatest of all blessings.
These auspicious verses
Bestow vitality, health,
Wealth, grain, cattle,
Abundant progeny,
And a long and healthy life
13 That spans one hundred years.

Here ends the *Lakṣmī Sūktam*.

Purāṇic Songs to Lakṣmī

Song for Lakṣmī, Gracious Bestower of Blessings
(Prasannavaradā Śrī Lakṣmī Stotram)

Attributed to the sage Agastya[1]

Victory to you of the lotus-petal eyes,
Beloved of the Lord of Auspiciousness.
Victory to you who carry us across
The restless ocean of life and death.
Victory, O Mother Mahālakṣmī! 1

Salutations, O Mahālakṣmī.
Salutations, O Queen of the Gods.
Salutations, O Beloved of Hari.
O Ocean of Compassion, salutations! 2

Salutations, O Lotus-dweller.
Salutations, O All-bestowing one.
May you ever send showers of wealth on all beings,
Drenching them with blessings of sweet delight. 3

Salutations, O Mother of the World.
Salutations, O Ocean of Mercy.
Salutations, O Tender One.
O Queen of the Universe, salutations! 4

Salutations, O Daughter of the Ocean of Milk.
Salutations, O Support of the Three Worlds.
Salutations to you of the propitious glance.
Protect me, for I come seeking refuge. 5

Protect me, O Queen of the Gods.
O Lakṣmī, Beloved of the Lord of the Gods,
Envelop me with your tender compassion.
6 Rescue me from poverty!

Salutations, O Mother of the Three Realms.
Salutations, O Purifier of the Three Realms.
O Bestower of Abundance,
7 O you who infuse the world with delight, salutations!

Salutations, O Beloved of Viṣṇu.
Salutations, O Support of the World.
Salutations to you who destroy pain and suffering.
8 Bless us with abundant, everlasting good fortune.

Salutations, O Lotus-dweller.
Salutations, O Sparkling One.
Salutations to you whose movements are graceful and charming.
9 Salutations to you, again and again.

Salutations to the Mother of the God of Love.
Salutations, O Mother,
Salutations to you again and again.
O Mother! Hear me, for I come seeking refuge.
10 Envelop me in your protective embrace.[2]

O Refuge!
O Lady of the Lotus!
O Mahālakṣmī!
O Final Resort!
In humility I come before you.
Rescue me! Rescue me!
11 Envelop me in your protective embrace.

O Mahālakṣmī,
Without you,
Nothing is precious or worthy of praise.
Without you,
The beauty of a person's good qualities
Cannot shine forth,

And the splendor of virtue,
Incapable of expression,
Can embellish nothing at all. 12

Wherever beauty is expressed,
Wherever virtue shines forth,
Wherever Nārāyaṇa is honored,
In those places is Lakṣmī greatly pleased. 13

O Lakṣmī, it is through you
That people are liberated from their debilitating vices,
That those without virtue become endowed with excellence,
And that those of ill repute
Come to earn the finest reputations. 14

O Lakṣmī, let beauty increase.
O Lakṣmī, let community increase.
O Lakṣmī, let wisdom increase.
O Lakṣmī, let prosperity increase in every direction. 15

O Lakṣmī, celebrated as Lady of the Lotus,
Neither Rudra, Ravi, Candra,
Nor the Lord of the Gods
Has words suitable to honor you fully.
O Mother of the Universe,
Who indeed is capable of describing
The true depths of your nature
And the many forms of your expression?
Quickly fulfill my desire, O Mother:
Envelop me with your protective embrace.[3] 16

Consumed by dire poverty
I am breathless with anxiety and fear.
In this impossibly painful state,
I am drawn to your side.
O Lakṣmī, Ocean of Compassion,
Bestow wealth,
And guide me to a state of prosperity. 17

O Mother, Beloved of Hari,
Behold me

As I come before you,
Lacking wealth or possessions.
O Lakṣmī, so beautifully arrayed
In garments of gold,
Extend to me your hand,
18 Right here and now.

O Lakṣmī, you are mother, you are father,
You are brother, and you are best friend.
19 So too, O Lakṣmī, are you supreme wisdom.

O Mahālakṣmī! Rescue! Rescue me!
O Queen of the Gods! Rescue! Rescue me!
O Mother of the Universe! Rescue! Rescue me!
Rescue me from poverty,
20 Right here and now.

Salutations, O Support of the World.
Salutations! Salutations to you.
Salutations, O Upholder of *Dharma*.
Salutations, O Bestower of Prosperity.
21 Salutations! Salutations to you.

I am drowning in a sea of poverty.
I am sinking
Further and further into the murky depths of hell.
O Goddess of Fortune,
Quickly extend your hand
22 And lift me out of this deep desperation.

O Lakṣmī, what solace could be greater
Than to recite again and again
The words of this prayer?
Truly, truly, O Beloved of Hari,
23 There is no greater refuge.

Hearing the words of Agastya's song,
Hari's Beloved was filled with delight.
She spoke to the sage
In a voice sweet as honey:
24 "I am pleased with you forever more.

Whoever recites or listens to this song of praise
So graciously composed by you
Becomes endowed with supreme good fortune
And obtains complete self-sovereignty." 25

Never does Lakṣmī abandon that person
Who recites this song regularly,
With sincere devotion.
Swiftly and surely, his debts disappear,
And never again does he suffer from want. 26

That person who recites it
Upon rising in the morning,
With an attitude of utmost devotion and faith
Enjoys a stable and happy home
With the Lady of Fortune ever by his side. 27

Such a person enjoys prosperity,
With the blessings of children,
Sterling virtues,
And a spotless reputation.
Endowed with happiness and well-being,
He grows to become learned and wise. 28

This highly auspicious song for Lakṣmī
Revealed by Agastya
Bears four types of fruit:
It instills one with the tranquility of Viṣṇu,
It creates triumph at the royal gates,
It ensures supreme victory over enemies,
And it vanquishes fear. 29–30

Never again shall one suffer from fear
Of tigers, ghosts,
Restless spirits, hellish fiends,
Swindlers, violent men with deadly weapons,
Nor indeed of many dangers unforeseen. 30–31

In order to pacify a debilitating habit
Or to expiate a heinous sin,
One should, with sincere intent and devotion,

Recite (this song) in a horse's stable
32 Or in a cow-shed among the cows.[4]

(This song of praise) bestows health and longevity,
And indeed creates every happiness.
It has been imparted by the sage Agastya
So that people may fulfill their hopes and desires
33 Now and for generations to come.

Here ends the *Lakṣmī Stotram* composed by Agastya.

Song for the Glorious Lotus Goddess
(Śrī Kamalā Stotram)

Attributed to Indra[5]

Salutations to the lotus-dweller.
Salutations to Nārāyaṇī.
Salutations to the one ever dear to Kṛṣṇa.
Salutations to Mahālakṣmī. 1

Salutations to the lovely lotus goddess
With eyes that curve like lotus leaves.
Salutations to the feminine aspect of Viṣṇu.
Salutations to the goddess seated on the lotus,
the gracious Padmiṇī. 2

Salutations to the essence of all true wealth.
Salutations to the one adored by all.
Salutations to the one who inspires devotion to Hari.
Salutations to the one who infuses the world with delight. 3

Salutations to the one who dwells on Kṛṣṇa's breast.
Salutations, O lovely lotus-jewel!
Salutations, O exquisite radiance of Kṛṣṇa.
Salutations, O luminous beauty of the moon. 4

To the great goddess of wealth and good fortune,
Salutations!
To the true essence of abundance,
To the bestower of abundance,
I offer salutations again and again. 5

You are Mahālakṣmī in Vaikuṇṭha
And Lakṣmī in the Ocean of Milk.
You are Svargalakṣmī in Indra's heaven
And Rājalakṣmī in the palaces of kings. 6

In homes, you are Gṛhalakṣmī, goddess of the household,
Manifest as the woman of the house.
You are Surabhi, Cow of Plenty,
And you are Dakṣiṇā, beloved consort of the fire sacrifice. 7

You are Aditi, mother of the gods,
And you are Kamalā, who dwells in the lotus.
In the sacrificial oblations, you are Svāhā
8 And in the ancestral offerings, you are Svadhā.

It is you who are the true essence of Viṣṇu.
You are the earth, the support of all.
Ever devoted to Nārāyaṇa,
9 You embody the essence of purity.[6]

There is no anger or violence about you,
For you are the embodiment of beauty and grace.
O Lovely One, Granter of Boons,
It is you who impart devotion to Hari
And you who grant fulfillment
10 Of the highest goal.

Without you, the entire universe
Would be reduced to ashes.
Without you, everything in the world
11 Would be suspended in a state of living death.[7]

You are the supreme mother of all,
And every woman is an embodiment of you.
So too do you express yourself in the forms
12 Of *dharma, artha, kāma,* and *mokṣa.*[8]

Just as a mother always takes
Her infant child to her breast,
So do you, Mother of All,
13 Ever protect and nourish all that exists.

A nursing infant who loses its mother
Might go on living through the force of its fate.
But most certainly, without you,
14 Not a single person could exist.

You have a most gracious nature.
Please, O Mother, be gracious to me.
O Eternal One, restore to me my own domain,
15 Now in the hands of enemies.

O beloved of Hari!
Since you have abandoned me,
I wander about like a beggar,
Homeless, without a friend,
Stripped of all wealth. 16

Grant me understanding and virtue!
Restore all of my cherished good fortune—
Majesty, power, and royal authority.
Grant me victory in battle,
And through this,
Supreme sovereignty. 17–18a

Nārāyaṇa spoke:

As he sang this, the great Lord Indra,
Surrounded by all of the other gods,
Bowed to the goddess again and again,
And all eyes were brimming with tears.
Brahmā, Śaṅkara, Śeṣa, Dharma, and Keśava
Joined together and repeatedly asked for the pardon
Of the chief of the gods.
Well pleased with those gods assembled before her,
Lakṣmī then answered their prayers
And draped a delightful garland of flowers
Upon the lovely-haired one.
Rejoicing, the assembled gods
Returned to their own realms,
O Nārada. 18b–21

In a happy state, the goddess returned to Hari,
Who was reclining upon the Ocean of Milk,
And Brahmā and Īśana, also extremely pleased,
Returned to their own abodes.[9] 22–23a

Whoever recites this highly auspicious song of praise
At the three twilights
Becomes like a king of kings
And attains wealth equal to that of Kubera.
By reciting this song five hundred thousand times,
One acquires its spiritual power.[10] 23b–24

Whoever recites this powerful song
Continuously for one month
Shall experience great happiness
And become, without a doubt,
A veritable Lord Indra.

Here ends the *Śrī Kamalā Stotram*.

Lord Indra's Song for Lakṣmī (Devarāja Indrakṛta Lakṣmī Stotram)[11]

Parāśara spoke:
Returning once more to the third heaven,
Taking his seat upon his splendid lion-throne
And exercising his sovereignty among the gods,
The Mighty One then addressed the lotus-bearing
goddess
With a song of praise:[12] 1

Indra sang:
I bow to Śrī, the ocean-born,
With soft and languid lotus-petal eyes.
Resting upon the chest of Lord Viṣṇu,
She is the mother of all that exists. 2

I sing the praises of the lotus-faced goddess,
With lotus hands and lotus-petal eyes.
Dwelling in the lotus,
She is the precious beloved
Of the one from whose navel springs a lotus.[13] 3

You are the success of any endeavor.
You are the sacred meals offered to the ancestors
And the oblations poured forth in the sacrifice.
You are divine nectar,
Purifier of the world,
The three twilights, and the depth of night.
You are radiance, wealth, intellect, and faith,
And you are goddess of letters, Sarasvatī. 4

O Auspicious One,
You are sacrificial knowledge,
Supreme knowledge,
And secret, mystical knowledge.
You are knowledge of the higher Self,
O Goddess,
And you are the one who confers liberation. 5

You are metaphysics,
You are the three Vedas,

You are the arts and sciences,
And you are the purveyor of justice.
O Goddess, the entire world,
With all of its pleasing and displeasing forms,
6 Consists of your essence.

Who other than you, O Goddess,
Is to be found resting upon that body,
Composed of all sacrifices,
Of the mace-wielding god of gods
7 Whom yogis contemplate in meditation?

Abandoned by you, O Goddess,
The three worlds were on the brink of destruction.
But now through your benevolence
8 They flourish once again.

O Most Fortunate One!
It is always through your propitious glances
That men obtain wives and children,
As well as homes,
Loyal friends,
Bountiful harvests,
9 And every type of prosperity.

O Goddess,
Those upon whom you cast your glance
Have little trouble attaining
Strong, healthy bodies,
Victory over enemies,
Sovereignty,
10 And supreme happiness.

You are the mother of all beings
And their father is Hari, god of gods.
This entire world
Of beings animate and inanimate
11 Is pervaded by you and Viṣṇu together.

O Purifier of All!
Never take leave of our treasuries,
Our cow-pens,

Our homes,
Our properties,
Our bodies,
Nor our spouses. 12

O you who abide on the chest of Viṣṇu, god of gods!
Never abandon our children,
Our circle of friends and attendants,
Our cows,
Nor our precious ornaments. 13

Those whom you abandon
Immediately lose their honor,
Truthfulness,
Purity,
Virtue,
And other excellent qualities. 14

Those upon whom you look with favor,
Even if lacking in good qualities,
Immediately become endowed
With honorable virtues
And a lineage of fine repute. 15

O Goddess,
Whosoever receives your gracious glance
Becomes praiseworthy,
Prosperous,
Of exalted family,
Learned and wise,
And lives life courageously. 16

O Sustainer of the Universe,
Beloved of Viṣṇu,
All of those excellent virtues and advantages
Lose their luster and strength
In those from whom you avert your gaze. 17

Even the tongue of Brahmā, the creator,
Is incapable of describing your magnificence.
Be gracious, O lotus-eyed goddess,
And never abandon me. 18

Parāśara spoke:
O Twice-born, thus being praised,
The delighted Śrī,
Who abides in all beings,
Responded to the god of one hundred rites,
19 And all of the gods listened.

Śrī spoke:
Extremely pleased am I,
O Lord of the Gods,
By your song of praise.
Ask of me what you desire,
20 For I have come to grant you a boon.

Indra replied:
If indeed I am worthy of your gifts, O Goddess,
I beg that you grant the following:
My first request
Is that the three worlds
21 Never again be deprived of your presence.

My second request,
O Ocean-born,
Is that you never abandon anyone
Who offers your praises
22 By chanting the words of this very song.

Said Śrī:
Most Excellent One!
Never again
Shall I forsake the three worlds.
I grant your first wish,
23 For I am well pleased by your song of praise.

And further,
Never shall I turn my face
From that person
Who offers morning recitations
24 Of the song you have sung to me.

Parāśara continued:
And that is how, O friend, in former times

The magnificent goddess of prosperity
Conferred those boons
Upon the chief of the gods,
Well pleased by his offering
Of laudatory song. 25

In her first birth, Śrī was born
As the daughter of Bhṛgu and Khyāti.
In a subsequent age,
When the gods and the anti-gods were churning the ocean,
She arose from the depths of those turbulent waters. 26

In a similar manner,
Janārdana, who is lord of the world
And king of the gods,
Makes his earthly descent
Accompanied each time by his divine partner, Śrī.[14] 27

Thus when Hari is born
As the son of Aditi
Śrī arises as the lotus flower.
When he is born as Rāma Bhārgava,
She is born as Dharaṇī.[15] 28

She is Sītā to Rāma Rāghava
And Rukmiṇī to Lord Kṛṣṇa.
Whenever Lord Viṣṇu descends to this realm,
It is she who incarnates as his companion. 29

If he embodies himself with a divine form,
So too is her form a heavenly one.
If he becomes human,
Then human is she.
Whatever type of form Viṣṇu assumes,
She assumes that shape accordingly. 30

Those who hear or recite
This birth story of Lakṣmī
Attract the presence of Śrī in their homes
For three generations. 31

Alakṣmī, repository of penury and strife,
Never gains entrance into those homes
32 Whose inhabitants offer songs to Śrī.

Thus, in answer to your inquiry, O brahman,
Have I narrated to you
The story of how Śrī,
Taking birth as the daughter of Bhṛgu,
Arose from the Ocean of Milk,
And how Alakṣmī may never take up residence
With those who recite Indra's verses
In praise of Lakṣmī,
The wellspring of abundance
33–34 And the means to all prosperity.

The Heavenly Gods' Praise-Song for Lakṣmī
(Śrī Daivakṛta Lakṣmī Stotram)

O Mother of Prosperity,
O you of patient disposition,
O you who have not a trace of anger,
O Supreme Goddess
Whose essence is truth and clarity,
Show compassion. 1

You are glorified in the highest
By all of the gods and sages.
Without you
The world has no savor
And feels like death. 2

You are the essence of all that exists,
The true essence of all prosperity.
You are the goddess
Who reigns supreme in the ecstatic *rasa* dance.
Every woman is an emanation of you. 3

On Mount Kailāśa you are Pārvatī.
In the Ocean of Milk, you are daughter of the sea.
You are Celestial Lakṣmī in heaven
And Mortal Lakṣmī on earth. 4

In Vaikuṇṭha, you are Mahālakṣmī,
Goddess of the gods.
In Brahmā's heavenly realm,
You are Sarasvatī, Gaṅgā, Tulasī, and Sāvitrī. 5

In Goloka,
You are the goddess more dear to Kṛṣṇa
Than life itself,
His own Rādhikā.
Deep in the forest,
Deep in the Vṛṇda forest,
You are mistress of the mesmerizing *rasa* dance.[16] 6

In the boughs of the sacred *bhandira* tree,
You are Kṛṣṇa's desire.

In the sandalwood forest you are Candrā,
In the grove of sweet yellow jasmine you are Virajā,
And on the hundred-peaked mountain you are the lovely
7 Sundarī.

In a thicket of lotuses, you are Padmāvatī,
In a wood where the *mālatī* flower blooms, you are
Mālatī,
In a forest of white jasmine, you are Kundadantī,
8 And in a grove of sweet *ketakī*. you are Suśilā.

So too do you exist as wreaths of *kadamba*
Gracing the bowers of a deep *kadamba* wood.
O Goddess, you are Royal Lakṣmī
In the palaces of kings,
And Lakṣmī of the Home
9 In ordinary households.

After chanting this song,
The gods, sages, and mortals
Bowed reverently.
Then with throats dried and choking
And eyes filled with tears,
10 They spoke these words:

This beautiful and auspicious song praising Lakṣmī
Has been composed by all of the gods.
Most assuredly, anything can be achieved
By one who recites it
11 Upon arising in the morning.

If single, one obtains a spouse
Who is loyal, accomplished,
Of admirable conduct,
Good-looking,
Delightful,
Sweet-speaking,
And exceedingly loving.
Such a spouse,
Born of an excellent family
And endowed with a pleasant disposition,
12–13 Shall foster an illustrious lineage.[17]

If childless, one is blessed with children.
Such a worshiper of Viṣṇu enjoys health and longevity,
And is endowed with wisdom,
Excellent reputation,
And great affluence.
If home and possessions have been lost,
They are regained.
If the goddess of prosperity has left his side,
He is blessed once again
With her auspicious presence. 13–14

Severed ties from friends and family are restored.
Lost wealth is replenished.
One whose reputation has suffered
Again enjoys great esteem,
And he reaps the blessing of steadfast security.
Most certainly this is true. 15

This wholly auspiciousness song of praise
Destroys anguish and distress
And generates bliss and delight.
Through this beneficent song,
One lives life with purpose and honor
And achieves final liberation. 16

Here ends the *Śrī Daivakṛta Lakṣmī Stotram.*

Eight Verses Praising Mahālakṣmī
(Mahalakṣmyaṣṭakam Stotram)

Indra spoke:

Salutations to you, O Supreme Enchantress,
Abode of good fortune,
Adored by all of the gods,
Holding in your hands a conch, discus, and mace.
1 O Mahālakṣmī, salutations to you.

Salutations to you, O Rider of the Eagle.
O terror of the hostile spirit Kola,
O destroyer of all iniquities,
O Goddess,
2 O Mahālakṣmī, salutations to you.

O you who know all,
O you who grant all boons,
O you who instill fear in the vicious and corrupt,
O Goddess, destroyer of all sorrows,
3 O Mahālakṣmī, salutations to you.

O Goddess, bestower of success and intelligence,
Bestower of worldly enjoyment and liberation,
O Goddess ever embodied in the sacred chant,
4 O Mahālakṣmī, salutations to you.

O Goddess without beginning or end,
O primordial cosmic energy,
O great queen born from yoga
And made manifest through yoga,
5 O Mahālakṣmī, salutations to you.

O great cosmic power of the mighty storm gods
Expressed as material and subtle forms,
O Goddess, womb of all,
Remover of all wrongdoings,
6 O Mahālakṣmī, salutations to you.

O lotus-seated Goddess,
Embodiment of Ultimate Reality,

O Supreme Lady, Mother of the Universe,
O Mahālakṣmī, salutations to you. 7

O Goddess clothed in white,
Adorned with a dazzling array of magnificent jewels,
You are the foundation of the world
And its divine mother.
O Mahālakṣmī, salutations to you. 8

Whoever recites this song to Mahālakṣmī
With great devotion
Achieves every type of success
And worldly attainment. 9

If recited regularly once a day,
It destroys great transgressions.
Recited regularly twice a day,
It brings abundant wealth and prosperity. 10

If recited regularly three times a day,
It destroys even the greatest enemy,
For if pleased regularly (with song),
Mahālakṣmī bestows gracious blessings of great good fortune. 11

Here ends the *Mahālakṣmyaṣṭakam*, composed by Lord Indra.

Tantric Songs to Lakṣmī

The Secret Heart of Lakṣmī
(Śrī Mahālakṣmī Hṛdayam)

Setting the Intention

Bhārgava is the seer of the garland of *mantra*s known as the most glorious *Secret Heart of Lakṣmī*. Its deity is the glorious Ādyādi Mahālakṣmī, source of all sources. It is composed in *anuṣṭubh* and other poetic meters. *Śrīṃ* is its seed-syllable, *hrīṃ* its power, and *aiṃ* its nail. Its purpose is to attract the favor of the glorious source of all sources, Primordial Mahālakṣmī.

Mantra Placements

Oṃ. On my head, salutations to the seer, Bhārgava.
Oṃ. On my face, salutations to *anuṣṭubh* and the other
poetic meters.
On my heart, salutations to the deity, the glorious
Ādyādi Mahālakṣmī, source of all sources,
On my genitals, salutations to the seed syllable, *śrīṃ*.
On my feet, salutations to the animating power, *hrīṃ*.
Over my entire body, salutations to the nail, *aiṃ*.

Mantra Placements on the Hands

Śrīṃ on my thumbs. Salutations!
Hrīṃ on my forefingers. Salutations!
Aiṃ on my middle fingers. Salutations!
Śrīṃ on my ring fingers. Salutations!
Hrīṃ on my little fingers. Salutations!
Aiṃ on the palms and tops of my hands. Salutations!

Mantra Placements on the Body

Śrīṃ on my heart. Salutations!
Hrīṃ on my head. *Svāhā.*
Aiṃ on the top back of my head. *Vaṣaṭ.*
Śrīṃ on the armor. *Huṃ.*
Hrīṃ on the third eye. *Vauṣaṭ.*
Aiṃ on the weapon. *Phaṭ.*
Śrīṃ. Hrīṃ. Aiṃ. Thus are the directions secured.[1]

Meditation for Visualization of the Deity

Let me contemplate the goddess Lakṣmī
Adorned with sparkling ankle bracelets
And charming toe-rings,
Playfully holding a lotus in her hand.
O Lakṣmī, bright one, exalted one,
Wielder of conch, discus, and mace,
Bestower of all success,
Grant me a boon.

Mantra

Oṃ śrīṃ hrīṃ aiṃ. (Salutations) to Mahālakṣmī, Lotus-bearer and Rider of the Lion. *Svāhā.*

Song of Praise

Oṃ. I sing the praises of Lakṣmī,
Whose essence is supreme auspiciousness
And whose body is formed of golden light.
Her entire being sparkles with the radiance of pure gold.
She bears the golden lotus
And the golden vessel filled with seeds.
Seated at the left side of Viṣṇu,
1 She is Śakti, mother of all creation.[2]

I sing the praises of Lakṣmī,
Beloved mother of auspiciousness,
The eternal one
Who confers delight,

Fulfills all desires,
And guides all endeavors to successful fruition. 2

With my mind focused
On her majestic sovereignty,
Ever do I call upon the queen of the gods.
Again and again I praise that supreme lady. 3

I sing the praises of Mahāśrī, source of wisdom,
Mahāśrī, source of every success and happiness,
Mahāśrī, source of all good fortune,
Mahāśrī, eternal source of auspiciousness. 4

I glorify Hari's beloved, source of prosperity,
The everlasting one
Who grants the delight of Self-recognition,
The charming one
Who gives birth to speech
And its amazing variegations.
I glorify that goddess
Who bestows happiness sweet and everlasting. 5

O Goddess, existing as the entire world,
You dwell in all beings as their essence.
O queen of endless bounty,
May your brilliance illumine the darkness of space
As you protect all of creation.
O Śrī, I bow to your lotus feet. 6

You are destroyer of poverty, sorrow,
And fruitless endeavor.
In my state of wretchedness and scarcity,
I place myself at your lotus feet.
O Śrī, anoint me with your merciful glance. 7

O Mother, be gracious.
Cast upon me your glance,
Moist with the nectar of compassion.
Let your mercy flow into my home.
Clinging to your lotus feet,
I bow to the one whose look

Destroys the pain that dwells in my heart.
8 I bow in reverence to you, O Śrī.

I bow to the gentle one,
Protectress of those who come seeking refuge.
I bow to the lovely one,
Abode of desirable virtues.
I bow to the serene one,
Resolver of difficulties.
I bow to that goddess who sustains the world,
9 Bestower of wealth, grains, and abundant good fortune.

Salutations to Cosmic Energy.
Salutations to the one whom poets laud
As the luster of the moon.
Salutations to Desire,
Who incites the passionate arising of nectar.
Salutations to Devotion.
Salutations to Intelligence.
Salutations to the one
Who carries us across the ocean of existence.
10 To the precious beloved of Madhu's foe, salutations.[3]

Homage to Lakṣmī,
The excellent one, the auspicious one.
Homage to Success,
Glorified as the perfection of auspiciousness.
Homage to Constancy,
Who shatters misfortune.
Homage to Refuge,
11 Bestower of happiness and good fortune.

Glory be to that goddess
Whom the gods worship in heaven.
Glory be to the goddess of abundance,
Vanquisher of the ills of humanity.
Glory be to the generous one,
Beloved of the earth-sustainer.
Glory be to Prosperity,
12 Beloved of Viṣṇu, most excellent of men.

Homage to you,
Destroyer of crushing poverty and woes.

Homage! Homage to you,
Pacifier of all fears,
Bestower of abundance,
Abiding on the chest of Lord Viṣṇu. 13

Glory! Glory be to Lakṣmī,
Who appears and disappears in the twinkling of an eye.
Glory! Glory be to Padmā,
Dearly beloved lady of the lotus.
Glory! Glory be to Wisdom,
Seated at Viṣṇu's left side.
Glory! May all offer glory and salutations to Śrī,
Wellspring of prosperity. 14

Glory! Glory be to the goddess
Worshiped reverently by the assembly of gods.
Glory! Glory be to the auspicious one,
Good fortune embodied as the daughter of Bhṛgu.
Glory! Glory be to the ever-spotless one,
Celebrated as supreme knowledge.
Glory! Glory be to the one
Who exists as the goodness
Inherent in all things. 15

Glory! Glory be to the delightful one
Who dwells in the magnificent depths of the sea.
Glory! Glory be to the golden one
Whose beautiful body sparkles with brilliant light.
Glory! Glory be to the charming one, the resplendent one.
Glory! Glory be to the tranquil one.
O auspicious goddess,
Arrive quickly! 16

The Thunder Beings and the Mighty One, chief of the gods,
Are but emanations of the Lotus-Born.
It is through her that they obtain
Their power, their excellence, their valor,
And indeed their entire existence.[4] 17

My forehead is anointed
With the ceremonial markings.

May the traces of those markings
Flow inward,
There to become manifest
As the fruit of inner wisdom.
O Śrī, O Lotus-dweller,
O most auspicious Daughter of the Ocean,
Reveal to me clearly
18 The full essence of this wisdom.

O Goddess,
With just a mere portion of your essence
You endow all things, animate and inanimate,
With their existence.
With similar ease
May you ever bestow your favor
19 And bless me with prosperity.

Just as Viṣṇu eternally projects
A portion of himself onto the earth,
So may Lakṣmī ever impart
20 A portion of herself unto me.

O Goddess,
Bestow complete happiness and well-being.
Infuse your worshipers with fearlessness.
Be unwavering
As that portion of yourself
21 Takes hold within me.

At the moment of awakening,
Let my body become Vaikuṇṭha,
From the seat to the forehead and in the crown of my head.
Grant that my eyes become an abode of Śrī.
Grant that my speech become anchored in the Realm of Truth.
O Lakṣmī, grant that by experiencing
A mere portion of your essence within me,
I may inhabit that glorious White Island
22 Illumined by its own splendor.[5]

Just as she dwells in the Ocean of Milk,
May a portion of Śrī ever dwell in my body.

Just as she exists in the sun and the moon,
May Śrī exist in me always
As Lakṣmī and her beloved lord. 23

O most glorious Mahālakṣmī,
Origin of origins,
Wholly auspicious,
Completely sovereign,
Establish a portion of yourself in me. 24

Establish a portion of yourself in me
As majesty,
For majesty is the illuminating light
Of pure knowledge
That destroys the darkness of ignorance. 25

Establish a portion of yourself in me
As auspiciousness,
For auspiciousness banishes Alakṣmī
As surely as the spreading of sunlight
Dispels the heavy darkness. 26

Endow me with just a portion of your majesty.
Endow me with just a portion of your auspiciousness.
For it is through these
That I am able to attain your state. 27

O Daughter of Bhṛgu,
How fortunate am I,
Deemed worthy of being possessed by you.
Through your grace I have become purified.
O Mother of the World, I bow to you. 28

You illumine my entire being
With just a portion of yourself.
O Śrī, show me your favor!
Draw near!
Reveal a mere fragment of your essence!
O Primordial Lakṣmī, absorb me completely,
Leaving nothing to remain. 29

O Lakṣmī, dwelling with Nārāyaṇa
In glorious Vaikuṇṭha,

Come into my presence.
30 Cast upon me your benevolent glance.

O Lakṣmī, dwelling with Vāsudeva
In the Realm of Truth,
Come into my presence.
31 Be gracious and grant me a boon.

O Lakṣmī, dwelling with Lord Viṣṇu
On the White Island,
Come quickly into my presence.
O Goddess, Virtuous One, Mother of the World,
32 Show me your favor.

O Lakṣmī, dwelling in the Ocean of Milk,
Come into my presence.
Ever shower me with the nectar
33 That flows from your merciful glance.

O Lakṣmī, dwelling in the bounteous sea,
Come into my presence.
Come, come, O Golden One!
34 Become manifest before me.

O Mahālakṣmī, be steadfast.
O Flawless One, waver not.
O gentle lotus goddess,
35 Be gracious and favor me in your heart.

O Abode of Good Fortune!
O Great and Auspicious Prosperity!
The supreme treasure lies within you.
Stir it up!
Bring it quickly to the surface
36 And let it be revealed!

O Source of Wealth,
Receptacle of Wealth,
Bestower of Wealth,
O Śrī most compassionate,
Reveal to me quickly
37 What is hidden within you.

O Auspicious One,
Beloved of Viṣṇu,
You who bring all to successful fruition,
Reveal!
Bring forth the precious treasures
Hidden deep within your womb. 38

O Mother Lakṣmī, though you have
Departed to the netherworlds,
Come to me quickly.
Reveal to me your supreme form. 39

O Mother, come close!
Care for me as tenderly
As a mother cow nurtures
Her needy young.
Become visible!
Come to me quickly,
With the speed of thought. 40

O Goddess,
Womb of the world,
Mother of the entire creation,
Impatiently I seek you.
Come to me quickly. 41

Arise!
Awaken within me!
Reveal the imperishable golden urn
That overflows with brilliant gold. 42

Essence of the inner treasure, awaken!
Essence of the inner treasure, arise!
Come forth!
Become clear!
Reveal yourself within me! 43

O Lakṣmī, be gracious.
Come before me
As the auspicious Cow of Plenty,
Bearing the intoxicating nectar
Whose essence is sweet compassion. 44

O Golden One,
Come to me here and now.
O Lakşmī,
Be firm,
Be steadfast,
Be fully pleased!
45 Grant me a boon!

Draw near, O Goddess!
Reveal to me the treasure!
Right now! In a flash!
And once this has been revealed,
46 Protect it in me always.

O Goddess!
Make me fearless
By settling firmly in my senses
And abiding with me at all times.
47 O Mahālakṣmī, salutations to you.

O Mahālakṣmī, draw near.
O Mistress of the White Island,
As I bow reverently before you,
48 Look upon me with abundant favor.

O Lakṣmī, though you have departed to the heavens,
Your golden essence remains everywhere.
Let me perceive your form
49 As all things, in all places.

O all-golden goddess,
You amuse yourself
By spreading wealth across the land.
May that graceful current of your abundance
50 Ever flow with steady ease.

O Lakṣmī,
Wherever you dwell
Reaps the fruits of good fortune.
O Mahālakṣmī, show me your favor!
51 Completely fulfill my heart's desires.

O magnificent goddess,
O you who dwell in Ayodhyā
And indeed in every city,
Come forth!
Display your powers mighty and diverse.[6] 52

O playful goddess,
Come! Come before me
And stay,
For your eyes are moist
With the nectar of compassion. 53

O Mahālakṣmī,
Be steadfast.
Place your hand on my head
And anoint me
With the sweet nectar of compassion. 54

O Lakṣmī, Delightful One!
O you who dwell in the palaces of kings,
Draw near.
Stand firmly and fully in me now.
Render me fearless
Through the power of your grace. 55

O Lakṣmī,
O you who dwell in the palaces of kings,
As I bow before you,
Stroke my head with tender mercy,
And establish a part of yourself in me. 56

O most glorious Primordial Mahālakṣmī,
Seated at the left side of Viṣṇu,
Reveal yourself before my eyes.
Envelop me in your protective embrace,
For I come to you seeking refuge. 57

O Mahālakṣmī, show me your favor.
O supremely auspicious one, bestow your sweet blessings.

Never wavering from your exquisite happiness,
58 Settle firmly in my home.

As long as the Vedas are upheld,
Even the mention of their name confers blessings.
And wherever Viṣṇu abides
There too are you present.
59 In light of these, grant me your compassion.

O luminous goddess!
Just as the moon's brilliance
Increases night by night,
So may your tender kindness toward me
60 Steadily unfold.

O Śrī, as surely as you abide
In the heavenly city of Vaikuṇṭha
Or deep in the Ocean of Milk,
So may you, together with Viṣṇu,
61 Settle firmly in my home.

O Śrī, as surely as you and Lord Viṣṇu
Ever dwell in the hearts of yogis,
So may you, together with Viṣṇu,
62 Settle firmly in my home.

As surely as you dwell in the heart of Nārāyaṇa,
So does Nārāyaṇa abide in your lotus heart,
For Nārāyaṇa, the eternally auspicious one,
Is none other than you.
O compassion-filled Śrī,
63 May you both settle firmly in my heart.

O Śrī, let understanding abound in my heart.
O Śrī, let good fortune abound in my household.
O Śrī, let compassion abound in my being.
64 O Śrī, let wealth and prosperity abound in my home.

May you never abandon me,
But rather, curl fast
Around your devoted worshiper

Like Kalpavalli, the fabulous vine
That satisfies all desires.
O Wish-fulfilling Jewel!
O Cow of Plenty!
O Mother of the Universe!
Bestow your sweet favor throughout my household,
Blessing every member of my family. 65

O Primordial Māyā,
You are the seed of the unborn egg.
You exist as the formed as well as the formless.
O Goddess, it is through the magnificent actions
Of you and Lord Viṣṇu
That the egg of existence
Is borne upon the waters. 66

Neither Brahmā nor Rudra
Nor any other of the Vedic gods
Is capable of extolling, in song,
Your full glory and majesty.
How, then, can I,
With my meager voice,
Hope to do so? 67

O Mother,
Your child lauds you
With reverent words and songs of praise.
O All-knowing One,
Please accept these offerings
With tender compassion. 68

Never have you failed me
When I've turned to you for help.
O most excellent lady,
With this thought filling my mind,
I come to you seeking refuge. 69

You are the supreme sanctuary,
Ever bestowing infinite happiness
Upon your worshipers.

O magnificent goddess,
With this thought filling my mind,
70 I come to you seeking refuge.

Solemnly have you promised
Never to abandon your devotees.
When I contemplate this,
71 It steadies my breath and calms my mind.

O Merciful One,
Ocean of Compassion,
Only you can know how much
I depend upon you.
Bestow upon me as much
72 As I am able to receive.

I cannot live even for an instant
Without your tender mercy.
Those who are separated from you
Do not flourish in this existence,
But are like fish caught in a net,
73 Dangling above the water.

Like a mother whose breasts swell with milk
At the very thought of her tender young,
You overflow with loving kindness
74 Toward all of your children born on this earth.

As I am your child
And you are my mother,
Anoint me with the nectar of your breasts,
75 Swelling with the milk of compassion.

Though I strive to overcome them,
My faults seem piled high as Mount Mandara.
May these failings dissolve through your grace,
Just as mounds of sand
76 Wash away in the rain.

Of the wretched I am surely foremost.
And among the merciful, you are supreme.

In all of the three worlds,
Who shows me greater compassion than you? 77

Even one who violates religious precept
Is not denied your tender mercy.
Do not healing herbs spring up
From even the harshest of soil? 78

Is it your compassion
Or is it my own sense of excitement
That draws me to you?
As I reflect on this,
Grant me understanding,
O Goddess, ocean of mercy. 79

You are mother,
You are father,
You are guru,
You are good fortune.
O Śrī, it is you
Who animate all of life.
What exists
That has not originated in your mind?
O my beloved goddess,
Essence of truth and mistress of the entire world,
Everything is you alone. 80

O Primordial Lakṣmī,
You who yield the sweet milk
Of happiness,
Of purity,
And of wise discernment,
Be well pleased.
Far surpassing the three qualities of nature,
You are the destroyer of ignorance.
O bright goddess of wisdom,
Be well pleased.[7] 81

O Destroyer of Dull and Idle Speech!
O Bestower of Sparkling Eloquence!
Adorned with vermilion

I stand trembling before you,
Offering my songs of praise.
82 O Śrī, be well pleased by my words.

You are the resplendent glow of success.
It is you who illumine all that is vigorous and bright.
O Beloved of Viṣṇu, awaken!
Send forth your splendor!
83 O Goddess of Speech, be well pleased!

O lovely one,
Bestower of all prosperity,
O you who pour forth streams of abundant compassion,
Fully reveal your glorious splendor.
O bestower of riches and bounty,
Smile upon me with sweet favor.
84 O golden Śrī, be pleased!

O bestower of every type of wealth,
O you who give birth to all the worlds,
Queen of the entire universe,
Vanquisher of every fear,
O most eminent of all,
Smile upon me with sweet favor.
85 O golden Śrī, be pleased!

You are resplendent
As you remove every obstacle
And uplift each one of your devotees.
O you who bestow endless good fortune and happiness,
86 O Golden One, be pleased!

The legions of gods glorify you
As their supreme leader,
For with your brilliant light
You guide them out of darkness.
Be well pleased, O Goddess.
87 Let fall your gracious glance upon my face.

O Mother,
Deeply embedded
Is my fear, my insecurity.

Have mercy, O Mother, on my wretched state.
Uproot it
With the joy that arises
From your sweet and compassionate glance.
O Mother of the Universe,
Infuse your children with fearlessness!
Plant in us the seed of auspiciousness
As we make our way in this world. 88

O Indirā, lady of the blue lotus,
Just a glance from you—
And my desires
Are satisfied here in this world,
For you are the Wish-fulfilling Jewel,
The celestial tree of the gods,
And the nine eternal treasures.
And yet, a marvelous elixir there is,
Distilled from the nectar of your compassion.
Secreted from just a portion of you,
It fulfills desires beyond imagination.
May this your nectar flow with steady ease. 89

O Kamalā, lady of the lotus,
Just as the touch of magic elixir
Transmutes iron into gold,
So, O Mother, does the touch of your gracious glance
Transform even the most inauspicious
Into a blessing of splendid good fortune. 90

"Give me . . .
There isn't any . . ."
In an anxious state
I intrude with these words,
Casting myself down before you for refuge.
Even as I fall before you,
I beg you to dwell securely within me
And bestow never-ending fearlessness. 91

O Śrī, in addition to the Wish-fulfilling Jewel
And the Tree of Paradise,
There exists a delightful, magic elixir
Formed from just a portion of you.

As this nectar moves through me,
Touching all of my parts from head to toe,
92 *Hak!* It transmutes them into a body of gold.[8]

O Ādyādi Lakṣmī,
Wife of Viṣṇu, upholder of *dharma,*
Establish yourself within me.
O primordial Lakṣmī,
Through your grace
May I perceive the nine treasures
93 At all times, in all places.

That person who recites *The Secret Heart of Primordial Lakṣmī, Source of All Sources*
Shall be blessed with the unwavering presence
Of Rājya Lakṣmī, goddess of kings.
Transforming even the most abject poverty
Into abundant wealth,
Śrī shall extend her blessings steadily
94 For generations to come.[9]

That person who continuously remembers the beloved of Viṣṇu
Becomes blessed with joyous contentment.
An adoring mother to her devotees,
95 The goddess lavishly grants their heart's desires.

If recited five thousand times
During the *puraścaraṇa* ceremony,
This secret book of divine knowledge
96 Grants the fulfillment of all desires.[10]

Yet indeed, that person who recites
Or even listens to this sacred song
Three times or even once,
While filled with complete devotion,
97 Is certain to attain Śrī.

By invoking Mahālakṣmī
With the recitation of this auspicious song
Five times during a night sacred to Bhārgavī,
98 One becomes endowed with wealth.[11]

A woman impregnated
With this scripture's sacred *mantras*
Gives birth to prosperity for her family,
And her husband becomes equal
To the lord of Śrī. 99

Misfortune never destroys
The lineage of a man
Whose woman immerses herself
In the sacred *mantras* of *The Secret Heart of Lakṣmī.* 100

That person who recites it with a devoted heart
While celebrating the festival of Rāma
During the bright half of the month of Āśvina
Will be showered
With a beautiful golden rain of exaltation
Upon uttering the final verse.[12] 101

That person who recites it faithfully for a year
Attains a completely purified mind.
After seventy recitations in a day,
He becomes victorious.
After one hundred recitations in a day,
He attains the might of Indra.
If even then misfortune should befall him,
Śrī will destroy it immediately
With just a glance. 102

O Śrī, beloved of Hari!
The purpose of these pleasing *mantras*
Is to become firmly established
In the remembrance of the spotless,
Awakened consciousness
Of the guru.
Bestow that supreme state, O Mother Śrī.[13] 103

You are Pṛthvī, Mother Earth,
And your husband is Most Excellent of Men.
You are the abode of abundance
And you are the acumen in obtaining wealth.
O Lakṣmī, grant me many years
Of enjoying prosperity and renown.[14] 104

O Daughter of Bhṛgu,
Endow me with the magical attainment
Of eloquence in speech,
Of good health and stability,
Of proficiency in worldly affairs,
Of progeny,
And of savoring every blessing of abundance
105 For all the days of my life.[15]

O Śrī, let wealth increase in my household.
O Śrī, let abundance increase in my home.

The chief mantra is *oṃ yaṃ haṃ kaṃ laṃ paṃ śrīṃ.*

Let us meditate on Lakṣmī,
The lovely one,
Clothed in streams of shimmering light,
Adorned with charming ornaments,
Her face sweet with laughter,
106 Sunrise-radiant with joy.

O Śrī, grant me fearlessness in every moment.
Let steadfastness ever be mine.
Let me always remain joined with the resplendent one
Who bears the lotus
107 And the brilliant golden vessel filled with seeds.

O Goddess, it is you who protect
This most secret of teachings,
A scripture brought into existence
For the benefit of householders.
Let its power flourish within me.
108 Let me always abide in your bounteous grace.

Here ends the *Mahālakṣmīhṛdaya Stotram*, located in the *Śrī Atharvaṇa Rahasya.*[16]

Praise-Song for the Bestower of Wealth (Dhanadā Stotram)[17]

Salutations to the one who exists as all things.
Salutations to the wellspring of auspiciousness.
O Goddess, grant us abundant prosperity.
Salutations, O Bestower of Wealth! 1

O Goddess, grant us supreme good fortune.
Completely fulfill our deepest desires.
O Goddess, grant us happiness and liberation.
Salutations, O Bestower of Wealth! 2

O you who exist as Brahmā,
O you who exist as everlasting bliss,
O Bliss Eternal!
O Goddess, quickly impart magical attainment.
Salutations, O Bestower of Wealth! 3

O you who exist as the rays of the sun,
O you who exist as the circle of heavenly beings,
O Goddess, impart success.
Salutations, O Bestower of Wealth! 4

O you who exist as Viṣṇu,
O you who exist as perfect harmony,
O compassionate, all-knowing protector of this world,
Salutations, O Bestower of Wealth! 5

O you who exist as Śiva,
O you who exist as the dissolution of the world,
O Bliss of Śiva,
O Bliss of Creation and Destruction!
Salutations, O Bestower of Wealth! 6

O you who exist as the five essential elements,
O you who always delight in the five practices,
O Goddess, so dear to the spiritual practitioner,
Salutations, O Bestower of Wealth! [18] 7

Song-Amulet of the Bestower of Wealth (Dhanadā Kavacam)[19]

Kubera is the seer
Of the *Song-Amulet for the Bestower of Wealth.*
Its meter is *paṅkti*
And its deity, Dhanadā,
1 Bestower of everlasting magical power.[20]

Its illustrious purpose is to acquire
2 Virtue, wealth, pleasure, and spiritual liberation.[21]

Let the seed-syllable *dhaṃ* protect my head.
(Let) the seed-syllable *hrīṃ* (protect) my forehead.
Let the seed-syllable *śrīṃ* protect my face.
3 Let the syllable *a* protect my heart.

Let the syllable *ti* protect my abdomen.
Let the syllable *pri* protect my back.
(Let) the syllable *ye* (protect) both of my legs.
(Let) the syllable *svā* (protect) the soles of my feet.
Let the syllable *hā* cast a mantle of protection over my
4 entire body.

Here ends the glorious *Dhanadā Kavacam.*

Praise-Song for the Lotus Goddess
(Kamalā Stotram)

O Goddess, you exist as the sounding of *oṃ*.
You exist as purity and equipoise.
From your essence you have given birth to the gods.
Be gracious, O Lovely One. 1

You exist as the senses and as the natural elements.
Your heart is the foundation of the Smṛti
And your essence permeates the Veda.
Be gracious, O Lovely One.[22] 2

O Lakṣmī, ever are you praised in song
By gods, demigods,
Celestial musicians,
Tree spirits, goblins, and centaurs.
Be gracious, O Lovely One. 3

O Mother of Wisdom,
So too are you lauded
By those who have transcended duality
And left behind their bondage to this world.
Be gracious, O Lovely One. 4

You exist as Brahmā and Sāvitrī.
You are the lamp that illumines the world,
For the entire creation is your own form.
Be gracious, O Lovely One. 5

You exist as the earth,
As the waters,
As fire,
As the winds,
And as the atmosphere.
It is you indeed who cause the five elements
To hold together in harmony.
Be gracious, O Lovely One. 6

You are the great queen,
You are the lady of the mountain,
You are the lotus goddess,

And you are the consort of the beautiful-haired one.
It is you indeed who are dear to the wise.
7 Be gracious, O Lovely One.

You exist as little girls in their childhood,
As young women in their youth,
And as elderly women in their old age.
8 Be gracious, O Lovely One.

You exist as the elements of nature
And you exist beyond those elements.
It is you who are the primordial wisdom
From which the entire world has sprung
And through which all moves in harmony.
9 Be gracious, O Lovely One.

You are practitioner of yogic austerities
And you are the magical powers produced through yoga.
Yours is the pure consciousness that animates this earth
And yours is the spiritual power of heaven.
10 Be gracious, O Lovely One.

You are the origin of the world,
You are its preservation,
And in the end, you are its dissolution.
O Goddess, these actions
11 Are simply expressions of your own desire.

O you who are fond of your devotees!
You illumine all that exists.
Whether animate or inanimate, visible or invisible,
12 All is permeated by your beautiful essence.

Through your power of illusion,
A person can become disconnected
From his Higher Self,
Wandering about from place to place,
Bereft of clear thought,
13 Lost in destructive behavior.[23]

It matters not how much truth
May shine forth in the world,

Illuminating the entire creation,
For one cannot acquire wisdom
Unless it is experienced
Through the opening of the heart.[24] 14

A person immersed in the depths of your wisdom
Enjoys the fullness of a happy life
Blessed with a spouse, home, family, good friends,
And the banishment of debilitating sorrow. 15

O Queen of the Gods,
It is only through your will
That the sun and moon
Grace the sky with their light.
Be gracious, O Lovely One. 16

O Queen of the Gods,
You are the mother of Brahmā, Īśa, and Viṣṇu.
Though *Brahmā* is the name designating Creator,
It is you who are the source
Of all things manifest and unmanifest.
Be gracious, O Lovely One.[25] 17

O Supreme Lady,
Source of all auspiciousness,
You are unwavering,
All-pervading,
Constant,
Eternal,
And beyond all illusion.
Be gracious, O Lovely One. 18

The entire universe is contained in your body.
You are queen of the lord of all that exists.
Endless you are,
And indivisible.
Be gracious, O Lovely One. 19

Mistress of all,
Adored by all,
Existing beyond thought,
You are the Supreme Self.
It is you who bestow both

Worldly enjoyment and spiritual liberation.
20 Be gracious, O Lovely One.

In Brahmā's realm [the center sector], you are Brāhmaṇī.
In Vaikuṇṭha [above], you are the wholly auspicious one.
In Amarāvati [Indra's abode, the east], you are Indrāṇī.
21 In Varuṇa's abode [the west], you are Ambikā.[26]

In Yama's abode [the south], you are the black-bodied.
In Kubera's palace [the north], you are Lady Prosperity.
In Agni's corner [the southeast], you are Great Bliss.
22 Be gracious, O Lovely One.

In Nairṛta's sector [the southwest], you are the red-toothed.
In Vāyu's sector [the northwest], you are the deer rider.
In the depths of murky Pātāla [below], you are Vaiṣṇavī.
23 Be gracious, O Lovely One.[27]

On the Island of Gems, you are the charming Surasā, mother of serpents.
In Īśana's northeast sector, you are the spear bearer.
So, too, in Lanka, you are Bhadrakālī.
24 Be gracious, O Lovely One.[28]

On the bridge leading toward Lanka, you are Rāma's queen.
In Siṃhala, you are she who fascinates the gods.
And in Śrī Kṣetram, you are the flawless one.
25 Be gracious, O Lovely One.[29]

In Kalighatta, you are Kālikā.
On the Blue Hill, you are Kāmākhyā.
In Oṅga country, you are Virajā.
26 Be gracious, O Lovely One.[30]

In Kurukṣetra, you are Bhadrakālī.
In Vraja, you are Kātyāyanī.
In Dvāraka, you are Mahāmayā.
27 Be gracious, O Lovely One.[31]

In Mathurā, you are the supreme queen.
It is you who offer solace to all living beings,

Carrying them across the ocean of existence.
Be gracious, O Lovely One. 28

You are Rāma's Jānakī,
Śiva's mind-bewitcher,
And Dakṣa's daughter.
Be gracious, O Lovely One. 29

By infusing Viṣṇu with your essence,
It was you who destroyed the demon Kaṃsa
And you who vanquished Rāvaṇa.
Be gracious, O Lovely One. 30

This auspicious song for Lakṣmī,
When recited with devotion,
Destroys all mental agitation
And allays all fears. 31

That person who recites it regularly,
Whether once a day
Or at the three twilights,
Generates great spiritual merit. 32

He is released from all wrongdoings,
Even the most debilitating,
And he achieves spiritual liberation,
Whether on earth, in heaven, or in a netherworld.
Of this there is no doubt.[32] 33

Whoever recites this song
With sincere devotion,
Whether in its entirety or just a verse at a time,
Overcomes all difficulties
And attains the highest state. 34

This song confers both worldly happiness and liberation.
Whoever recites it with complete devotion
Receives blessings
Equal to the fruits of thousands of pilgrimages.
Of this there is no doubt. 35

Kamalā, the One Goddess,
Always becomes pleased (with its recitation).

Is there anything more powerful
In all the three worlds
Than to receive the blessings
36 Of the Queen of the Gods?[33]

What on earth, then, cannot be accomplished
By those who recite this song of praise?
It is for this reason
That this excellent song is so highly esteemed.
37 This is true, O Pārvatī, most certainly this is true.[34]

Here ends the glorious *Kamalā Stotram.*

108 Names of the Glorious Lotus Goddess
(Śrī Kamalā Aṣṭottaraśatanāma Stotram)

Lord Śiva spoke:
O Lovely One, I shall now reveal
The 108 names of the glorious lotus goddess.
Though these names surely invoke her presence,
They can never describe fully
The mysterious depths of her being:[35] 1

Great Illusion
Supreme Goddess of Wealth
Supreme Speech
Magnificent Queen
Great Goddess
Great Cosmic Night
Slayer of the Demon King 2

Obsidian Night
Lady Kubera
Slender-waisted
Full of Delight
Primordial
Auspicious
Night
Victory
Open Space
Supreme Cosmic Energy
Mother of the Gods 3

Mother of the Great Boar
She Who Arouses the God of Love
Wide Earth
Indra's Power
Indra's Queen
Lauded by Indra
Dear to Śiva
Beloved[36] 4

She Who Delights the Lord of Vaikuṇṭha
She Who Dwells on Viṣṇu's Chest
Queen of the Universe

Mother of the Universe
Bestower of Boons
Bestower of Fearlessness
5 Consort of Śiva[37]

Ma
Spear-bearer
Discus-bearer
Noose-bearer
Conch-bearer
Mace-bearer
She Who Wears a Necklace of Severed Heads
Lady of the Lotus
6 Abode of Compassion

Lotus-eyed
Gracious Mother
She Who Sweetly Dotes on Mahāviṣṇu
She Who Frolics with the Lord of the Cow Realm
7 She Who Is Worshiped by the Lord of the Cow Realm[38]

Rider of the Eagle
The (river) Gayā
The (river) Gaṅgā
The (river) Yamunā
The (river) Gomatī
The (river) Gaṇḍakī
The (river) Sarayū
The (river) Taptī
The (river) Revā
8 The (river) Payasvinī [39]

The (river) Narmadā
The (river) Kāverī
She Who Dwells in the High Himalaya
Maiden
She Who Is Lauded by the Beautiful-haired One
9 She Who Is Gloriously Praised by Lord Indra[40]

She Who Is Celebrated in the Vedas
Mother of Brahmā and the Other Gods

She Who Dwells in the Center of Brahmā's Cosmic Egg
Creatrix of Brahmā's Cosmic Egg 10

Embodiment of the Veda
Source of the Veda
Resplendence of Veda and Smṛti
Beauty
Daughter of the Waters
Mother of the Elephants
Origin of the World 11

She Who Gives Birth to the Three Worlds
She Whose True Form Is Expressed as Tantric Scriptures
She Whose True Form Is Expressed as Tantric *Mantra*s
She Who Dispels Illusion Quickly
Youthfulness
Auspiciousness
Abode of Auspiciousness 12

Slayer of Madhu and Kaitabha
Vanquisher of Śumbha the Demon
Destroyer of Niśumbha and His Armies
Mother
Adored by Hari and Śaṅkara[41] 13

Entirety
She Who is Filled with the Essence of All the Gods
Shelter
Protectress of Those Seeking Refuge
Adored by Śambhu
She Who Dwells by the Waters' Edge[42] 14

She Who Delights in the Songs of the Celestial Musicians
She Who is Celebrated in the *Gītāgovinda*
Protector of the Three Worlds
She Who Exists as the Elements
She Who is Filled with the Prime of Youth 15

Moon
Mistress of the Lunar Dynasty
Moon-faced
Moonlight

Sister of the Moon
Adored by the Moon
Praised in Song
16 Final Refuge[43]

She Who Exists as Cosmic Creation
She Who Expands the World into Being
She Who Surges Forth the Entire Universe and Contracts
It Inward Once Again

Thus do I praise you, O Goddess,
17 With the recitation of your hundred and eight names.

By reciting this collection (of names)
With sincere devotion
At dawn, noon, and dusk,
A person obtains
Whatever may be desired.
18 Of this there is no doubt.

Whoever recites this song
Shall receive abundant blessings
From the goddess of prosperity
During this lifetime,
And at the time of death
That person shall be delivered from even the deepest
level of hell
19 By the heavenly queen of Vaikuṇṭha.

Here ends the *Śrī Kamalā Aṣṭottaraśatanāma Stotram.*

Song-Amulet of the Lotus Goddess
(Kamalātmikā Kavacam)[44]

O Great Lady, I shall now impart
The song-amulet that fulfills all desires.
When its mantras are applied with proper skill,
The Eternally Auspicious One
Appears before one's eyes.[45] 1

O Queen of the Gods,
By reciting its *mantra*s,
One becomes a son of Pārvatī,
Fully mastering the power in all of the scriptures. 2

It grants that Kamalā, beloved of Viṣṇu,
Ever dwell with those who pursue wealth,
And moreover, it bestows the wealth of eternal wisdom
Upon those who seek the highest truth. 3

Setting the Intention

The Lord is the seer of the four-syllabled song-amulet of Viṣṇu's Beloved. *Anuṣṭubh* is its poetic meter. *Vāgbhavī* is its power and its deity. *Vāgbhavaṃ* is its seed-syllable. *Lajjāramā* is its nail. Its purpose is to furnish a person abundantly with every spiritual power by forming a protective covering of wise words and beautiful poetry, whose core essence consists of desire.

Song-Amulet

With the pronunciation of *aiṃ,*
Let Vāgbhavī, bestower of all spiritual powers,
Bless my head with a mantle of protection.
Hrīṃ. Let Śaṅkarī protect my two eyes
And the space between my eyes. 1

(And let also her protect) my tongue,
The inside of my mouth,
My ears, teeth, nose,
Upper and lower lips,
Upper and lower jaws,
And cheeks. 2

Let Viṣṇu's beloved lady bless me with a mantle of
  protection.
Let Lakṣmī, beautiful embodiment of Viṣṇu's splendor,
Protect my two ears.
Let Pārvatī protect my two arms
3 And my two breasts.

Let her also protect my heart,
Wrists, neck, rib cage, back,
Feminine private parts,
Left and right hips and buttocks,
4 Navel, and both thighs.[46]

(Let her also bless with a mantle of protection)
Both knees, both feet,
Both ankles, and the soles of my feet.
And then, following the course of the life-breath
Up through the constituent elements of my body,
5 (Let her protect) the hair-part on my head.[47]

Let Vijayā protect me in my home.
Let Jayā protect me wherever I travel.
Let Kāmeśī, Mahādevī, and Sarasvatī protect my entire
6 body.[48]

Let Mahāmāyā protect contentment.
Let Mahādevī protect prosperity.
Let Śambhu's Beloved protect excellence at all times, in
7 all places.

Let Vāgbhavī protect me everywhere.
Let the one who dwells with Hara protect me.
Let the Goddess of Fortune protect me.
Let the Eternal Goddess protect me with her heavenly
8 splendor.[49]

Let Lakṣmī, Viṣṇu's mysterious creative power, protect
  my entire body.
Let Sureśvarī protect (my entire body).
Let Śivadūtī always protect me.
9 Let Sundarī protect me at all times, in all places.[50]

Let Bhairavī always protect me.
Let Bheruṇḍā protect me at all times.
Let Tvaritā always protect me.
Let Mugutārā protect me at all times. 10

Let Kālikā always protect me.
Let Kālarātrī protect me at all times.
Let the nine Durgās always protect me.
Let Kāmākṣī protect me at all times. 11

Let the Legions of Divine Mothers
And the Circle of Celestial *Yoginīs* protect me at all times.
Let the Enchanted Ones protect me at all times.
Let the female spirits of the sacred seals protect me
At all times, in all places.[51] 12

Let Lakṣmī, goddess of the gods
And bestower of all prosperity, protect me
At all times
In all places
In all matters
Under all circumstances. 13

Thus has been revealed the divine song-amulet
Comprised entirely of spiritual powers.
If one desires to obtain its benefits,
It should not be spoken of carelessly or with
disparagement. 14

The Supreme Lady
Never reveals herself
To a person lacking in spiritual devotion,
Nor to one who cheats or is abusive,
Who is severely disfigured,
Or who has an extra finger or toe.[52] 15

This sacred song has been revealed
For the benefit of those dedicated to the *kula* path
And for any other sincere devotees
Who greatly desire a vision of the Auspicious One.[53] 16

So too may this most excellent song-amulet
Be imparted to devotees of Viṣṇu,
To those who are virtuous and wise,
Who are dedicated spiritual seekers,
17 And who are blessed with a peaceful disposition.

Reciting this song-amulet
18a Is equal to reciting all of the Tantras.

On Tuesdays and Saturdays,
One may inscribe its *mantra*s
In red sandalwood paste,
With beautiful wildflowers.
Inscribing this divine song-amulet (in this way)
18b–19 Is equal to inscribing all of the Tantras.

(It may also be inscribed)
With one's own sexual juices or those of another,
Mixed with various fragrances
And red or yellow sandalwood paste.
(This should be done) on Sundays
During the bright phase of the moon
Or during an auspicious constellation
Within the months of Śrāvaṇa, Āśvina,
20–21 Kārttika, or Phālguṇa. [54]

On Tuesdays in the early part of Bhādrapada,
The song should be inscribed;
During an auspicious constellation,
Especially during those of Āyuṣ, Prīti,
Brahmā, Indra, Śubha, and Śukra,
22–23 It should be recited in a temple.[55]

During the constellations of Kaulava, Bālava, and Vaṇija
It is best (to recite it)
In desolate burning grounds,
Or in any particularly deserted places,
24 Far from other people.

One should worship the eternal goddess
By first offering prayers to a young girl.
Then the supreme goddess should be offered
25 A savory stew of fish, meat, and greens.

The Supreme Lady should be worshiped
And brahmans should be feasted
With fried sweet lentil-cakes prepared with ghee
And served with a sauce of various spicy ingredients. 26

One should perform the described practices
Flawlessly, three times a day,
As is held in the supreme teaching
Declared by Lord Śaṅkara. 27

[By observing these practices,] a person is protected
From hatred, murder, and other types of violence.
One becomes a son of Pārvatī,
Fully mastering the power in all of the scriptures.
Of this there is no doubt. 28

One soon acquires the spiritual power
By which he can rejoice in the realization
That one's spiritual master is no different than Hara
And that one's wife is the embodiment of Hara's
Beloved.[56] 29

Whoever recites this song regularly
From the depths of one's being
Receives, while still living in this world,
Manifold fruits of those recitations.
One becomes endowed with every success,
And Lakṣmī bestows upon that person the crown of a
king. 30

Here ends the *Kamalātmikā Kavacam*, from the *Viśvasāra Tantra*.

Song for the Lakṣmī of Spiritual Power (Śrī Siddhalakṣmī Stotram)[57]

Setting the Intention

Oṃ. Hiraṇyagarbha is the seer of the *mantras* of the *Song for the Lakṣmī of Spiritual Power* (*Śrī Siddhalakṣmī Stotram*). Its poetic meter is *anuṣṭubh,* the glorious Mahākālī, Mahālakṣmī, and Mahāsarasvatī are its deities, *śrīṃ* is its seed-syllable, *hrīṃ* its animating power, and *klīṃ* its nail. The *Song for the Lakṣmī of Spiritual Power* is recited in order to completely destroy all afflictions and suffering, to remove the anxiety of poverty, and to achieve spiritual power of attainment in all endeavors.

Mantra *Placements of the Seer and Other Preliminaries*

On my head, salutations to the seer, Hiraṇyagarbha.
On my face, salutations to the poetic meter, *anuṣṭubh.*
On my heart, salutations to the deities, the glorious Mahākālī, Mahālakṣmī, and Mahāsarasvatī.
On my feminine private parts, salutations to the seed-syllable, *śrīṃ.*
On my feet, salutations to the animating power, *hrīṃ.*
On my navel, salutations to the nail, *klīṃ.*
Over my entire body, salutations to the intention.

Mantra *Placements on the Hands*

Śrīṃ. On my thumbs, salutations to Siddhalakṣmī.
Hrīṃ. On my forefingers, salutations to Viṣṇu's Effulgence.
Klīṃ. On my middle fingers, salutations to Immortal Bliss.
Śrīṃ. On my ring fingers, salutations to the demon-garlanded goddess.
Hrīṃ. On my little fingers, homage to Resplendent Light.
Klīṃ. On the palms and tops of my hands, salutations to Brāhmaṇī, Vaiṣṇavī, and Rudrāṇī.
Śrīṃ. On my heart, salutations to Siddhalakṣmī.
Hrīṃ. On my head, salutations to Viṣṇu's Effulgence. *Svāhā.*
Klīṃ. On the top back of my head, salutations to Immortal Bliss. *Vaṣaṭ.*

Śrīṃ. On the armor, salutations to the demon-garlanded goddess. *Huṃ*.
Hrīṃ. On my eyes, salutations to Resplendent Light. *Vaṣaṭ*.
Klīṃ. On the weapon, salutations to Brāhmaṇī, Vaiṣṇavī, and Rudrāṇī. *Phaṭ*.[58]

Securing the Directions[59]

Oṃ śrīṃ hrīṃ klīṃ śrīṃ. Salutations to Siddhalakṣmī.

Meditation for Visualization of the Deity

That goddess
Who is the consort of Brahmā, Viṣṇu, and Śiva,
Who has six arms, four faces, and three eyes,
Wielder of sword and trident,
Bearer of lotus, discus, and mace,
Revealing herself as an alluring young woman
Dressed in bright yellow garments
And adorned with a dazzling array of jewels—
Upon that resplendent goddess
Let us meditate.

Song of Praise

The syllable *oṃ* is Lakṣmī,
Embodiment of the imperishable heart of Viṣṇu.
The syllable *hrīṃ* is Lakṣmī,
Embodiment of the unfathomable bliss of Viṣṇu. 1

Klīṃ is the bright and auspicious one
Who bestows immortal bliss.
Śrīṃ is the demon-destroying Śakti,
Garlanded with enemies she has slain. 2

That goddess who is divine resplendence,
Bestower of boons,
Source of auspiciousness,
And the feminine aspect of Brahmā, Viṣṇu, and Śiva,
Embodies herself as the beautiful Kālikā. 3

The primordial sound of the goddess is enunciated
In the syllable *a*, embodiment of Lakṣmī,

In the syllable *u*, embodiment of the imperishable Viṣṇu,
And in the syllable *m*, embodiment of the unfathomable
4 Puruṣa.[60]

(The primordial sound)
Resembles the disc of the sun
And the crescent moon,
And radiates the same exquisite luster.
In between (the sun and moon) is embedded
The hidden treasure,
5 The essence of *brahman*.[61]

The syllable *oṃ*,
Greatest bliss of all,
Is none other than the lovely goddess,
Essence of happiness and well-being.
O Siddhalakṣmī, Mokṣalakṣmī, Ādyalakṣmī,
6 Salutations to you![62]

To the auspicious source
Of all auspiciousness,
To the feminine aspect of Śiva,
To the one who guides all endeavors to successful attainment,
To the one who grants refuge,
To the bright, three-eyed goddess,
To the feminine aspect of Nārāyaṇa,
7a Salutations!

The first (syllable pronounced) is
Gaurī, the three-eyed.
7b And the second is Vaiṣṇavī.[63]

The third (syllable) pronounced is Kamalā,
The fourth is the beautiful one,
The fifth is the animating power of Viṣṇu,
8 And the sixth is Kātyāyanī.

The seventh (syllable) pronounced is Vārāhī,
The eighth is Hari's beloved,
The ninth is the sword-bearer,
9 And the tenth is Devakī.

The eleventh is Siddhalakṣmī,
And the twelfth is the rider of the swan.[64] 10a

That person who recites
This most excellent song
For one to six months,
Continuously and diligently,
Without allowing outside distractions,
Becomes liberated from the bonds of existence.
It should be recited three times a day
By those brahmans burdened with troubles
And the stressful bane of poverty. 10b–12

One who is childless
Shall be blessed with children,
And one bound in poverty
Due to all the offenses of former lives
Shall, after one thousand recitations,
Attain Lakṣmī. 13

Resplendent with glory,
The Auspicious One
Easily destroys one's enemies.
She roams about on a tiger,
Protector against thieves,
Subjugator of ghosts and demons,
And slayer of vampires. 14

The collected revenue is held secure
Within the royal palace gates.[65]

This song was composed by the gods
For the benefit of all living beings. 16

Let it always be recited by brahmans
So as never to be harassed by poverty,
For Lakṣmī is the destroyer of every affliction
And the bestower of every success. 16

Here ends the *Śrī Siddhalakṣmī Storam*, located in the *Brahmā Purāṇa*.

Song for the Glorious "Eyes of Indra" *(Śrī Indrākṣī Stotram)*[66]

Oṃ. The Lord of the Thousand Eyes is the seer of the mantras of the *Song for the Glorious "Eyes of Indra"* (Śrī Indrākṣī Stotram). Its deity is Indrākṣī, *anuṣṭubh* is its meter, Mahālakṣmī its seed, Bhuvaneśvarī its animating power, and Bhavānī its nail. Its seed-syllables are *oṃ, śrīṃ, hrīṃ,* and *klīṃ*. The purpose of reciting the *Song for the Glorious "Eyes of Indra"* is to achieve success in whatever is desired.[67]

Oṃ. On my thumbs, salutations to the glorious Eyes of Indra.
Oṃ. On my forefingers, salutations to Mahālakṣmī.
Oṃ. On my middle fingers, salutations to the Supreme Lady.
Oṃ. On my ring fingers, salutations to the Lotus-eyed.
Oṃ. On my little fingers, salutations to Kātyāyanī.
Oṃ. On the palms and tops of my hands, salutations to the Maiden.
Oṃ. On my heart, salutations to the glorious Eyes of Indra.
Oṃ. On my head, (salutations to) Mahālakṣmī. *Svāhā*.
Oṃ. On the top back of my head, (salutations to) the Supreme Lady. *Vauṣaṭ*.
Oṃ. On the armor [torso], (salutations to) the Lotus-eyed. *Huṃ*.
Oṃ. On the third eye, (salutations to) Kātyāyanī. *Vauṣaṭ*.
Oṃ. On the weapon [hands], (salutations to) the Maiden. *Phaṭ*.

Oṃ bhūr bhuvaḥ svarom.[68]
Thus have the directions been secured.

Herein the mantra*:*

Oṃ aiṃ hrīṃ śrīṃ klīṃ klūṃ. Salutations to Indrākṣī.

Indra spoke:

I celebrate Indrākṣī,
That goddess
Whom the gods glorify with many names:

Brightness
Bearer of the Conch
Formidable
Devī 1

Red-clad Widow
Great Goddess
Moonglow
Great Heat of Austerity
Sāvitrī
Splendor of Meditation
Gāyatrī
Lady Brahmā
Sound-essence of the Wisdom Books 2

Lady Narāyaṇa
Auspicious Darkness
Lady Rudra
Black-hued
Flame of the Sacred Fire
She of the Terrifying Face
Black Night
Mistress of Yogic Austerities 3

Raincloud-dark
Thousand-eyed
Wild-haired
Water-bellied
Great Goddess
She of Unbound Hair
She of Terrifying Form
She of Tremendous Might 4

Invincible
Bestower of Auspiciousness
Felicity
Destroyer of Disease
Beloved of Śiva
Attendant of Śiva
Sword-flame of Agni's Fire
She Who Reveals Herself Clearly Before One's Eyes
Supreme Lady 5

Eternal
Bewitching
Goddess
Beautiful
Queen of the Universe
Indra's Eyes
Indra's Splendor
Indra's Cosmic Power
6 Final Refuge

Destroyer of the Demon King
Vanquisher of Camuṇḍa
Womb of the Gods
Lady of the Great Boar
Lady of the Man-lion
Ferocious
7 She of the Terrifying Roar

Sacred Revelation
Sacred Remembrance
Constancy
Intelligence
Knowledge
Lakṣmī
Sarasvatī
Infinity
Victory
Abundance
Mother of the Mind
8 Unrivalled

Bhavānī
Pārvatī
Durgā
Daughter of the Himalaya
Ambikā
9 Lady Śiva.

Thus has Lord Indra sung the praises of the goddess,
Lauding her with these hundred divine names.[69]

By reciting (this song) one thousand times
While standing waist-deep in water,

One obtains health, longevity, sovereignty,
Wisdom, esteem, and might. 10

The words of this song are *mantra*s
That bestow spiritual power.
Therefore by chanting it
With devotion,
One acquires the power of those *mantra*s. 11

The goddess is pleased
When this song is recited conscientiously.
A person who completes one hundred thousand
recitations
Attains liberation,
Without a doubt. 12

After one thousand recitations,
A person obtains whatever is desired.
If recited one hundred times every evening,
Its spiritual power is realized
Within six months. 13

This song releases a person
From the fear of disease and mental anxiety.
After abiding in it for a full year,
One successfully attains all desired goals. 14

Even after six months,
A servant becomes equal to a king.
Of this there is no doubt. 15

Here ends the *Śrī Indrākṣī Stotram*.

Song-Formulary of the Glorious Mahālakṣmī (Śrī Mahālakṣmī Pañjara Stotram)

Setting the Intention

Oṃ. Brahmā is the seer of the supreme *mantras* of the *Song-Formulary of the Glorious Lakṣmī* (*Śrī Mahālakṣmī Pañjara Stotram*). *Paṅkti* is its meter, *svāhā* its animating power, and *śriyai* its nail. Desires of all kinds may be fulfilled through the recitation of the *Lakṣmī Pañjara Stotram.*[70]

Mantra *Placements on the Hands*

Oṃ śrīṃ hrīṃ. On my thumbs, salutations to Viṣṇu's Beloved.
Oṃ śrīṃ hrīṃ. On my forefingers, salutations to the Mother of the Universe.
Oṃ śrīṃ hrīṃ. On my middle fingers, salutations to the one who is honored as Spiritual Power.
Oṃ śrīṃ hrīṃ. On my ring fingers, salutations to the Bestower of Spiritual Power.
Oṃ śrīṃ hrīṃ. On my little fingers, salutations to the one who fulfills desires.
Oṃ śrīṃ hrīṃ śrīṃ śriyai namaḥ. On the palms and tops of my hands, salutations to the Goddess of the Sacred Flame.[71]

Mantra *Placements on the Body*

Oṃ śrīṃ hrīṃ. On my heart, salutations to Viṣṇu's Beloved.
Oṃ śrīṃ hrīṃ. On my head, salutations to the Mother of the Universe. *Svāhā.*
Oṃ śrīṃ hrīṃ. On the top back of my head, salutations to the one who is honored as Spiritual Power. *Vaṣaṭ.*
Oṃ śrīṃ hrīṃ. On my eyes, salutations to the one who fulfills desires. *Vauṣaṭ.*
Oṃ śrīṃ hrīṃ śrīṃ śriyai namaḥ On the weapon [hands], salutations to the Goddess of the Sacred Flame. *Phaṭ.*

Meditation for Visualization of the Deity

Oṃ. I sing the praises of Lakṣmī,
Whose essence is supreme auspiciousness

And whose body is formed of golden light.
Her entire being sparkles with the radiance of pure gold.
She bears the golden lotus
And the golden vessel filled with seeds.
Seated at the left side of Viṣṇu,
She is Śakti, mother of all creation.[72] 1

O Mahālakṣmī, beloved of Hari,
I come to you seeking refuge.
O Queen of the Gods,
Be patient with my shortcomings
And show me your favor. 2

To the wholly auspicious one
Who graciously confers auspiciousness,
To the glorious Ramā,
Who is more enticing
Than millions of charming love-gods,
I bow, seeking refuge. 3

Six Verses on the Root Mantra (Mūlamantra Ṣaṭkam)[73]

Oṃ śrīṃ hrīṃ aiṃ klīṃ.
Homage to Viṣṇu's beloved, Mahāmāyā.
Kaṃ khaṃ gaṃ ghaṃ ṅaṃ.
Homage! Homage to you.
Protect! Protect me.
Shield! Shield my wealth, grains, and prosperity.
Bestow! Bestow glorious success.
Homage to Śrī. *Svāhā.* 1

Oṃ śrīṃ hrīṃ aiṃ klīṃ.
Homage to the Mother of the Universe,
Ocean of maternal compassion.
Caṃ chaṃ jaṃ jhaṃ ñaṃ.
Homage! Homage to you.
Protect! Protect me.
Shield! Shield the prosperity and stability of my home.
Bestow! Bestow the magical power of speech.
Homage to Śrī. *Svāhā.*[74] 2

Oṃ śrīṃ hrīṃ aiṃ klīṃ.
Homage to the one who is honored as Spiritual Power.

Homage to the indivisible one,
The one who fulfills desires,
The one embodied as spiritual initiation.
Ṭaṃ ṭhaṃ ḍaṃ ḍhaṃ ṇaṃ.
Homage! Homage to you.
Protect! Protect me.
Shield! Shield me from every type of fear.
Bestow! Bestow prosperity.
3 Homage to Śrī. *Svāhā.*

Oṃ śrīṃ hrīṃ aiṃ klīṃ.
Homage to the Bestower of Spiritual Power.
Homage to the *śakti* of the one who surpasses all thought.
Taṃ thaṃ daṃ dhaṃ naṃ.
Homage! Homage to you.
Protect! Protect me.
Keep watch! Keep watch over me.
Grant me prosperity!
Grant the fulfillment of all my desires.
4 Homage to Śrī. *Svāhā.*[75]

Oṃ śrīṃ hrīṃ aiṃ klīṃ.
Homage to the one who fulfills all desires,
To the one who is the core essence
Of all spiritual power and success.
Paṃ phaṃ baṃ bhaṃ maṃ.
Homage! Homage to you.
Protect! Protect me.
Keep watch! Keep watch over me.
Bestow! Bestow the successful fulfillment
Of all of my heart's desires.
5 Homage to Śrī. *Svāhā.*[76]

Oṃ śrīṃ hrīṃ aiṃ klīṃ.
O Kamalā, lady of the lotus,
Be gracious! Be gracious to me.
O Mahālakṣmī, I offer you obeisance.
Homage to you, O support of the world.
Yaṃ raṃ laṃ vaṃ śaṃ ṣaṃ saṃ haṃ kṣaṃ.
Homage! Homage to you.

Protect me! Keep me in your care.
O most beguiling goddess,
Śakti of the one who surpasses all thought,
Grant me majestic power.
Grant me prosperity.
Homage to Śrī. *Svāhā.* 6

Oṃ śrīṃ hrīṃ aiṃ klīṃ. Salutations to the Mother. *Svāhā.*
Oṃ śrīṃ hrīṃ aiṃ klīṃ. Salutations to the one embodied in the seed-syllable. *Svāhā.*
Oṃ śrīṃ hrīṃ aiṃ klīṃ. Salutations to Viṣṇu's Beloved. *Svāhā.*
Oṃ śrīṃ hrīṃ aiṃ klīṃ. Salutations to Spiritual Power. *Svāhā.*
Oṃ śrīṃ hrīṃ aiṃ klīṃ. Salutations to Intellect. *Svāhā.*
Oṃ śrīṃ hrīṃ aiṃ klīṃ. Salutations to Constancy. *Svāhā.*
Oṃ śrīṃ hrīṃ aiṃ klīṃ. Salutations to Mind. *Svāhā.*
Oṃ śrīṃ hrīṃ aiṃ klīṃ. Salutations to Feminine Beauty. *Svāhā.*
Oṃ śrīṃ hrīṃ aiṃ klīṃ. Salutations to Peace. *Svāhā.*
Oṃ śrīṃ hrīṃ aiṃ klīṃ. Salutations to the Auspicious Essence of All Things. *Svāhā.*
Oṃ śrīṃ hrīṃ aiṃ klīṃ. Salutations to Śrī. *Svāhā.*

Oṃ. I bow to the lady of Brahmā and the other gods, mother of sacred knowledge, origin of sacred knowledge, womb of sacred knowledge, creative power of all, the supreme Śrī.

O Beloved of Hari,
Fulfill! Fulfill my desires.
Transmute! Transmute me into a receptacle of Spiritual Power.
Bring forth! Bring forth the immortal nectar.
Instill! Instill fearlessness.
Kindle! Kindle! Blaze! Blaze through every thought and deed.
Illumine! Illumine me, a child of cosmic energy.
Vanquish! Vanquish debilities.
Make perfect! Make perfect all imperfection.
Hrīṃ hrīṃ hrīṃ glauṃ glauṃ śrīṃ. Salutations to Śrī. *Svāhā.*

Song-Amulet of Lakṣmī (Lakṣmī Kavacam)

Oṃ. Let the goddess Padmā, the lotus-bearer,
Bless my head with protection.
Let Lakṣmī, the lotus-dweller, mother of the world,
1 Bless my forehead with protection.

(Let) Mahāmāyā (bless) my mouth (with protection).
(Let) the daughter of Bhṛgu (bless) my cheeks.
(Let) the daughter of the ocean (bless) my nose.
2 (Let) Viṣṇu's Beloved (bless) my eyes.

Let the Maiden bless my throat with protection.
(Let) Hari's Beloved (bless) my shoulders.
Let the source of all creative power always bless my
3 heart.

Let the Queen of the Universe bless my navel.
Let the one who dwells in all things bless my genitals.
Let the lotus goddess bless my hips.
Let the one honored by Brahmā and the other gods
4 (bless) my thighs.

Let the one whose body is the whole world bless my
shins.
Let the source of all delight (bless) my feet.
Let the Self-born One bless my entire body with the
5 seed-syllable of Śrī.

In any difficulty, adversity, or dangerous situation,
Whether seen or unseen,
May the sky-dweller bless me
6 With her all-pervading auspiciousness.

This song-formulary is a great secret
That has been mystically revealed by Lakṣmī herself.
7 One should guard it with diligence.

That person who recites it continuously
With sincere devotion
Receives the blessing of conquering the senses.
By meditating upon these verses for Lakṣmī

With a loving heart,
Nothing at all is difficult to obtain. 8

That person who recites the *Thousand Names of Viṣṇu*
And then with great devotion
Completes five cycles (of the *Lakṣmī Pañjara*)
Attains the perfection of Hari. 9

One should inscribe a six-angled *yantra*
With the corresponding mantras
Upon a *bilva* pedestal.
There, the goddess may be worshiped
With the recitation (of this composite invocation).[77] 10

One should count the recitations
On a rosary of turmeric.
That person who continually recites this esteemed (song)
Most certainly acquires the spiritual power
To achieve whatever may be desired.[78] 11

Here ends the *Lakṣmī Pañjara Stotram*, from the *Śrī Atharvaṇa Rahasya*.

Secret Lakṣmī Incantation That Yields Immediate Results (Sadyaḥ Phaladā Lakṣmīstava Hṛdayam)[79]

I sing the praises of Lakṣmī, the eternal one,
Most glorious mother of auspicious good fortune,
Whose worship generates delight
1 And the fulfillment of all desires.

O Lakṣmī, dwelling with Nārāyaṇa
In glorious Vaikuṇṭha,
Come into my presence.
2 Cast upon me your benevolent glance.[80]

O Lakṣmī, dwelling with Vāsudeva
In the Realm of Truth,
Come into my presence.
3 Be gracious and grant me a boon.

O Lakṣmī, dwelling with Lord Viṣṇu
On the White Island,
Come quickly into my presence.
O Goddess, Virtuous One, Mother of the World,
4 Show me your favor.

O Lakṣmī, dwelling in the Ocean of Milk,
Come into my presence.
Ever shower me with the nectar
5 That flows from your merciful glance.

O Lakṣmī, dwelling in the bounteous sea,
Come into my presence.
Come, come, O Golden One!
6 Become manifest before me.

O Mahālakṣmī, be steadfast.
O Flawless One, waver not.
O gentle lotus goddess,
7 Be gracious and favor me in your heart.

O Abode of Good Fortune!
O Great and Auspicious Prosperity!
The supreme treasure lies within you.

Stir it up!
Bring it quickly to the surface
And let it be revealed! 8

O Source of Wealth,
Receptacle of Wealth,
Bestower of Wealth,
O Śrī most compassionate,
Reveal to me quickly
What is hidden within you. 9

O Auspicious One,
Beloved of Viṣṇu,
You who bring all to successful fruition,
Reveal!
Bring forth the precious treasures
Hidden deep within your womb. 10

O Lakṣmī, reveal yourself here and now.
Stand firmly, O Golden One.
Be steadfast, O Delightful One.
Be gracious and grant a boon. 11

O Lakṣmī,
O you who dwell in the palaces of kings,
As I bow before you,
Stroke my head with tender mercy,
And establish a part of yourself in me.[81] 12

O Śrī, as surely as you abide
In the heavenly city of Vaikuṇṭha
Or deep in the Ocean of Milk,
So may you, together with Viṣṇu,
Settle firmly in my home.[82] 13

O Primordial Mahālakṣmī,
Seated at the left side of Viṣṇu,
Reveal yourself to me.
Protect me, for I come seeking refuge. 14

O Mahālakṣmī,
Abundant with wealth and grains,

Draw near!
As I bow humbly before you,
15 Look upon me with favor.

O Śrī, bestow upon me your merciful glance.
O Śrī, cover my home in a shower of gold.

By invoking Mahālakṣmī
With the recitation of this secret and auspicious song
On a night sacred to Bhārgavī,
16 One receives the blessing of a long and prosperous life.[83]

Here ends the glorious *Sadyaḥ Phaladā Lakṣmīstava Hṛdayam.*

EPILOGUE

The Goddess Returns Home

Invoking Lakshmi begins with the circumstances of a ceremony inviting the goddess to visit our human realm. Throughout this book we have considered how she is invoked and how she makes herself manifest. We have seen a fluidity in her manifestations: She fills the form that we provide for her through our capacities for perception. In the undifferentiated state of her source-essence, she has no form, for there is no form to be had—she is expansiveness itself. Is this not the very definition of abundance, of resplendence, of Śrī?

We have considered just a few of the infinite ways that the goddess presents herself; all of these are expressions of the vessels we have created for her to fill. Of course, in the highest sense, the goddess, as creator and mother of all, has provided the substance for even our own imaginations. As humans dwelling in the differentiated state of a time-space continuum, we construct vessels that fit the size of our own expectations and abilities to greet the goddess. How we invoke her, whether she arrives, and what we do to maintain our relationship with her all play a part in the continuous journey of spiritual exploration. What begins as a prayer for one type of wealth might evolve into yet another level of expanded awareness of the magnificent gifts that the goddess of prosperity is ready to bestow. As we consider the ever-changing nature of Lakṣmī and our abilities to perceive her on our terms and in our territories, we can't help but wonder: What are the goddess's terms and territories? We are reminded of a question posed at the beginning of this book: If the goddess has arrived, then where has she come from?

In the Farewell (*Namaskāra*) section at the conclusion of the *Lakṣmī Pūjā*, the goddess is seen off, to return "home." From our vantage point in our world, we don't really know what that is, other than to envision it, somehow, as an undifferentiated state of pure, unlimited consciousness. However, the songs throughout this volume indicate that the goddess has quite a few other "homes." There is more to the picture than her simply moving from a primordial state of pure expansiveness into the limited arena of name-and-form (*nāma-rūpa*) that characterizes our worldly constructions of reality.

We learn that the goddess inhabits each of the eleven cosmic directions—the eight cardinal directions on the earth plane, plus the central point, and then the various levels stretching "above" into the heavenly realms and "below" into the strata of the netherworlds. When she is not "here," she might be in the heavenly abode of Vaikuṇṭha, where she dwells with Viṣṇu in his form as Nārāyaṇa, or she could be in the paradisiacal Cow Realm (Goloka), where she dwells with Viṣṇu in his form as Kṛṣṇa. So too may she be found on one of her sacred islands within the cosmic Ocean of Milk, such as the White Island (Śvetadvīpa) or the Island of Gems (Maṇidvīpa). Even in Pātāla, the lowest level of the netherworlds, whose murky waters are home to poisonous snakes, Lakṣmī reigns as beneficent queen.

All of the realms that Lakṣmī inhabits exceed the time-space matrix of our ordinary conceptual capacities. They may be visited, however, by those who can meet the specific dimensions of the consciousness prevalent in those realms. This is why the poets beseech the goddess to bring their own consciousness into resonance with hers. How amazing to bask in the exquisite presence of the goddess, having convinced her to arrive. How much more amazing might it be to follow her home, to experience the splendors of Vaikuṇṭha or Maṇidvīpa or Śvetadvīpa. Simply to experience the states of conscious that one would have to develop in order to prepare for such journeys would constitute a spiritual transformation of its own. From that state, the entire universe would call to us. Even the serpent-beings who dwell in Pātāla at the very root of the body of the universe might entice us to wonder: Are these not primordial forms of the Kuṇḍalinī that dwells at the very root of our own human body? As the Tantric sources suggest, the realms of the goddess exist outward, beyond the earth, and they also exist within us. Accessing the heavenly states of the goddess's supreme consciousness has as much to do with our own spiritual preparation as it does with a gracious invitation from the goddess.

As we have seen in the songs in our collection, there are two basic types of prayers to the goddess of wealth: One is to ask for prosperity in any of its forms. The other is to ask for access to the *source* of that prosperity. For the first, the goddess comes to us, meets us in our place, on our terms, and works within our limitations. For the other, the goddess may meet us partway, but if we want access to the *source*, we need to be able to make that journey alongside her. Here, the roles become reversed. For the first type of prayer, we are the ones who do the invoking. For the other, it is the goddess who calls to us, inviting us to make a pilgrimage to experience her heavenly abodes, her exquisitely expansive state. In this book we have focused on *Invoking Lakshmi*, calling her into our realm. As marvelous as this has been, how much more exciting to anticipate the next great adventure, to be able to accept the challenge should the goddess, on departing from our glorious meeting, suggest, "Next time, *my* place."

Transliterated Sanskrit Texts

Unless otherwise specified, all Sanskrit texts are from *Śrī Lakṣmī Upāsanā*, ed. Dixit.

Lakṣmī Pūjā Text

Svasti-vācana

oṃ svasti na indro vṛddhaśravaḥ svasti na pūṣā viśvavedāḥ / svastinastārkṣaryo ariṣṭanemiḥ svastino bṛhaspatirdadhātu // oṃ payaḥ pṛthivyām payaḥ oṣadhīṣu payo divyantarikṣe payodhāḥ / payasvatīḥ pradiśaḥ santu mahyam // [ ] oṃ agnirdevatā vāto devatā sūryo devatā candramā devatā vasavo devatā rudro devatā'dityādevatā marutodevatā viśvedevā devatā bṛhaspatirdevatendro devatā varuṇo devatā // oṃ dhyau śāntirantarikṣam śāntiḥ pṛthivī śāntirāpaḥ śāntiroṣadhayaḥ śāntiḥ vanaspatayaḥ śāntirviśvedevāḥ śāntirbrahma śāntiḥ sarvam śāntiḥ śāntireva śāntiḥ sāmā śāntiredhi/ [ ] śāntiḥ śāntiḥ śāntirbhavatu //

Pavitrīkaraṇa

oṃ apavitraḥ pavitrovā sarvāvasthāṃgato'pivā
yaḥ smaretpuṇḍarīkākṣam sa bāhyābhyantaraḥ śuciḥ

Bhūta-śuddhi

oṃ apasarpantu te bhūtā ye bhūtā bhuvi saṃsthitā
ye bhūtā vighnakartāraste naśyantu śivājñayā

Srī Gaṇeśa Dhyāna Mantra

om̩ sumukhaścaikadantaśca kapilo gajakarṇakaḥ
lambodaraśca vikaṭo vighnanāśo vināyakaḥ
dhūmraketurgaṇādhyakṣo bhālacandro gajānanaḥ
dvādaśaitāni nāmāni yaḥ paṭhecchṛṇuyādapi
vidhyārambhe vivāhe ca praveśe nirgame tathā
saṃgrāme saṃkaṭe caiva vighnastasya na jāyate
śuklāmbaradharaṃ devaṃ śaśivarṇaṃ caturbhujam
prasannavadanaṃ dhyāyetsarvavighnopaśāntaye

Saṃkalpa-vākya

Dhyāna

namaste'stu mahāmaye śrīpīṭhe surapūjite
1 śaṅkhacakragadāhaste mahālakṣmi namo'stute
namaste garuḍārudhe kolāsura bhayaṃkari
2 sarvapāpa hare devi mahālakṣmi namo'stute
padmāsanasthite devi parabrahmasvarūpiṇi
3 parameśi jaganmātarmahālakṣmi namo'stute
śvetāmbaradhare devi nānālaṅkārabhūṣite
4 jagatsthite jaganmātarmahālakṣmi namo'stute
yā śrīḥ padmāsanasthāvipulakaṭi taṭī padmapatrāpatākṣī
gambhīrāvarttanābhitanubharanamitā śubhravastrottarīyā
yā lakṣmīdivyarūpair maṇigaṇakhacitaiḥ stāpitāṃ
hemakuṃbhaiḥ
sā nityam padmahastā mama vasatugṛhe sarvamāṅgalya
5 yuktā

Āvāhana

oṃ sarvalokasya jananī padmahastāṃ sulocanām
1 sarvadevamayīmīśāṃ devīmāvāhayāmyaham
tattakāñcanavarṇābhām muktāmaṇi virājitam
2 amalaṃ kamalaṃ divyamāsanaṃ pratigṛhyatām
sarvatīrtha samudbhutaṃ padyam gandhādibhiryutam
3 mayādattaṃ gṛhānedaṃ bhagavatibhaktavatsale
aṣṭagandha samāyuktaṃ svarṇapātra prapūritam
4 arghyam gṛhānamaddattam mahālakṣmyai namo'stute

sarvalokasya yā śaktirbrahmaviṣṇuśivādibhiḥ
stutā dadāmyācamanaṃ mahālakṣmyai namoharam 5
pañcāmṛta samāyuktaṃ jāhnavī salilaṃ śubham
gṛhāna viśva janani snānārthaṃ bhakta vatsale 6
divyāmbaram nūtanaṃ hi kṣaumaṃtvati manoharam
dīyamānam matā devi gṛhana jagadambike 7
kāpilam dadhi kundedudhabalaṃmadhusaṃyutam
svaṛṇapātrasthitaṃ devi madhuparka gṛhāṇa me 8
ratna kaṅkaṇavaidūrya muktāhārādikāni ca
suprasanne gamaṇasādattāni svīkuruṣvame 9
śrīkhaṇḍāgarukarpūramṛganābhi samanvitam
vilepanaṃ gṛhāṇatvaṃ namo'stute bhaktavatsale 10
raktacandana sammiśraṃ pārijātasamudbhavam
mayādattagṛhānāśu candanaṃ gandhasaṃyutam 11
sindūram raktavarṇam ca sindūratilakam priye
bhaktyādattammayā devi sindūram pratigṛhyatām 12
kuṃkumaṃ kāmadam divyam kuṃkumaṃ kāmarūpiṇam
akhaṇḍakāma saubhāgyaṃ kuṃkumaṃ pratigṛhyatām 13
tailāni ca sugandhīnidravyāṇi vividhāni ca
mayādattāni lepārthaṃ gṛhāṇa parameśvari 14
mandārapārijātadīnpāṭalaṃ ketakīṃ tathā
meruvāmogaraṃ caiva gṛhāṇāśu namo'stute 15
viṣṇvādi sarvadevānāṃ priyāṃ sarva suśobhanām
kṣīrasāgarasambhūtāṃ dūrvā svīkuru sarvadā 16
vanaspatirasodbhūto gadhāḍhyaḥ sumanoharaḥ
āghreyaḥ sarvadevānāṃ dhūpo'yaṃ pratigṛhyatām 17
karpūravarttisaṃyuktaṃ ghṛtayuktaṃ manoharam
tamonāśakaraṃ dīpam gṛhāṇa parameśvari 18
naivedyaṃ gṛhyatāmdevi bhakṣyabhojya samanvitam
ṣaḍrasairanvitaṃ divyam lakṣmi devi namo'stute 19
śītalam nirmalaṃ toyam karpūreṇa suvāsitam
ācamanyatāṃ mama jalaṃ prasīda tvaṃ maheśvari 20
elālavaṅga karpūra nāgapatrādibhiryutam
pūgīphalena saṃyuktam tāmbūlaṃ pratigṛhayatām 21
phalena phalitaṃ sarvam trailokyaṃ sacarācaram
tasmātphalapradānena pūrṇāḥ santu manorathaḥ 22
hiraṇyagarbha garbhasthaṃ hemabījaṃ vibhāvasoḥ
anantapuṇya phaladam ataḥ śānti prayaccha me 23
caturdasarvalokānāṃ timirasya nivāraṇam
ārtikyaṃ kalpitam bhaktyā gṛhāṇa parameśvari 24

yāni kāni ca pāpāni brahmahatyāsamāni ca
25 tāni tāni vinaśyanti pradakṣiṇāṃ pade pade
ketakījāti kusumairmallikā mālatībhavaiḥ
26 puṣpañjalirmayādattātāvatprapyai namo'stute
namaste sarvadevānāṃ varadāsi hariḥpriye
27 yāgatistva prapannāmāṃ sāme bhūyāttvadarpanāt

Vedic Texts

Hymn to Śrī
(Śrī Sūktam)[1]

hiraṇyavarṇām hariṇīm suvarṇa-rajata-srajām
candrām hiraṇmayīṃ lakṣmīm jātavedo ma āvaha 1
tāṃ māvaha jātavedo lakṣmīṃ-anapagāminīm
yasyāṃ hiraṇyam vindeyaṃ gāmaśvam puruṣānaham 2
aśvapurvāṃ rathamadhyāṃ hastināda prabodhinīm
śriyaṃ devīm upāhvaye śrīr mā devi juṣatām 3
kām so'smitām hiraṇya-prākārām ārdrām jvalantīm
tṛptām tarpayantīm
padme-sthitām padma-varṇām tām ihopahvaye śriyam 4
candrām prabhāsām yaśasā jvalantīm śriyaṃ loke
devajuṣṭām udārām
tām padmanemīm śaraṇam aham prapadye'alakṣmīr me
naśyatām tvām vṛṇe 5
ādityavarṇe tapaso'dhijāto vanaspatis tava vṛkso'tha
bilvaḥ
tasya phalāni tapasā nudantu mā yāntara yāś ca bāhyā
alakṣmiḥ 6
upaitu mām devasakhaḥ kīrtiś ca maniṇā saha
prādurbhūto'smi rāṣṭre'smin kīrtim ṛddhim dadātu me 7
kṣutpipāsāmalām jyeṣṭhām alakṣmīm nāśayāmy'aham
abhūtim asamṛddhim ca sarvān nirṇuda me gṛhāt 8
gandhadvārām durādharṣāṃ nityapuṣṭām karīṣiṇīm
īśvarīm sarva bhūtānām tām ihopahvaye śriyam 9
manasa kāmam ākutim vācas satyam aśīmahi
paśunāṃ rūpam annasya mayi śrīḥ śrayatām yaśaḥ 10
kardamena prajābhūtā mayi sambhava kardama
śriyam vāsaya me kule mātaram padmamālinīm 11
āpaḥ sṛjantu snigdhāni ciklīta vasa me gṛhe
ni ca devīm mātaraṃ śriyam vāsaya me kule 12
ārdrām puṣkariṇīm puṣṭim piṅgalām padmamālinīm
candrām hiraṇmayīṃ lakṣmīm jātavedo ma āvaha 13
ārdrām yaḥ kariṇīm yaṣṭim suvarṇām hemamālinīm
sūryām hiraṇmayīm lakṣmīm jātavedo ma āvaha [2] 14
tām ma āvaha jātavedo lakṣmīm anapagāminīm
yasyām hiraṇyaṃ prabhutam gāvo dāsyo'śvān vindeyam
puruṣān aham 15

Hymn to Lakṣmī
(Lakṣmī Sūktam)[3]

padmānane padmini padmapatre padmapriye
padmadalāyatākṣi
viśvapriye viśvamano'nukūle tvatpādapadmam mayi
1 sannidhatsva
padmānane padma ūrū padmākṣi padmasaṃbhave
2 tanme bhajasi padmākṣi yena saukhyaṃ labhāmyaham
aśvadayi godāyi dhanadāyi mahādhane
3 dhanaṃ me labhatāṃ devi sarvakāmaṃśva dehime
putrapautradhanaṃ dhānyaṃ hastyaśvādi gave ratham
4 prajānāṃ bhavasī mātā āyuṣmaṃtam karotu me
dhanamagnirdhanaṃ vāyurdhanaṃ sūryo dhanam vasuḥ
5 dhanamindro bṛhaspatirvaruṇam dhanamaśvinau
vainateya somaṃ piba somam pibatu vṛtrahā
6 somam dhanasya somino mahyaṃ dadātu sominaḥ
na krodho na ca mātsaryaṃ na lobho nāśubhā matiḥ
7 bhavanti kṛtapuṇyānāṃ bhaktānāṃ śrīsūktaṃ japet
sarisijanilaye sarojahaste dhavalatarāṃśukagandhamālya
śobhe
bhagavti harivallabhe manojñe tribhuvanabhūtikari
8 prasīda mahyam
viṣṇupatnīm kṣamāṃ devīṃ mādhavīṃ mādhavapriyām
9 viṣṇupriyām sakhīṃ devīm namāmyacyutavallabhām
oṃ mahālakṣmīm ca vidmahe viṣṇupatnīṃ ca dhīmahi
10 tanno lakṣmīḥ pracodayāt
ānandaḥ kardamaḥ śrīdaḥ ciklīta iti viṣrutāḥ
11 ṛṣayaścaḥ śriyaḥ putrā mayi śrīrdevī devatā
ṛṇarogādidāridryaṃ pāpañca apamṛtyavaḥ
12 bhayaśokamanastāpā naśyantu mama saravadā
śrīrvacasvamāyuṣyamārogyamāvidhātpavāmanaṃ
mahīyate
dhanam dhānyam paśuṃ bahuputralābhaṃ
13 śatasaṃvatsaraṃ dīrghamāyuḥ

iti lakṣmīsūktaṃ samāptam

Purāṇic Texts

Song for Lakṣmī, Gracious Bestower of Blessings
(Prasannavaradā Śrī Lakṣmī Stotram)

jaya padmapalāśākṣi jaya tvam śrīpati priye
jaya mātarmahālakṣmi samsārārṇava tāriṇi 1
mahālakṣmi namastubhyaṃ namastubhyaṃ sureśvari
haripriye namastubhyaṃ namastubhyaṃ dayānidhe 2
padmālaye namastubhyaṃ namastubhyaṃ ca sarvade
sarvabhūtahitārthaya vasuvṛṣtim sadā kuru 3
jaganmātarnamastubhyaṃ namastubhyaṃ dayānidhe
dayāvati namastubhyaṃ viśveśvari namostu te 4
namaḥ kṣirārṇavasute namastrailokya dhāriṇi
vastuḍṛste namastubhyaṃ rakṣa māṃ śaraṇāgatam 5
rakṣa tvam devadeveśi devadevasya vallabhe
daridryāttrāhi māṃ lakṣmi kṛpā kuru mamopari 6
namastrailokya janani namastrailokya pāvani
brahmādaye namaste tvāṃ jagadānanda dāyinīm 7
viṣṇupriye namastubhyaṃ namastubhyaṃ jagaddhite
ārti hantri namastubhyaṃ samṛddhi kuru me sadā 8
abjavāse namastubhyaṃ capalāyai namo namaḥ
caṇvalāyai namastubhyaṃ lalitāyai namo namaḥ 9
namaḥ pradyumna janani mātastubhyaṃ namo namaḥ
paripālaya bho mātarmāmṃ tubhyaṃ śaraṇāgatam 10
śaraṇya tvām prapanno'smi kamale kamalālaye
trāhi trāhi mahālakṣmi paritrāṇa parāyane 11
pāṇitam śobhate naiva na śobhanti guṇā nare
śīlatvam naiva śobheta mahālakṣmi tvayā vinā 12
tāvadvirājate rūpam tāvacchīlam virājate
tāvad guṇā nārāyaṇāñca yāvallakṣmi prasīdate 13
lakṣmi tvayā tvaṃkṛta mānavā ye
    pāpairvimuktā nṛpa lokamānyaḥ
guṇairvihīnā guṇino bhavanti
    duḥśīlinaḥ śīlavatāṃ variṣṭhaḥ 14
lakṣmīrbhūṣayate rūpaṃ lakṣmīrbhūṣayate kulam
lakṣmīrbhūṣayate vidyāṃ sarvallakṣmīrviśiṣyate 15
lakṣmi tvadguṇakīrtanena kamalā
    bhūyātyalaṃ jihyatām
rudrādyā ravicandra devapatayo
    vaktuñca naiva kṣamāḥ

asyābhistava rūpa lakṣaṇa guṇāṃ
vaktuṃ kathaṃ śakyate
mātārmāṃ paripāhi viśvajanani
16 kṛtvā mameṣṭam dhruvam
dīnārtibhītaṃ bhavatāpa pīḍitaṃ
dhanairvihīnam tava parśvamāgataḥ
kṛpānidhitvanmama lakṣmi satvaraṃ
17 dhana pradānāddhana nāyakam kuru
māṃ vilokya janani haripriyeḥ
nirdhanaṃ tava samīpamāgatam
dehi me jhaṭiti lakṣmi karāgraṃ
18 vastra kañcana varānna yadbhutam
tvameva jananī lakṣmi pītā lakṣmi tvameva ca
19 bhrātā tvaṃ ca sakhā lakṣmi vidyā lakṣmi tvameva ca
trāhi trāhi mahālakṣmi trāhi trāhi sureśvari
20 trāhi trāhi jaganmātardaridryāttrāhi vegataḥ
namastubhyaṃ jagaddhātri namastubhyaṃ namo namaḥ
21 dharmādhare namastubhyaṃ namaḥ sampatti dāyinī
daridrārṇava magno'haṃ nimagno'ham rasātale
majjantaṃ māṃ kare dhṛtvā sūddhara tvaṃ rame
22 drutam
kiṃ lakṣmi bahunoktena jalpitena punaḥ punaḥ
23 anyame śaraṇam nāsti satyaṃ satyaṃ haripriye
etacchrutvā'gasti vākyaṃ hṛsyamāṇya haripriyā
24 uvāca madhurā vāṇīṃ tuṣṭāhaṃ tava sarvadā
yattvayoktamidaṃ stotraṃ yaḥ paṭhiṣyati māṇavaḥ
25 śṛnoti ca mahābhāgastasyāha vaśavartinī
nityam paṭhati yo bhaktyā lakṣmītasya na naśyati
26 ṛṇaśca naśyate tīvraṃ viyogam naiva paśyati
yaḥ paṭhetprātaruttāya śraddhābhakti samanvitaḥ
27 gṛhe tasya sadā sthāsye nityaṃ śrīpatinā saha
sukha saubhāgya sampanno manasvī buddhimān bhavet
28 putravān guṇavān śreṣṭho bhoga bhoktā ca mānavaḥ
idaṃ stotram mahāpuṇyaṃ lakṣmyagasti prakīrtitam
29 viṣṇu prasāda jananaṃ caturvargaṃ phalāpradam
rājaddvāre jayaścaiva śatroścaiva parājayaḥ
30 bhūtapreta piśācānāṃ vyāghrāṇāṃ na bhayaṃ tathā
na śastrānalato yaudyād bhayaṃ tasya prajāyate
31 durvṛttānām ca pāpānāṃ bahuhānikaraṃ param
mandarākariśālāsu gavāṃ goṣṭhe samāhitaḥ
32 paṭhettaddoṣa śāntyartham mahāpātaka nāśanam

sarva saukhyakaraṃ nṛṇāmāyurarogyadaṃ tathā
agasti muninā proktaṃ prajānāṃ hitakāmyayā 33

ityagasti viracitaṃ lakṣmī stotraṃ samāptam

Song for the Glorious Lotus Goddess
(Śrī Kamalā Stotram)

namaḥ kamalavāsinyai nārāyanyai namo namaḥ
1 kṛṣṇa priyāyai satatamṃ mahālakṣmyai namo namaḥ
padmapatrekṣanāyai ca padmāsyayai namo namaḥ
2 padmāsanāyai padminyai vaiṣṇavyai ca namo namaḥ
sarvaṃ sampatsvarūpinyai sarvarāddhyai namo namaḥ
3 haribhakti pradātryai ca harṣadātryai namo namaḥ
krṛṣṇa vakṣaḥ sthitāyai ca kṛṇośāyai namo namaḥ
4 candraśobhā svarūpāyai ratnapadme ca śobhane
sampatyadhiṣṭhātṛdevyai mahādevyai namo namaḥ
5 namo vṛddhisvarūpāyai vṛddhidāyai namo namaḥ
vaikuṇṭhe yā mahālakṣmīryā lakṣmīḥ kṣīra sāgare
6 svargalakṣmīrindragehe rājalakṣmīrnṛpālaye
gṛhalakṣmīśca gṛhiṇī gehe ca gṛhadevatā
7 surabhiḥ sāgare jātā dakṣiṇā yajña kāminī
aditirdeva mātā tvaṃ kamalā kamalālayā
8 svāhā tvaṃ ca havirdāne kavyādane svadhāsmṛtā
tvaṃhi viṣṇusvarūpā ca sarvādhāra vasundharā
9 śuddhasatvasvarūpā tvaṃ nārāyaṇa parāyaṇa
krodhahiṃsāvarjita ca varadā śāradā śubhā
10 paramārtha pradā tvāṃ ca haridāsya pradā parā
yayā vinā jagatsarvam bhasmībhūtamasārakam
11 jīvanmṛtam ca viśvaṃ ca śāśvatsarvayayā vinā
sarveṣāṃ ca parā mātā sarvabāndhavarūpiṇī
12 dharmārtha kāmamokṣāṇāṃ tvaṃ ca kāraṇa rūpiṇī
yathā mātā stanāṃdhānāṃ śiśūnāṃ śaiśave sadā
13 tathā tvaṃ sarvadā mātā sarveṣāṃ sarvarūpataḥ
mātṛhīnaḥ stanāṃdhastu sa ca jīvati daivataḥ
14 tvayāhīno janaḥ ko'pi na jīvatyena niścitam
suprasannasvarūpā tvaṃ māṃ prasannā bhavāmbike
15 vairigrastaṃ ca viṣayam dehi mahyaṃ sanātani
ahaṃ yāvattvayā hīno bandhuhīnaśca bhikṣukaḥ
16 sarvasaṃpaddhihīnāśca tāvadeva haripriye
jñānaṃ dehi ca dharmaṃ ca sarvaṃ saubhāgyamīpsitam
17 prabhāvaṃ ca pratāpaṃ ca sarvādhikārameva ca
jayam parākramaṃ yuddhe paramaiśvaryam eva ca
śrī nārāyaṇa uvāca—
18 ityuktvā ca mahendraśca sarveḥ suragaṇauḥ saha
praṇanāma sāśrunetro mūrdhna caiva punaḥ punaḥ
19 brahmā ca śaṅkaraścaiva śeṣo dharmaśca keśavaḥ

sarve cakruḥ parīhāraṃ surārthe ca punaḥ punaḥ
devebhyaśca varaṃ datvā puṣpamālāṃ manoharām 20
keśavāya dadau lakṣmīḥ saṃtuṣṭāḥ surasaṃsadi
yayurdevāśca saṃtuṣṭā svaṃ svaṃ sthānaṃ ca nārada 21
devī yayau hare sthānaṃ hṛṣṭā kṣīrodaśāyinaḥ
yayatuścaiva sva sva gṛhaṃ brahmeśānau ca nārada 22
datvā śubhāśiyaṃ tau ca devebhyaḥ prītipūrvakam
idaṃ stotraṃ mahāpuṇyaṃ trisandhyaṃ yaḥ paṭhennaraḥ 23
kuberatulyaḥ sa bhavedrājarājeśvaro mahān
pañcalakṣa japenaiva stotrasiddhirbhavennṛṇām 24
siddha stotraṃ yadi pathenmāsamekaṃ tu santatam
mahāsukhī ca rājendro bhaviṣyati na saṃśayaḥ 25

iti śrī kamalā stotraṃ samāptam

Lord Indra's Song for Lakṣmī
(Devarāja Indrakṛta Lakṣmī Stotram)[4]

pārāśara uvāca—
siṃhāsana gataḥ śakraḥ saṃprāpta tridivaṃ puraḥ
1 devarājye sthitā devīṃ tuṣṭāvābjakarāṃ tataḥ
indra uvāca—
namaste sarvabhūtānāṃ jananīmabdhi saṃbhavām
2 śrīyakunnidrapadmākṣī viṣṇu vakṣasthalasthitāṃ
padmālayāṃ padmakarāṃ padmapatra nivekṣaṇām
3 vande padmamukhīṃ devīṃ padmanābha priyāmaham
tvaṃ siddhistvaṃ svadhā svāhā sudhātvaṃ lokapāvanī
4 sandhyā rātri prabhā bhūtirmedhā śraddhā sarasvatī
yajñavidyā mahāvidyā guhyavidyā ca śobhane
5 ātmavidyā ca devi tvaṃ vimukti phaladāyinī
ānvikṣikī trayī vārtā daṇḍanītistvameva ca
6 saumyāsaumyair jagadrūpaistvayaitad devi pūritam
kā tvanyā tvāmṛte devi sarvayajñamayaṃ vapuḥ
7 adhyāste devadevasya yogicintyaṃ gadābhṛtaḥ
tvayādevi parityaktaṃ sakalaṃ bhuvanatrayam
8 vinaṣṭaprāpamabhavat tvayedānīṃ samedhitam
dārāḥ putrāstathā'gara suhṛddhānyu dhanādikaṃ
9 bhavatyetanmahābhāge nityaṃ tvaddīkṣanānnṛnān
śarīrārogyamaiśvaryamari pakṣa kṣayaḥ sukham
10 devi tvaddṛṣṭidṛṣṭānāṃ puruṣānāṃ na durlabham
tvamambā sarvabhūtānāṃ devadevo hariḥ pitā
11 tvayaitadviṣṇunā cāmba jagaddyāptaṃ carācaram
mā naḥ kośaṃ tathā goṣṭhaṃ mā gṛham ma paricchadam
12 mā śarīram kalatra ca tyajethāḥ sarvapāvani
mā putrānmā suhṛdvargānmā paśūnmā vibhūṣaṇam
13 tyajethā mama devasyaviṣṇorvakṣa sthalāśraye
satvena satyaśaucābhyāṃ tathā śīlādibhirguṇaiḥ
14 tyajyaṃte te narāḥ sadhya saṃtyaktā ye tvayā'male
tvayā'valokitāḥ sadyaḥ śīlācyairakhilairguṇaiḥ
15 kulaiśvaryaśca yujyante puruṣā nirguṇā api
sa ślaghyaḥ saguṇī dhanyaḥ sa kulīnaḥ sabhuddhimān
16 sa sūraḥ sa ca vikrānto yastvayā devi vikṣitaḥ
sadyo vaiguṇyamāyāṃti śīlādyaḥ sakalā guṇaḥ
17 parāñmukhī jagaddhātrī yasya tvaṃ viṣṇuvallabhe
na te varṇayitam śaktā guṇān jihvāpi vedhasaḥ
18 prasīda devi padmākṣi nāsmāṃstyākṣīḥ kadācana

pārāsara uvāca—
evaṃ śrī saṃstutā saṃyak prāha hṛṣṭhā śatakratum
śṛṇvatāṃ sarvadevānāṃ sarvabhūtasthitā dvija 19
śrīruvāca—
parituṣṭāsmi deveśa stotreṇānena te hare
varaṃ vṛṇīṣva yo'bhīṣṭaḥ varadāhaṃ tavāgatā 20
indra uvāca—
varada yadi me devi varārho yadi vāpyaham
trailokyaṃ na tvayā tyājyameṣa me'stu varaḥ paraḥ 21
stotreṇa yastavaitena tvāṃ stoṣyatyabdhisambhave
sa tvāṃ na parityajyo [ ] dvitīyostu varo mama 22
śrīruvāca—
trailokyaṃ tridaśa śreṣṭha na saṃtyakṣyāmi vāsava
dattā varo mayā'yaṃ te stotrārādhana tuṣṭayā 23
yaśca'āyam tathā prātaḥ stotreṇānena mānavaḥ
māṃ stoṣyati na tasyāhaṃ bhaviṣyāmi parāṅmukhī 24
pārasara uvāca—
evam varaṃ dadau devī devarājāya vai purā
maitraya śrīrmahābhāga stotrārādhana toṣitā 25
bhṛgoḥ khyātyāṃ samutpannā śrīḥ pūrvamudadheḥ punaḥ
devadānava yatnena prastūtā'mata maṃthane 26
evaṃ yathā jagatsvāmī devarājo janārdanaḥ
avatāraṃ karotyeṣā tathā śrīstatsahāyinī 27
punaśca padmasambhūtā tathā'dityo'bhavaddhari
yadā ca bhārgavo rāmastadā'bhūddharaṇī tviyam 28
rāghavatve'bhavassītā rukmiṇī kṛṣṇa janmani
anyeṣuravatāreṣu viṣṇoreṣā'napāyinī 29
devatve devadeheyaṃ mānusatve ca mānuṣī
viṣṇo dehānurūpāṃ vai karotyeṣā'tmanastanum 30
yaścaittacchṛṇuyājjanma lakṣmya yaśca paṭhennaraḥ
śriyo na vicyutistasya gṛhe yāvatkulatrayam 31
paṭhyate veṣu caitreṣu gṛhaṣu śrīstavo mane
alakṣmī kalahādhārā na teṣvāste kadācana 32
etatte kathitaṃ brahman yanmāṃ tvaṃ paripṛcchasi
kṣīrābdhau śrīryathā jātā pūrvaṃ bhṛgusutā satī 33
iti sakala vibhutyavāpti hetuḥ stutiriyamindramukhodgatā hi lakṣmyaḥ
anudhinmiha paṭhyate nabhiyarvasati na teṣu kadācidapyalakṣmīḥ 34

The Heavenly Gods' Praise-Song for Lakṣmī
(Śrī Daivakṛta Lakṣmī Stotram)[5]

kṣamasva bhagavatyaṃba kṣamāśile parātpare
1 śuddha sattvasvarūpe ca kopādiparivarjite
upame sarvasādhvīnāṃ devīnāṃ deva pūjite
2 tvayā vinā jagatsarva mṛtatulyaṃ ca niṣphalam
sarva sampatsvarūpā tvaṃ sarveśāṃ sarvarūpiṇī
3 rāseśvaryadhidevī tvaṃ tvatkalāḥ sarva yoṣitaḥ
kailaśe pārvatī tvaṃ ca kṣīrode sindhukanyakā
4 svarge ca svargalakṣmīstvaṃ martya lakṣmīścabhūtale
vaikuṇṭhe ca mahālakṣmīrdaivadevī sarasvatī
5 gaṅgā ca tulasī tvam ca sāvitrī brahmalokataḥ
kṛṣṇaprānādhidevi tvaṃ goloke rādhikā svayam
6 rāse rāseśvarī tvaṃ ca vṛndāvana vane vane
kṛṣṇapriyā tvaṃ bhāṇdire candrā candana kānane
7 virajā campaka vane śataśṛṅge ca sundarī
padmāvatī padmavane mālatā mālatī vane
8 kundadantī kundavane suśīlā ketakī vane
kadaṃbamālā tvaṃ devī kadaṃba kānane'pi ca
9 rājalakṣmī rājagehe gṛhalakṣmī gṛhe gṛhe
ityuktva devatāḥ sarve munayo manavastathā
10 rurudurnamravadanāḥ śuṣkakaṇṭhoṣṭhatālukā
iti lakṣmī stavaṃ puṇyaṃ sarvadevaiḥ kṛtaḥ śubham
11 yaḥ paṭhetprātarutthāya sa vai sarva labheddhruvam
abharyo labhate bhāryaṃ vinītam ca sutāṃ satīm
12 suśīlam sundarīṃ ramyāmatisupriya vādinām
putrapautravatīṃ śuddhāṃ kulajāṃ komalāṃ varam
13 aputro labhate putraṃ vaiṣṇavaṃ cirajīvanam
paramaiśvaryayuktaṃ ca vidyāvatam yaśasvinam
14 bhraṣṭarājyo labhedrājyaṃ bhraṣṭa śrīrlabhate śriyam
hatabandhurlabhedbandhuṃ dhanabhraṣṭo dhanaṃ labhet
15 kīrtihīno labhetkīrtiṃ pratiṣṭhāṃ ca labheddhruvam
sarva maṅgaladaṃstotram śoka santāpanāśanam
16 harṣānandakaraṃ śāśvaddharma mokṣa suhṛtpradam

iti śrī lakṣmī stotram samāptam

Eight Verses Praising Mahālakṣmī
(Śrī Mahālakṣmyaṣṭakam Stotram)[6]

indra uvāca—
namaste'stu mahāmaye śrīpithe surapūjite
śaṅkhacakragadāhaste mahālakṣmī namo'stute 1
namaste garuḍārūdhe kolāsura bhayaṅkari
sarvapāpa hare devi mahālakṣmi namo'stute 2
sarvajñe sarvavarade sarvaduṣṭabhayaṅkari
sarva duḥkha hare devi mahālakṣmi namo'stute 3
siddhi buddhiprade devi bhukti mukti prādayini
mantramūrte sadā devi mahālakṣmi namo'stute 4
ādyantarahite devi ādyaśakti maheśvari
yogaje yogasambhūte mahālakṣmi namo'stute 5
sthūla sūkṣma mahāraudre mahāśakti mahodare
mahāpāpa hare devi mahālakṣmi namo'stute 6
padmāsana sthite devi parabrahma svarūpiṇi
parameśi jaganmātarmahālakṣmi namo'stute 7
śvetāmbaradhare devi nānālaṅkāra bhūṣite
jagatsthite jaganmātarmahālakṣmi namo'stute 8
mahālakṣmyaṣṭakamstotram yaḥ paṭhedbhaktimānnaraḥ
sarvasiddhim avāpnoti rājyam prāpnoti sarvadā 9
eka kale paṭhennityaṃ mahāpāpa vināśanam
dvikālaṃ yaḥ paṭhennityaṃ dhanadhānya samanvitaḥ 10
trikālaṃ yaḥ paṭhennityaṃ mahāśatru vināśanam
mahālakṣmīrbhavennityaṃ prasannā varadā śubhā 11

iti śrī indrakṛta mahālakṣmyaṣṭakam samāptam

Tantric Texts

The Secret Heart of Lakṣmī
(Śrī Mahālakṣmī Hṛdayam)

Viniyoga

ādyādi śrī mahālakṣmī hṛdayamālā mantrasya bhārgava ṛṣi ādyādi śrīmahālakṣmīrdevatā anuṣṭubādinachandāṃsi śrīṃ bījaṃ / hrīṃ śaktiḥ aiṃ kīlakaṃādyādimahālakṣmīprasādasiddhyartha jape viniyogaḥ /

Nyāsa

oṃ bhārgava ṛṣaye namaḥ śirasi
oṃ anuṣṭupādi nānāchandebhyonamaḥ mukhe
ādyādi mahālakṣmyaidevatāyai namo hṛdaye
śrīṃ bījaya namaḥ guhye
hrīṃ śaktaye namaḥ padayoḥ
aiṃ kīlakāya namaḥ sarvāṅge

Karanyāsa

śrīṃ aṅguṣṭhābhyāṃ namaḥ
hrīṃ tarjanībhyāṃ namaḥ
aiṃ madhyamābhyāṃ namaḥ
śrīṃ anāmikābhyāṃ namaḥ
hrīṃ kaniṣṭhikābhyāṃ namaḥ
aiṃ karatalakara pṛṣṭhābhyāṃ namaḥ

Saṭaṅganyāsa

śrīṃ hṛdayāya namaḥ
hrīṃ śirase namaḥ
aiṃ śikhāyai vaṣaṭ
śrīṃ kavacāya huṃ
hrīṃ netra trayāya vauṣaṭ
aiṃ astrāya phaṭ

śrīṃ hrīṃ aiṃ iti digbandhaḥ

Dhyāna

hastadvayena kamale dhārayantīṃ svalīlayā
hāra nūpura saṃyuktāṃ lakṣmīṃ devī vicintaye
śaṅkhacakra gadā haste śubhravarge suvāsinī
mama dehi varaṃ lakṣmi sarvasiddhi pradāyini

Mantra

oṃ śrīṃ hrīṃ aiṃ mahālakṣmyai kamaladhāriṇyai siṃhavāhinyai svāhā

Stotra

vande lakṣmīṃ paraśivamayīṃ śuddhajāmbūnadābhāṃ
tejorūpāṃ kanankavasanāṃ sarvabhūṣojjvalāngīm
bījāpūraṃ kanaka kalaśaṃ hemapadma
dadhānāmādhyāṃ
śakti sakala jananīṃ viṣṇuvāmāṅga saṃsthām 1
śrimatsaubhāgyajananīṃ staumilakṣmīṃ sanātanīm
sarvakāma phalāvāpti sādhanaika sukhāvahām 2
smarāmi nityaṃ deveśi tvayā prerita mānasaḥ
tvadājñām śirasā dhṛtvābhajāmi parameśvarīm 3
samasta sampatsukhadāṃ mahāśriyam,
samasta saubhāgyakarīm mahāśriyam
samasta kalyāṇakarīṃ mahāśriyam,
bhajāmyahaṃ jñānakarīṃ mahāśriyam 4
vijñanasaṃvatsukhadāṃ sanātanīṃ,
vicitra vāgbhūtikarīṃ manoharām
ananta sāmodasukha pradāyinīṃ,
namāmyahaṃ bhūtikarīm haripriyām 5
samasta bhūtāntara saṃsthitā tvaṃ,
samasta bhoktrīśvari viśvarupe
trāsti yattadvayatiriktavasatu,
tvatpādapadmaṃ praṇamāmyahaṃ śrīḥ 6
dāridryaduḥkhaudyatamoghahantri,
tvatpādapadma mayi sannidhatsva
dīnātivicchedana hetubhūtaiḥ,
kṛpākaṭakṣairabhiṣiñca māṃ śrīḥ 7
amba prasīda karuṇāsudhayardra dṛṣṭyā,
māṃ tvatkṛpā dravitha gehamimnaṃ kuruṣva

ālokaya praṇata hṛdgataśoka hantri-,
8 tvatpādapadma yugalaṃ praṇamāmyahaṃ śrīḥ
śāntyai namostu śaraṇāgatarakṣaṇāyai,
kāntyai namostu kamanīyaguṇāśrayāyai
śāntyai namostu durita kṣayakāraṇāyai,
9 dhātryai namostu dhanadhānyasamṛddhidāyai
śaktyai namostu śaśiśekhara saṃstutāyai,
ratyai namo'stu rajakaṃ rasodarāyai
bhaktyai namostu bhavasāgaratārakāyai,
10 matyai namostu madhusūdana vallabhāyai
lakṣmyai namostu śubhalakṣaṇa lakṣitāyai,
siddhayai namostu śivasiddhasupūjitāyai
dhṛtyai namostvamita durgati bhañjanāyai,
11 gatyai namostu varasadgati dāyakāyai
devyai namostu divi devagaṇorcitāyai,
bhūtyai namostu bhuvatātivināśanāyai
dātrayi namostu dharaṇīdhara vallabhāyai,
12 puṣṭyai namostu puruṣottama vallabhāyai
sutīvra dāridrya viduḥkha hantryai,
namo'stu te sarvabhayāpahatryai
śrī viṣṇu vakṣasthala saṃsthitāyai,
13 namo namassarva vibhūtidāyai
jayatu jayatu lakṣmīrtya kṣaṇālaṃ kṛtāngī,
jayatu jayatu padmā padmasapadmābhivandyā
jayatu jayatu vidyā viṣṇu vāmāṅka saṃsthā,
14 jayatu jayatu samyaksarva saṃpatkarī śrīḥ
jayatu jayatu devi devasaṅghabhipūjyā,
jayatu jayatu bhadrā bhārgavī bhāgyarūpā
jayatu jayatu nityā nirmala jñānavedyā,
15 jayatu jayatu satyā sarvabhūtāntarasthā
jayatu jayatu ramyā ratnagarbhāntarasthā,
jayatu jayatu śuddhā suddha jāmbunadābhā
jayatu jayatu kāntā kāntimadbhāsitāṅgī,
16 jayatu jayatu śāntāśīghramāgaccha saumye
yasyāḥ kalādyaḥ kamalodbhavādyā,
rudrāśca śakra pramukhāśca devāḥ
jīvanti sarvā api śaktayatāḥ,
17 prabhutvamāptāḥ paramāyuṣaste
lilekha niṭile vidhirmama lipi visṛjyāntaram,
vilikhitavyamediti tatphala prāptaye
tadantaraphale sphuṭam kamalavāsinī śrīrimāṃ,
18 samarpayasamudrikāṃ sakalabhāgyasaṃsūcikam

kalayā te yathā devi jīvanti sacarācaram
tathā sampatkarelali sarvadā samprasīdame 19
yathā viṣṇurdhruvenityaṃ svakalāṃ sannaya śayat
tathaiva svakalāṃ lakṣmi mayi samyak samarpaya 20
sarvasaukhya prade devi bhaktānāmabhayaprade
acalāṃ kuru yatnena kalāṃ mayi niveśitām 21
gudāstāṃmadbhale paramapadalakṣmīḥ sphuṭakalā,
sadā vaikuṇṭha śrīnivāsatu kalā me nayanayoḥ
vasetsatye loke mama vacasi lakṣmī varakalā,
śriyaśśvetadvīpe nivasatu kalā me svakarayoḥ 22
tavannityaṃ mamāṅgeṣu kṣirābdhau śrīkalāvaset
sūryācandramasau yāvadyāvallakṣmīpatiḥ śriyā 23
sarvamaṅgalasampūrnā sarvaiśvarya samanvitā
ādyādi śrīmahālakṣmi tvatkalā mayi tiṣṭhatu 24
ajñāna timiraṃ hantuṃ śuddhajñāna prakāśikā
sarvaiśvaryapradāmestu tvatkalā mayi saṃsthitā 25
alakṣmīṃ haratu kṣipraṃ tamaḥ sūryaprabhā yathā
vitanotu mama śreyastvatkalā mayi saṃsthitā 26
aiśvarya maṅgalotpattisvatkalāyāṃ nidhīyate
mayi tasmātkṛtārthe'sminpātramasmi sthitestava 27
bhavadāveśabhāgyārho bhāgyavānasmi bhārgavi
tvatprasādātpavitrohaṃ lokamātarnamostu te 28
punāsi māṃ tvaṃ kalayaivayasmā [ ]
datuḥ samāgaccha mamāgratastvam
parampadaṃ śrīrbhavatu prasannā,
mayyacyutena praviśādi lakṣmi 29
śrīvaikuṇṭhasthite lakṣmi samāgaccha mamāgrataḥ
nārāyaneṇa saha māṃ kṛpādṛṣṭyā vilokaya 30
satyaloka sthite lakṣmi tvam mamāgaccha sannidhim
vāsudevena sahitā prasīda varadā bhava 31
śvetadvīpasthite lakṣmi śīghramāgaccha suvrata
viṣṇunā sahite devi jaganmātaḥ prasīda me 32
śrīrāmbudhisthite lakṣmi samāgaccha samādhave
tvatkṛpādṛṣṭisudhayā satataṃ māṃ vilokaya 33
ratnagarbhasthite lakṣmi paripūrṇa hiraṇmayi
samāgaccha samāgaccha sthitvāśu [?] purato mama 34
sthirābhava mahālakṣmi niścalā bhava nirmale
prasanne kamale devi prasanna hṛdaya bhava 35
śrīdhare śrīmahābhute tvadanta sthaṃ mahānidhim
śīghramuddhṛtya purataḥ pradarśaya samarpaya 36
vasundhare śrī vasudhe vasudogdhra kṛpāmayi
tvatkukṣigata sarvasvaṃ śīghram me sampradarśaye 37

viṣṇu priye ratnagarbhe samastaphalade śive
38 tvadgarbhagatahemadiīn sampradarśaya darśaya
rasātalagate lakṣmi śīghramāgaccha me puraḥ
39 na jāne paramaṃ rūpaṃ mātarme sampradarśaya
āvirbhava manovegācchīghramāgaccha me puraḥ
40 māvatsa bhairihetyuktyā kāmaṃ gauriva rakṣamām
devi śīghram samāgaccha dharaṇīgarbha saṃsthite
41 mātastvadbhṛtyabhṛtyohaṃ mṛgaye tvam kutūhalām
uttiṣṭha jāgṛhi tvam me samuttiṣṭha sujāgṛhi
42 akṣayan hemakalaśān suvarṇena supūritam
nikṣepan me samakṛsya samuddhatya mamāgrataḥ
43 samunnātānanā bhūtvā samodhedhi dharāntarāt
matsannidhi samāgaccha madāhita kṛpārasāt
44 prasīda śreyasāndogdhri lakṣmi me nayanāgrataḥ
atropaviśa lakṣmi tvaṃ sthirā bhava hiraṇmayi
45 susthirābhava samprītyā prasīda varadā bhava
ānīya tvaṃ tathā devi nidhīm me sampradarśaya
46 adya kṣaṇena sahasā datvā saṃrakṣa māṃ sadā
mayi tisṣṭha tathā nityaṃ yathendrādiṣu tiṣṭhasi
47 abhayaṃ kuru me devi mahālakṣmi namo'stute
samaāgaccha mahālakṣmi śuddhājāmbūnadaprabhe
48 prasīda purataḥ sthitva praṇatam māṃ vilokaya
lakṣmi bhuvam gatā āsi yatra yatra hiraṇmayī
49 tatra tatra sthitā tvaṃ me tava rūpaṃ pradarśaya
krīḍase bahudhā bhūmau paripūrṇahiranmayī
50 samamūrddhani te hastamavilambitamarpaya
phalādbhagyodaye lakṣmi samastapura vāsini
51 prasīda me mahālakṣmi paripūrṇa manorathe
ayodhyādiṣu sarveṣu nagareṣu samāsthite
52 vaibhavairvividhairyuktā samāgaccha balānvite
samāgaccha samāgaccha mamāgre bhava susthirā
53 karuṇarasaniṣyanda netra dvaya vilāsinī
sannidhatsva mahālakṣmi tvatpāṇi mama mastake
54 karuṇaśudhayā māṃ tvamabhiṣiñca sthirī kuru
sarvarājagṛhe lakṣmi samāgaccha mudānvite
55 sthitavāśu purato me prasādenābhayaṃ kuru
sādaram mastake hastaṃ mama tvam kṛpayārpaya
56 sarvarājagṛhe laksmi tvatkalā mayi tiṣṭhatu
ādyādi śrīmahālakṣmi viṣṇuvāmāṅka saṃsthite
57 pratyakṣam kuru me rūpaṃ rakṣa māṃ śaraṇāgatam
prasīda me mahālakṣmi suprasīda mahāśive
58 acalā bhava samprītyā susthirā bhava madgṛhe

yāvattiṣṭhanti vedāśca yāvatvannāma tiṣṭhati
yāvadvisṣṇuśca yāvattvaṃ tāvatkuru kṛpā mayi 59
cāndrī kalā yathā śukle varddhate sā dine dine
tathā dayā te mayyeva varddhatāmabhivarddhatām 60
yathā vaikuṇṭha nagare yathā vai kṣira sāgare
tathā madbhavane tiṣṭha sthira śrī viṣṇunāṃ saha 61
yogināṃ hṛdaye nityaṃ yathā tiṣṭhasi viṣṇunā
tathā madvane tiṣṭha sthiraṃ śrī viṣṇunā saha 62
nārāyaṇasya hṛdaye bhavati yathāste,
nārāyaṇopi tava hṛtkamale yathāste
nārāyaṇastvamapi nityasubho tathaiva,
tau tiṣṭhatam hṛdi mamāpi dayāvati śrīḥ 63
vijñāna vṛddhiṃ hṛdaye kuru śrīḥ,
saubhāgya vṛddhiṃ kuru me gṛhe śrīḥ
dayā suvṛddhiṃ kurutām mayi śrīḥ,
suvarṇavṛddhiṃ kuru me gṛhe śrīḥ 64
mamāṃ tyajethāḥ śrita kalpavalli,
sadbhakta citrāmaṇi kāmadheno
viśvasya mātarbhava suprasannā,
gṛhe kalatreṣu ca putravarge 65
ādyādi māye tvamajāṇḍa bījaṃ,
tvameva sākāra nirākṛti stvam
tvayā dhṛtāścābjabhavāṇḍa saṅghān,
citraṃ caritraṃ tava devi viṣṇoḥ 66
brahmarudrādayo devā vedāścāpi na śaknuyuḥ
mahimānaṃ tava stotuṃ mando'haṃ śaknuyāṃ katham 67
ambatvadvatsa vākyāni sūktā sūktāni yāni ca
tāni svīkuru sarvajñe dayālutvena sādaram 68
bhavatīm śaraṇaṃ gatvā kṛtārthāḥ syuḥ purātanāḥ
iti sañcintya manasā tvāmahaṃ śaraṇaṃ vraje 69
anantā nityasukhinastvadbhaktāstvatparāyaṇāḥ
iti veda pramāṇāddhi devi tvam śaraṇam vraje 70
tava pratijñā madbhaktānanaśyantītyapi kvacit
iti sañcintya sañcintya prāṇānsandhārayāmyaham 71
tvadadhīna stvahaṃ mātastvakṛpā mayi vidyate
yāvatsampūrṇakāmaḥ syāttāvaddehi dayānidhe 72
kṣanamātram na śaknomi jīvitum tvatkṛpāṃ vinā
na jīvantīha jalajā jalaṃ tyaktvā jalāgrahāḥ 73
yathāhi putra vātsalyajjananī prasnutastanī
vatsaṃ tvanaritamātya samprīrṇayati vatsalā 74
yadi syāntava putro'ham mātā tvam yadi māmakī
dayā payodharastanya sudhābhirabhiṣiñca mām 75

mṛgyo na guṇaleśopi mayi doṣaikamandare
76 pāṃsunāṃ vṛṣṭi bindūnāṃ doṣāṇāñca namemiti
pāpināmahamevāggre dayālunām tvamāgraṇīḥ
77 dayanīyo madanyo'sti tava kotra jagattraye
vidhi hanna sṛṣṭaścennasyāttava dayālutā [ ]
78 āmayo vā na sṛṣṭaścedauṣadhasya vṛthodayaḥ
kṛpā madaguṇā kiṃ te ahaṃ kiṃ vā tadagrajaḥ
79 vicārya dehi ye vittam tava devi dayānidhe
mātā pitā tvaṃ guru sadgati
śrīstvameva sañjīvana hetubhūta
anyanna manye jagadeka nāthe,
80 tvameva sarva mamadevi satye
ādyādilakṣmīrbhava suprasannā,
viśuddha vijñāna sukhakaṃdoghrī
ajñānahantrī triguṇātiriktā,
81 prajñānanetrī bhava suprasannā
aśep vāg jaḍyamalāya hantrī,
navannavam spaṣṭa suvāk pradāyinī
mameha vihvāgra suraṅga narttakī,
82 bhava prasannā vadena ca me śrīḥ
satasta sampatsu virājamānā,
samastatejaśca ya bhāsamānā
viṣṇu priye tvam bhava dīpyamānā,
83 vāgdevatā me nayane prasannā
sarva pradarśe sakalārthade tvam
prabhā sulāvanya dayā pradogdhrī
suvarṇade tvam sumukhī bhava śrī,
84 hiraṇmayī me nayane prasannā
sarvārthadā sarvajagatsūtiḥ
sarveśvarī sarvabhayāya hantrī
sarvonnatā tvaṃ sumukhī bhava
85 śrīrhiraṇmayīme nayane prasannā
samasta vighnaugha vināśakāriṇī,
samastabhaktoddharaṇo vicakṣanā
ananta saubhagya sukha pradāyinī,
86 hiraṇmayī me nayane prasannā
devi prasīda dayanīya tamāya yahyan,
devādhināthabhava devagaṇabhivandhye
mātastathaiva sannihitā dṛśorye,
87 patyā samam maya mukye bhava suprasannā
mā vatsa bhairabhayadāna karo'rpitaste,
maulo mayeti mama dīnadayānukampe

mātahḥ samarpaya mudā karuṇā kaṭākṣaṃ,
    māṅgalya bījamiha naḥ sṛja janmamātaḥ 88
katākṣa iha kāma bhuktava manastu cintāmaṇiḥ karaḥ
  surataruḥ sadā navanidhistvamevendire
bhavettava dayārasomama rasāyanaṃ cānvahaṃ sukham
  tava kalānidhi vividha vāñchatārthapradam 89
yathā rasasparśana to'yasopi,
    suvarṇatā syātkamale tathā te
kaṭākṣasaṃsparśanato janāna,
    mamaṅgalānāmapi maṅgala tvam 90
dehīti nāstīti vacaḥ praveśād,
    bhīto rame tvām śaranaṃ prapadye
ataḥ sadāsminna bhayapradā tvaṃ,
    sadaiva patyā mayi sannidhehi 91
kalpadrumeṇa maṇinā sahitā suramyā,
    śrīste kalāmayi rasena rasāyanena
āstāṃ yato mama ca hak śirayānipād,
    spṛṣṭāḥ suvarṇavapuṣaḥ sthirajaṅgamā syuḥ 92
ādyādi viṣṇoḥ sthiradharmapatnī,
    tvameya patyā mayi sannidhehi
ādyādi lakṣmī tvadanugraheṇa,
    pade pade me nidhi darśanaṃsyāt 93
ādyādi lakṣmī hṛdayaṃ paṭhedyaḥ,
    sa rājya lakṣmīmacalaṃ tanoti
mahādaridropi bhaved dhanādhyaḥ,
    tadanvaye śrīḥ sthiratāṃ prayāti 94
yasya smaraṇamātreṇa tuṣṭā syād viṣṇuvallabhā
tasyābhiṣṭaṃ dadātyāśu taṃ pālayati putravat 95
idaṃ rahasyaṃ hṛdayaṃ sarvakāma phala padam
japaḥ pañcasahasraṃ tu puraścaraṇamucyate 96
trikālameka kālaṃ vā naro bhakti samanvitaḥ
yaḥ paṭhecchṛṇuyādvāpi sa yāti paramāṃ śriyam 97
mahālakṣmīm samuddiśya niśi bhārgavavāsare
idaṃ śrī hṛdayam japtvā pañcavaraṃ dhanī bhavet 98
anena hṛdayenānnaṃ garbhiṇyā abhimantritam
dadāti tatkule putro jāyate śrīpatiḥ svayam 99
nareśa vāthavā nāryā lakṣmīṃ hṛdaya mantrite
jale pīte ca tadvaṃśe mandabhāgyo na jāyate 100
ya aśvine māsi ca śuklapakṣe,
    rāmotsave sannihitaikabhaktyā
paṭhettathaikottaravāra vṛddhayā,
    labhetsa sauvarṇamayīṃ suvṛṣtim 101

ya ekabhaktonvahameka varṣa,
viśuddhadhīḥ saptativārajāyī
sa mandabhāgyopi rayākaṭākṣāt,
102 bhavadet sahasrākṣaśatādhika śrīḥ
śrī śāṃghri bhaktiṃ haridasadāsyaṃ,
prasannamantrārtha dṛḍhaikaniṣṭhām
guroḥ smṛtiṃ nirmalabodhabuddhim,
103 pradehi mātaḥ paramaṃ padaṃ śrīḥ
pṛthvīpatitvaṃ puruṣottamatvaṃ,
vibhūtivāsam vivadhārtha siddhim
sampūrṇa kīrtiṃ bahuvarṣa bhogaṃ,
104 pradehi me lakṣmi punaḥ punastvam
vādārthasiddhiṃ bahulokavaśyam,
vayaḥ sthiratvaṃ lalanāsubhogam
pautrādi labdhiṃ sakalārtha siddhiṃ,
105 pradehi me bhārgavi janma janmani
suvarṇavṛddhiṃ kuru me gṛhe śrī,
vibhūtivṛddhiṃ kuru me gṛhe śrīḥ
śirobījam—oṃ yaṃ haṃ kaṃ laṃ paṃ śrīṃ
dhyāyellakṣmī prahasita mukhī,
koṭi bālārkamīsāṃ
vidyuddharṇāmbara paradharāṃ,
106 bhūṣanādhyāṃ suśobhām
bījāpuraṃ sarasijayugaṃ,
vibhratīṃ svarṇapātraṃ
bhartrāyuktāṃ muhurabhayadāṃ,
107 mahyamapyacyuta śrīḥ
guhyātiguhyagoptrī tvaṃ,
gṛhāṇāsmatkṛtaṃ japam
siddhirbhavatu me devi,
108 tvatprasādānmayi sthitā

iti śrī atharvaṇarahasye śrīmahālakṣmīhṛdayastotraṃ samāptam

Praise-Song for the Bestower of Wealth
(Dhanadā Stotram)

namaḥ sarvasvarūpe ca namaḥ kalyāṇa dāyike
mahāsampatprade devi dhanadāyai namo'stute 1
mahābhoga prade devi mahākāma prapūrite
sukha mokṣaprade devi dhanadāyai namo'stute 2
brahmarūpe sadānande sadānanda svarūpiṇi
drutasiddhi prade devi dhanadāyai namo'stute 3
udyansūrya prakāśāye udyadāditya maṇḍale
śiktatva [ ] prade devi dhanadāyai namo'stute 4
vissṇu rupe viśvamate viśvapālana kāriṇi
mahasattvaguṇātrānte dhanadāyai namo'stute 5
śivarupe śivānande kāraṇānanda vigrahe
viśvasaṃhāra rūpe ca dhanadāyai namo'stute 6
pañcatattva svarūpe ca pañcācāra sadārate
sādhakābhiṣṭaye devi dhanadāyai namo'stute 7

Song-Amulet of the Bestower of Wealth
(Dhanadā Kavacam)

dhanadā kavacasyāsya kubera ṛṣirīriti
1 paṅktiśchando devatā ca dhanadā siddhidā sadā
2 dharmārthakāma mokṣeṣu viniyogaḥ prakīrttitaḥ
dhaṃ bijaṃ me śiraḥ pātu hrīṃ bījaṃ me lalāṭakam
3 śrīṃ bījaṃ me mukhaṃpāturakāra hṛdaya me'vatu
tikāra pātu jaṭharaṃ prikāraṃ pṛṣṭhato'vatu
ye kāraṃ jaṅghayoryugme svākāraṃ pāda mūlake
4 śīrṣādi pāda paryanta hākāraṃ sarvato'vatu

iti śrī dhanadā kavacam samāptam

Praise-Song for the Lotus Goddess
(*Kamalā Stotram*)[7]

oṃkārarūpiṇī devi viśuddhasattvarūpiṇī
devānāṃ jananī tvaṃ hi prasannā bhava sundari 1
tanmātraṃcaiva bhūtāni tava vakṣaḥsthalaṃ smṛtam
tvamevaṃ vedagamyā tu prasannā bhava sundari 2
devadānava gandharva yakṣa rākṣasa kinnaraiḥ
stūyate tvaṃ sadā lakṣmi prasannā bhava sundari 3
lokātītā dvaitātitā samastabhūta veṣṭitā
vidyajjana kīrtitā ca prasannā bhava sundari 4
brahmarūpā ca sāvitrī tvaddīptya bhāsate jagat
viśvarūpā vareṇyā ca prasannā bhava sundari 5
kṣityaptejo marudvyoma pañcabhūtasvarūpiṇī
bandhādeḥ kāraṇaṃ tvaṃ hi prasannā bhava sundari 6
maheśe tvaṃ hemavatī kamalā keśave'pi ca
brāhmanaḥ preyasī tvaṃ hi prasannā bhava sundari 7
bālye ca bālikā tvaṃhi yauvane yuvatīti ca
sthāvire vṛddharūpā ca prasannā bhava sundari 8
guṇamayī guṇātītā ādya vidyā sanātatī
mahattattvādi saṃyuktā prasannā bhava sundari 9
tapasvinī tapaḥ siddhiḥ svargasiddhistadarthiṣu
cinmayī prakṛtistvaṃ tu prasannā bhava sundari 10
tvamādirjagatāṃ devi tvameva sthiti kāraṇam
tvamante nidhana sthānaṃ svecchācārā tvameva hi 11
carācarāṇāṃ bhūtānāṃ bahirantastvamevahi
vyāpyāpaka rūpeṇa tvaṃ bhāsi bhaktavatsale 12
tvanmāyāya hṛtajñānā nāṣṭātmāno vicetasaḥ
gatāgataṃ prapadyante pāpapuṇya vaśātsadā 13
tāvansatyaṃ jagadbhāti śuktikārajataṃ yathā
yāvanna jñāyate jñānaṃ cetasānānvagāminī 14
tvajjñānāttu sadā yuktaḥ putradaragṛhādiṣu
ramante viṣayānsarvvānante duḥkha pradān dhruvam 15
tvadājñayā tu deveśi gagane sūryamaṅgalam
candraścabhramate nityaṃ prasannā bhava sundari 16
brahmeśa viṣṇujananī brahmākhyā brahmasaṃśraya
vyaktāvyaktā ca deveśi prasannā bhava sundari 17
acalā sarvagā tvaṃ hi māyātītā maheśvari
śivātmā śāśvatā nityā prasannā bhava sundari 18
sarvakāya niyantrī ca sarvabhuteśvareśvari
anantā niṣkalā tvaṃ hi prasannā bhava sundari 19

sarveśvarī sarvavandyā acintyā paramātmikā
20 bhukti muktipradā tvaṃ hi prasannā bhava sundari
brahmāṇī brahmaloke tvaṃ vaikunṇṭhe sarvamaṅgalā
21 indrāṇi amarāvatyām ambikā varuṇālaye
yamālaye kālarūpā kuberabhavane śubhā
22 mahānandāgnikoṇe ca prasannā bhava sundari
nairṛtyāṃ raktadantā tvaṃ vāyavyāṃ mṛgavāhinī
23 pātale vaiṣṇavīrūpa prasannā bhava sundari
surasā tvaṃ maṇidvīpe aiśānyāṃ śuladhāriṇī
24 bhadrakālī ca laṅkāyāṃ prasannā bhava sundari
rāmeśvarī setubandhe siṃhale devamohinī
25 vimalā tvaṃ ca śrī kṣetre prasannā bhava sundari
kālikā tvamṃ kālighaṭṭe kāmākhyā nīla pārvate
26 virajā oṅgadeśe tvaṃ prasannā bhava sundari
bhadrakālī kurukṣetre tvaṃca kātyāyanī vrate
27 mahāmāyā dvārakāyāṃ prasannā bhava sundari
kṣudhā tvaṃ sarvajīvānāṃ velā ca sāgarasyahi
28 maheśvarī mathurāyāṃ prasannā bhava sundari
rāmasya jānakī tvaṃca śivasya manamohinī
29 dakṣasya duhitā caiva prasannā bhava sundari
vissṇubhaktipradā tvaṃ ca kāmsāsura vināśinī
30 rāvaṇanāśinī caiva prasannā bhava sundari
lakṣmīstotramidaṃ puṇyaṃ yaḥ paṭhed bhaktisaṃyutaḥ
31 sarvajvarabhayaṃ naśyetsarva vyādhi nivāraṇam
idaṃ stotraṃ mahāpuṇyamāpaduddhārakāraṇam
32 trisaṃdhyamekasandhyaṃ vā yaḥ paṭhetsatataṃ naraḥ
mucyate sarva pāpebhyo tathā tu sarva saṅkaṭāt
33 mucyate nāma sandehī bhuvi svarge rasātale
samastaṃ ca tathā caikaṃ yaḥ paṭhedbhaktitatparaḥ
34 sasarvaṃ duṣkaraṃ tīrtvā labhate paramāṃ gatim
sukhadaṃ mokṣadaṃ stotraṃ yaḥ paṭhedbhakti
saṃyutaḥ
35 sa tu koṭi tīrtha phalaṃ prāpnoti nāma saṃśayaḥ
ekā devī tu kamalā yasmiṃstuṣṭā bhavetsadā
36 tasyā'sādhyam tu deveśi nāsti kiṃcijjagatraye
paṭhanādapi stotrasya kiṃ na siddhyati bhūtale
37 tasyātstotravaraṃ proktaṃ satyaṃ satyaṃ hi pārvati

iti śrī kamalā stotraṃ samāptam

108 Names of the Glorious Lotus Goddess
(Śrī Kamalā Aṣṭottaraśatanāma Stotram)

śrī śiva uvāca—
śatamaṣṭottaram nāmnāṃ kamalāyā varānane
pravakṣāmyati guhyaṃ hi na kadāpi prakāśayet 1
mahāmāyā mahālakṣmīrmahāvāṇī maheśvarī
mahādevī mahārātrirmahiṣāsura mardinī 2
kālarātrīḥ kuhaḥ pūrṇānandādyā bhadrikā niśā
jayā riktā mahāśaktirdevamātā kṛśodarī 3
śacīndrāṇī śakranutā śaṅkarapriya vallabhā
mahāvarahajananī madanonmathinī mahī 4
vaikuṇṭhanātharamaṇī visṣṇuvakṣaḥsthala sthitā
viśveśvarī viśvamātā varadābhayadā śivā 5
śūlinī cakriṇī mā ca pāśinī śaṅkhadhāriṇī
gadinī muṇḍamālā ca kamalā karuṇālayā 6
padmākṣadhāriṇī hyambā mahāviṣṇu priyaṅkarī
golokanātharamaṇī golokeśvara pūjitā 7
gayā gaṅgā ca yamunā gomatī garuḍāsanā
gaṇḍakī sarayū tāpī revā caiva payasvinī 8
narmadā caiva kāverī kedārasthala vāsinī
kiśorī keśavanutā mahendraparivanditā 9
brahmādi deva nirmāṇa kāriṇī veda pūjitā
koṭi brahmāṇḍamadhyasthā koṭi brahmāṇḍa kāriṇī 10
śrutirūpā śrutikarī śrutismṛti parāṣanā
indirā sindhutanayā mātaṅgī loka mātṛkā 11
trilokajananī tantrā tantra mantra svarūpiṇī
taruṇī ca tarohantrī maṅgalā maṅgalāyanā 12
madhukaitabhamathanī śumbhāsura vināśinī
niśumbhādiharā mātā hariśaṅkarapūjitā 13
sarvadevamayī sarvā śaraṇāgatapālinī
śaraṇyā śambhuvanitā sindhutīra nivāsinī 14
gandharvagāyarasikā gītā govinda vallabhā
trailokyapālinī tattvarūpatāruṇyapūritā 15
candrāvalī candramukhī candrikā candrapūjitā
candrā śaśaṅka bhaginī gītavādya parāyaṇā 16
sṛṣṭirūpā sṛṣṭikarī sṛṣtisaṃhārakāraṇī
iti te kathitaṃ devi samānāma śataṣṭakam 17
trisandhyaṃ prayatobhūtvā paṭhedetatsamāhitam
yaṃ yaṃ kāmayate kāmaṃ taṃ taṃ prāpnotyasaṃśayam 18

imaṃ stavaṃ yaḥ paṭhetīha martyo vaikuṇṭhapatnya
paramādareṇa
dhanādhipadyaiḥ parivanditaḥ prayāsyati śrīpadamanta
19 kāle

iti śrī kamalāyā aṣṭottaraśatanāma stotraṃ samāptam

Song-Amulet of the Lotus Goddess
(*Kamalātmikā Kavacam*)[8]

athavakṣye maheśāni kavacaṃ sarvvakāmadam
yasya vijānamātreṇa bhavetsākṣātsadā śivaḥ 1
nārcyanantasya deveśi mantra mātrañjapennaraḥ
sabhavetpārvvatī putraḥ sarvvaśāstra viśāradaḥ 2
vidyārthināṃ sadā vidyā dhanadātṛ viśeṣataḥ
dhanārthibhissadāsevyā kamalā viṣṇuvallabhā 3

[Viniyogaḥ]

asyāścaturakṣarī viṣṇuvallabhāyāḥ kavacasya bhagavān ṛṣiranuṣṭup chando vāgbhavī śaktiddevatā vāgbhavaṃ bījaṃ lajjāramā kīlakaṃ kāmabījātmakaṅkavacamasupāṇḍitya kavitva sarvvasiddhi samṛddhaye viniyoga

[Kavacam]

aiṃkāroṃ mastake pātu vāgbhavī sarvvasiddhidā
hrīṃ pātu cakṣuṣormmadhye cakṣuyyugme ca śāṅkarī 1
jihvāyāmmukha vṛtte ca karṇṇayorddantayornnasi
auṣṭhādhare danta paṅktau taralūmūlehanaupunaḥ 2
pātumāṃ vviṣṇu vanitā lakṣmīḥ śrīviṣṇurūpiṇī
karṇṇayugme bhuja dvandve stanadvandve ca pārvvatī 3
hṛdaye maṇibandhe ca grīvāyāmpārśśvayoḥ punaḥ
pṛṣṭhadeśe tathā guhye vāme ca dakṣine tathā
upasthe ca nitambe ca nābhaujaṅghadvayepunaḥ 4
jānucakre padadvande ghuṭike guli mūlike
svādhatuprāṇāśktyātma sīmante mastake punaḥ 5
vijayā pātu bhavane jayāpātu sadāmama
sarvāṅge pātu kāmeśī mahādevī sarasvatī 6
tuṣṭiḥ pātu mahāmāyā utkṛṣṭiḥ sarvvadāvatu
ṛddhiḥ pātu mahādevī sarvvatra śambhuvallabhā 7
vāgbhavī sarvvadāpātu pātu māṃ haragehinī
ramāpātu sadādevī pātumāyā svarāṭsvayam 8
sarvvāṅge pātu māṃllakṣmīrviṣṇumāyā sureśvarī
śivadutī sadāyātu sundarī pātu sarvvadā 9
bhairavī pātu mānnitya bheruṇḍā sarvvadāvatu
tvaritā pātu mānnitya mugutārā sadāvatu 10
pātumāṅkālikānityaṅkāla rātriḥ sadāvatu
navadurggā sadā pātu kāmākṣī sarvvadāvatu 11

yogityaḥ sarvvadā pāntu mudrāḥ pāntu sadā mama
12 mātrāḥ pāntu sadā devyaścakrasthāyoginī gaṇāḥ
sarvvatra sarvva kāryyeṣu sarvva karmāsu sarvvadā
13 patumāndeva devī ca lakṣmīḥ sarvva samṛddhidā
itite kathitaṃ divyaṅkavacaṃ sarvva siddhaye
14 yatra tatraṃ na vaktavyaṃyyadīcchetātmanohitam
śaṭhāya bhaktihīnāya nindakāya maheśvarī
15 nyunānge cātiriktāṅge darśayenna kadācana
nastavandarśśaye divyaṃ sandarśśya śivahābhavet
16 kulīnāya mahecha ya durggābhakti parāya ca
vaiṣṇavāya viśuddhāya dadyātkavacamuttamam
17 nija śiṣyāya śāntāyadhanine jñānine tathā
padyāt kavacamityuktaṃ sarvatantra samanvitam
18 śanaumaṅgala vāreca raktacandana kaistathā
yāvakena likhenmantraṃ sarvvatantra samanvitam
19 vilikhya kavacandivyaṃ svayambhukusumaiḥ subhaiḥ
svaśukraḥ para śukrairvā nānāgandha samanvitaiḥ
20 gauro canākuṅkumena rakta candanakena vā
sutithau śubhayoge vā śrāvaṇāyāṃ raveddine
21 aśvinyākṛttikāyaṃvvā phalgunyāvvāmadyāsu ca
purvvabhādrapadāyoge svātyāmmaṅgalavāsare
22 vilikhetprapaṭhetstotraṃ śubhayoge surālaye
āyuṣmatprīti yoge ca brahmayoge viśeṣataḥ
23 indrayoge śubheyoge sukrayoge tathaiva ca
kaulave bālave caiva vaṇije caiva sattamaḥ
24 śūnyāgora śmaśāne ca vijane ca viśeṣataḥ
kumārīmyūjayitvādau yajeddevīṃ sanātanīm
25 matsyair mmāsaiḥ śāka sūpaḥ pūjayetparadevatām
ghṛtādyaiḥ sopakaraṇaiḥ pūpasūpairvviśeṣataḥ
26 brahmaṇānbhojanayitvā ca pūjayetparameśvarīm
akheṭakam upākhyānaṃ tatra kuyyāddinatrayam
27 tadādharenmahā vidyāṃ śaṅkareṇa prabhāṣitām
māraṇa dveṣaṇādīni labhate nātra saṃśayaḥ
28 sambhavetpārvatī putraḥ sarvaśāstra puraskṛtaḥ
gururddevoharaḥ sākṣātpatnī tasya harapriyā
29 abhedena bhajedyastu tasya siddhiradūrataḥ
paṭhati yaṃ ihaṃmartyo nityamaddrāntarātmā,
japa phalam anumeyaṃllapsyateya dvidheyam
sa bhavati padamuccaissampadāpādanamra,
30 kṣitipa mukuta lakṣmīrllakṣaṇānāñcirāya

iti śrī viśvasāra tantre kamalātmikā kavacaṃ samāttam

Song for the Lakṣmī of Spiritual Power
(Śrī Siddhalakṣmī Stotram)

Viniyoga

oṃ asya śrīsiddhalakṣmī stotra mantrasya hiraṇyagarbhaṛṣiḥ anuṣṭupchandaḥ śrīmahākālī mahālakṣmī mahāsarasvatyo devatāḥ śrīṃ bījaṃ hrīṃ śaktiḥ klīṃ kīlakaṃ mama sarvakleśapīḍāparihārārtha sarva duḥkhadāridryanāśanārtha sarva kāryasiddhyartha ca śrī siddhalakṣmī stotra pāṭhe viniyogaḥ

Ṛṣyādinyāsa

hiraṇyagarbha ṛṣaye namaḥ śirasi
anuṣṭupchandase namo mukhe
śrī mahākālī mahālakṣmī mahāsarasvatī devatābhyo
namo hṛdi
śrīṃ bījāya namaḥ guhye
hrīṃ śaktaye namaḥ pādayoḥ
klīṃ kīlakāya namo nābhau
viniyogāya namaḥ sarvāṅge

Karanyāsa

śrīṃ siddha lakṣmyai aṅgusthābhyāṃ namaḥ
hrīṃ viṣṇu tejaḥ tarjanībhyāṃ namaḥ
klīṃ amṛtānandāyai madhyamābhyāṃ namaḥ
śrīṃ daityamālinyai anāmikābhyāṃ namaḥ
hrīṃ tejaḥ prakāśinyai kaniṣṭhikābhyāṃ namaḥ
klīṃ brāhmaṇai vaiṣṇavyai rudrāṇyai karatalakara
pṛṣṭhābhyāṃ namaḥ
śrīṃ siddhalakṣmyai hṛdayāya namaḥ
hrīṃ viṣṇutejase śirase svāhā
klīṃ amṛtānandāyai śikhāyai vaṣaṭ
śrīṃ daityamālinyai kavacāya huṃ
hrīṃ tejaḥ prakāśinyai netratrayāya vauṣaṭ
klīṃ brāhmau vaiṣṇavyai rudrāṇyai astrāya phaṭ

Digbandhana Mantra

oṃ śrīṃ hrīṃ klīṃ śrīṃ siddhalakṣmyai namaḥ

Dhyāna Mantra

brāhmī ca vaiṣṇavīṃ bhadrā ṣaḍbhujāṃ ca caturmukham
1 trinetrām khadgatriśūlam padmacakragadādharām
pītāmbaradharāṃ devīṃ nānālaṃkāra bhūṣitām
2 tejaḥ puñjadharīṃ śreṣtṭhāṃ dhyāyed bālakumārikām

Stotra

oṃkāraṃ lakṣmīrūpaṃ tu viṣṇu hṛdayamavyayam
1 viṣṇumānandamavyaktaṃ hrīṃkāra vājarūpinīm
klīṃ amṛtānandinīṃ bhadrā sadātmānandadāyinīm
2 śrīṃ daityaśamanīṃ śaktiṃ mālinīṃ śatrumardinīm
tejaḥ prakāśinīṃ devīṃ varadāṃ śubhakāriṇīm
3 brāhmīṃ ca vaiṣṇavīṃraudrīṃ kālikārūpa śobhinīm
akāre lakṣmīrūpaṃ tu ukāre viṣṇumavyayaṃ
4 makāraḥ puruṣo'vyakto devīpraṇava ucyate
sūrya koṭi pratīkāśaṃ candrakoṭi samāprabham
tanmadhye nikaraṃ sūkṣmaṃ brahmarūpaṃ
5 vyavasthitam
oṃkāraṃ paramānandaṃ sadaiva sukha sundarīm
6 siddhalakṣmi mokṣalakṣmi ādyalakṣmi namo'stute
sarvamaṅgala māṅgalye śive sarvārtha sādhike
śaraṇye tryambake gauri nārāyaṇi namo'stute
7 prathamaṃ tryambakā gaurī dvitīyaṃ vaiṣṇavī tathā
tṛtiyaṃ kamalā proktā caturthaṃ sundarī tathā
8 pañcamaṃ viṣṇuśaktiśca ṣaṣṭhaṃ kātyāyanī tathā
vārāhī saptamaṃ caivaṃ hyaṣṭamaṃ harivallabhā
9 navamī khaḍginī proktā daśamaṃ caiva devikā
ekādaśaṃ siddhalakṣmī dvādaśaṃ haṃsa vāhinī
10 etatstotravaraṃ devyā ye paṭhantiḥ sadā naraḥ
sarvāpadbhyo vimucyante nātra kāryā vicāraṇā
11 ekamāsaṃ dvimāsaṃ ca trimāsaṃ ca catuṣṭakam
pañcamāsaṃ ca ṣaṭmāsaṃ trikālaṃ yaḥ sadā paṭhet
12 brāhmaṇaḥ kleśito duḥkhī dāridryāmaya pīḍitaḥ
janmāntara sahasrarthamucyate sarva kilviṣaiḥ
13 daridro labhate lakṣmīmaputraḥ putravān bhavet
dhanyo yaśasvī śatrughno bahlī caurabhayeṣu ca
14 śākinībhūta vetāla saṃvavyāghra nipātana
rājadvare sabhā sthāne kārāgṛha nibandhane
15 īśvareṇa kṛtaṃ stotraṃ prāṇināṃ hitakārakam

stuvantu brāhmaṇā nityam dāridryaṃ na ca bādhate
sarvapāpaharā lakṣmī sarvasiddhi pradāyinīm 16

iti śri brahmapurāṇe śrī siddha lakṣmī stotraṃ
samāptam

Song for the Glorious "Eyes of Indra"
(*Śrī Indrākṣī Stotram*)[9]

oṃ asya śrīndrākṣī stotra mantrasya sahasrākṣa ṛṣiḥ / indrākṣī devatā / anuṣṭup chandaḥ / mahālakṣmī bījam / bhuvaneśvarī śaktiḥ / bhavānīti korakaṃ oṃ śrīṃ hrīṃ klīṃ iti bījāni mama sarvābhīṣṭa siddhyarthe śrīmadindrākṣī stotra jape viniyogaḥ /

oṃ indrākṣī ityaṅguṣṭhābhyāṃ namaḥ
oṃ mahālakṣmīriti tarjanībhyāṃ namaḥ
oṃ maheśvarīti madhyamābhyāṃ namaḥ
oṃ ambujākṣītyanāmikābhyāṃ namaḥ
oṃ kātyāyanīti kaniṣṭhikābhyāṃ namaḥ
oṃ kaumārīti karatalakarapṛṣṭhābhyāṃ namaḥ
oṃ indrākṣīti hṛdayāya namaḥ
oṃ mahālakṣmīrīti śirase svāhā
oṃ maheśvarīti śikhāyai vauṣaṭ
oṃ ambujākṣīti kavacāya hum
oṃ kātyāyanīti netratrayāya vauṣaṭ

oṃ kaumārītyastrāya phaṭ
oṃ bhūrbhuvaḥsvarom iti digbandhanam

atha mantraḥ
oṃ aiṃ hrīṃ śrīṃ klīṃ klūṃ indrākṣyai namaḥ

indra uvāca—
indrākṣī namaḥ sa devī daivataiḥ samudāhṛtā
1 gaurī śaṅkabharī devī durgānāmnīti viśrutā
kātyāyanī mahādevī candraghaṇṭā mahātapā
2 sāvitrā sā ca gāyatrī brahmāṇī brahmāvādinī
nārāyaṇī bhadrakālī rudrāṇī kṛṣṇapiṅgalā
3 agnijvālā raudramukhī kālarātristapasvinī
meghaśyāmā sahasrākṣī muktakeśī jalodarī
4 mahādevī muktakeśī ghorarūpā mahābalā
ajitā bhadradā nandā rogahaṃtrī śivapriyā
5 śivadūtī karālī ca pratyakṣā parameśvarī
sadā sammohinī devī sundarī bhuvaneśvarī
6 indrākṣī indrarūpā ca indraśakti parāyaṇā
mahiṣāsura saṃhartrī cāmuṇḍā garbhadevatā
7 vārāhī nārasiṃhī ca bhīmā bhairava nādinī

śruti smṛti dhṛtirmedhā vidyā lakṣmīḥ sarasvatī
anantā vijayā pūrṇā mānastokā'parājitā 8
bhavānī pārvatī durgā haimavatyambikā śivā
etairnāmaśatairdivyaiḥ stutā śakreṇa dhīmatā 9
āyurārogyamaiśvaryaṃ vittaṃ jñānaṃ yaśobalam
nābhimātrajale sthitvā sahasra parisaṃkhyayā 10
japetstotramidaṃ mantraṃ vācāṃ siddhirbhavettataḥ
anena vidhinā bhaktyā mantrasiddhiśca jāyate 11
santuṣṭa ca bhaveddevī pratyakṣā samprajāyate
śatamavartayedyastu mucyate nāma saṃśayaḥ 12
āvartana sahasreṇa labhyate vāñchataṃ phalam
sāyam śataṃ paṭhennityam ṣaṣmāsātsiddhirucyate 13
coravyādhibhayasthāne manasāhyanucintayam
saṃvatsaram upāśritya sarvakāmārtha siddhaye 14
rājānaṃ vaśyamāpnoti ṣaṇmāsānnatra saṃśayaḥ 15

iti śrīndrākṣī stotraṃ samāptam

Song-Formulary of the Glorious Mahālakṣmī
(Śrī Mahālakṣmī Pañjara Stotram)

Viniyoga

oṃ asya śrī lakṣmī pañjara mahāmantrasya brahmā ṛṣiḥ paṅktiśchandaḥ śrīmahālakṣmīrdevatā śrīṃ bījaṃ svāhā śaktiḥ śriyai iti kīlakaṃ mama sarvābhīṣṭa siddhyarthe lakṣmī pañjara stotra jape viniyogaḥ

Karanyāsa

oṃ śrīṃ hrīṃ viṣuvallabhāyai aṅguṣṭhābhyāṃ namaḥ
oṃ śrīṃ hrīṃ jagajjananyai tarjanībhyāṃ namaḥ
oṃ śrīṃ hrīṃ siddhisevitāyai madhyamābhyāṃ namaḥ
oṃ śrīṃ hrīṃ siddhidātryai anāmikābhyāṃ namaḥ
oṃ śrīṃ hrīṃ vāñchitapūritāyai kaniṣṭhikābhyāṃ namaḥ
oṃ śrīṃ hrīṃ śrīṃ śriyai namaḥ svāheti karatala karapṛṣṭhābhyāṃ namaḥ

Ṣaḍaṅganyāsa

oṃ śrīṃ hrīṃ viṣṇuvallabhāyai hṛdayāya namaḥ
oṃ śrīṃ hrīṃ jagajjananyai śirase svāhā
oṃ śrīṃ hrīṃ siddhisevitāyai śikhāyai vaṣaṭ
oṃ śrīṃ hrīṃ vāñchitapūrikāyai netrābhyāṃ vauṣaṭ
oṃ śrīṃ hrīṃ śrīṃ śriyai namaḥ svāhetyastrāya phaṭ

Dhyāna

oṃ vandelakṣmīṃ paramaśivamayīṃ śuddha jāṃbūnadābhyāṃ
tejorūpāṃ kanakavasanāṃ sarva bhūṣojjvalāṅgīm
bījāpuraṃ kanaka kalaśaṃ hemapadmaṃ dadhānā
mādhyāṃśaktiṃ sakala jananīṃ viṇuvāmāṅka
1 saṃsthām
śaraṇaṃ tvāṃ prapanno'smi mahālakṣmi haripriye
2 prasādaṃ kuru deveśi mayi duṣṭe'parādhini
koṭi kandarpa lāvaṇyāṃ saundaryyaika svarūpatām
3 sarvamaṅgala māṅgalyāṃ śrīrāmāṃ śaraṇaṃ vraje

Mūlamantra Ṣaṭkam

oṃ śrīṃ hriṃ aiṃ klīṃ namo viṣṇuvallabhāyai
mahāmāyāyai kaṃ khaṃ gaṃ ghaṃ ṅaṃ namaste
namaste māṃ pāhi pāhi rakṣa rakṣa dhanaṃ dhānyaṃ
śriyaṃ samṛddhiṃ dehi dehi śrīṃ śriyai namaḥ svāhā 1
oṃ śrīṃ hrīṃ aiṃ klīṃ namo jagajjananyai
vātsalyanidhaye caṃ chaṃ jaṃ jhaṃ ñaṃ namaste
namaste māṃ pāhi pāhi rakṣa rakṣa śriyaṃ pratiṣṭhāṃ
vāksiddhiṃ me dehi dehi śrīṃ śriyai namaḥ svāhā 2
oṃ śrīṃ hrīṃ aiṃ klīṃ namaḥ siddhisevitāyai
sakalābhiṣṭhadāna dīkṣitāyai ṭaṃ ṭhaṃ ḍaṃ ḍhaṃ
ṇaṃ namaste namaste māṃ pāhi pāhi rakṣa rakṣa
sarvato'bhayaṃ dehi dehi śrīṃ śriyai namaḥ svāhā 3
oṃ śrīṃ hrīṃ aiṃ klīṃ namaḥ siddhidātryai mahā acintya
śaktikāyai taṃ thaṃ daṃ dhaṃ naṃ namaste namaste
māṃ pāhi pāhi rakṣa rakṣa me sarvābhiṣṭasiddhi dehi
dehi śrīṃ śriyai namaḥ svāhā 4
oṃ śrīṃ hrīṃ aiṃ klīṃ namaḥ vāñchita pūritāyai
sarvasiddhimūlabhūtāyai paṃ phaṃ baṃ bhaṃ maṃ
namaste namaste māṃ pāhi pāhi rakṣa rakṣa me
manovāñchitāṃ sarvārthabhūtāṃ siddhiṃ dehi dehi
śrīṃ śriyai namaḥ svāhā 5
[oṃ] śrīṃ hrīṃ aiṃ klīṃ kamale kamalālaye madyam
prasīda prasīda mahālakṣmi tubhyaṃ namo namaste
jagaddhitāyai yaṃ raṃ laṃ vaṃ śaṃ ṣaṃ saṃ haṃ
kṣaṃ namaste namaste māṃ pāhi pāhi rakṣa me
vaśyākarṣaṇa mohanastaṃbhanoccāṭanatāḍanācintya-
śakti vaibhavaṃ dehi dehi śrīṃ śriyai namaḥ svāhā 6

oṃ śrīṃ hrīṃ aiṃ klīṃ dhātryai namaḥ svāhā
oṃ śrīṃ hrīṃ aiṃ klīṃ śrīṃ bījarūpāyai namaḥ svāhā
[oṃ] śrīṃ hrīṃ aiṃ klīṃ viṣṇuvallabhāyai namaḥ svāhā
[oṃ] śrīṃ hrīṃ aiṃ klīṃ siddhayai namaḥ svāhā
oṃ śrīṃ hrīṃ aiṃ klīṃ buddhayai namaḥ svāhā
oṃ śrīṃ hrīṃ aiṃ klīṃ dhṛtyai namaḥ svāhā
oṃ śrīṃ hrīṃ aiṃ klīṃ matyai namaḥ svāhā
oṃ śrīṃ hrīṃ aiṃ klīṃ kāntyai namaḥ svāhā
oṃ śrīṃ hrīṃ aiṃ klīṃ śāntyai namaḥ svāhā
oṃ śrīṃ hrīṃ aiṃ klīṃ sarvatobhadrarūpāyai namaḥ
svāhā
oṃ śrīṃ hrīṃ aiṃ klīṃ śrīṃ śriyai namaḥ svāhā

oṃ namo bhagavatī brahmādi vedamātarvedodbhave
vedagarbhe sarvaśakti śiropaṇe śrī harivallabhe
mamābhiṣṭaṃ pūraya pūraya māṃ siddhibhājanaṃ
kuru kuru amṛtaṃ kuru kuru abhayaṃ kuru kuru
sarvaṃ kāryeṣu jvala jvala prajvala prajvala me
sutaśaktiṃ dīpaya dīpaya mamāhitān nāśaya nāśaya
asādhya kāryaṃ sādhaya sādhaya hrīṃ hrīṃ hrīṃ
glauṃ glauṃ śrīṃ śriye namaḥ svāhā

Lakṣmī Kavacam

oṃ śiro me rakṣatād devī padmā paṅkajadhāriṇī
1 bhālaṃ pātu jaganmātā lakṣmī padmālayā ca me
mukhaṃ pāpānmahāmāyā haśo me bhṛgukanyakā
2 ghṛāṇaṃ sindhi sutā pāyānnetre me viṣṇuvallabhā
kaṇṭham rakṣatu kaumārī skandhau pātu haripriyā
3 hṛdayaṃ me sadā rakṣet sarva śakti vidhāyinī
nabhiṃ sarveśvarī pāyātsarvabhūtālaya ca me
4 kaṭiśva kamalā pātū ūrū brahmādi devatā
jaṅghe jaganmayī rakṣet pādau sarva sukhāvahā
5 śrī bīja vāsa niratā sarvāṅge janakātmajā
sarvatobhadrarūpā māmavyād dikṣu vidikṣu ca
6 viṣame saṅkaṭe durge pātu māṃ vyoma vāsinī
itīdaṃ pañjaraṃ lakṣmyā guhyād guhyataraṃ mahat
7 gopaniyaṃ prayatnena daśādyasya kasya ca
yaḥ paṭhetprayato nityaṃ phalāhāri jitendriyaḥ
8 dhyāyellakṣmīpadaṃ prītyā tatya kiñcanna durlabhaṃ
viṣṇornāmnā sahasreṇa sampuṭīkṛtya yaḥ paṭhet
9 pañcāyuta prayatnena sa siddhasyādyathā hari
bilva pīṭhe likhedyantraṃ ṣaṭkoṇaṃ mantra saṃyutam
10 tatra sampūjayendevīṃ tadagre pāṭhamācaret
haridrā mālayā samkhyāṃ kurvannityamatadritaḥ
11 sarvasiddhim avāpnoti yadyadvāñchati satvara

iti śrī atharvaṇa rahasye lakṣmī pañjara stotraṃ
samāptam

Secret Lakṣmī Incantation That Yields Immediate Results
(Sadyaḥ Phaladā Lakṣmistava Hṛdayam)

śrīmatsaubhāgya jananīṃ staumi lakṣmī sanātanīm
sarvakāma phalāvāpti sādhanaika sukhāvahām 1
śrī vaikuṇṭhasthite lakṣmi samāgaccha mamaāgrataḥ
nārāyaneṇa saha māṃ kṛpā dṛṣṭāvalokaya 2
satyalokasthite lakṣmi tvaṃ samāgaccha sannidhim
vāsudevena sahitā prasīda varadā bhava 3
śvetadvīpa sthite lakṣmi śighramāgaccha suvrate
viṣṇunā sahitedevi jaganmātaḥ prasīda me 4
kṣīrābdhi saṃsthite lakṣmi samāgaccha samādhave
tvatkṛpādṛṣṭi sudhayā satataṃ māṃ vilokaya 5
ratnagarbhasthite lakṣmi paripūrṇa hiraṇmayi
samāgaccha samāgaccha sthtivā sapurato mama 6
sthirābhava mahalakṣmi niścalābhava nirmale
prasanno kamale devi prasannā varadā bhava 7
śrīdhare śrīmahābhūme tvadantastha mahānidhim
sīghramuddhṛtya purataḥ pradarśaya samāpaya 8
vasundhare śrīvasudhe vasudogdhe kṛpāmayi
tvatkukṣigataṃ sarvasvaṃ śīghram me pradarśaya 9
viṣṇu priye ratnagarbhe samasta phalade śive
tvadgarbhagata hemādan sampradarśaya darśaye 10
atropaviśya lakṣmi tvaṃ sthirābhava hiraṇmayi
susthirābhava saprītyā prasannā varadā bhava 11
sādare mastake hasta mama tava kṛpārpaya
sarva rājagṛhe lakṣmi tvatkalā mayi tiṣṭhatu 12
yathā vaikuṇṭhanagare yathaiva kṣīrasāgare
tathā madbhavanatiṣṭhasthiraṃ śrīviṣṇunāsaha 13
ādyādi mahālakṣmi viṣṇuvāmāṅga saṃsthite
pratyakṣam kuru me rūpaṃ rakṣaṃ māṃ śaraṇāgatam 14
samāgaccha mahālakṣmi dhanadhānya samanvite
prasīda purataḥ sthitvā praṇataṃ māṃ vilokaya 15
dayā sudṛṣṭiṃ kurutāṃ mayi śrīḥ
suvarṇa vṛṣṭiṃ kuru me gṛhe śrīḥ
mahālakṣmī samuddhiśya niśibhārgava vāsare
idaṃ śrīhṛdayaṃ japtvā śatavāraṃdhanī bhavet 16

iti śrī sadyaḥ phaladā lakṣmīstava hṛdayam samāptam

Notes

Introduction

1. Śāradā is the Sanskrit word for autumn and is also a name of the goddess.

2. Dīvālī is the vernacular name for Dīpāvalī, a Sanskrit name meaning "rows" (*āvalī*) of "lamps" (*dīpa*).

3. *Ghee* is clarified butter.

4. For a fascinating study of popular worship of Hanumān that includes *paddhati*s, see Lutgendorf, "Five Heads and No Tale."

5. For further discussion of this feature of Sanskrit texts, particularly in the *Śrī Sūktam* and in the *Devī Māhātmyam*, see Coburn, *Devī Māhātmya: Crystallization of the Goddess Tradition*, 1–86.

Chapter 1

1. Detailed discussions of the early iconography of the Indian lotus goddess may be found in a number of excellent sources, such as (listed alphabetically): Coomaraswamy, *Yakṣas*, 155–160; Gupta, *Elephant in Indian Art and Mythology*, 19–24; Kinsley, *Goddesses' Mirror*, 53–70; Kinsley, *Hindu Goddesses*, 19–22; Maury, *Folk Origins of Indian Art*, 101–126; Shaw, *Buddhist Goddesses of India*, 94–109; *Vāstu Śāstra*, ed. Shukla, 311–312; Singh, *Iconography of Gaja-Lakshmī*, 24–58; Sircar, *Studies*, 94–104; and Zimmer, *Myths and Symbols*, 90–102.

2. *Hymn to Lakṣmī* (*Lakṣmī Sūktam*) 1.

3. Qtd. in Slocum and Robinson, *Water Gardening: Water Lilies and Lotuses*, 13.

4. One of the first Europeans to master Sanskrit, British scholar Sir William Jones (1746–1794) was a key figure in advancing the academic study of Sanskrit in the West.

5. It has generally been held that the *Ṛg*, *Sāma*, and *Yājur Veda*s date from 1500 to 1200 BCE, and that the *Athārva Veda* dates from 1200 to 1000 BCE, though these have not been determined with certainty. Recent investigations argue for much earlier dates for all four Vedas. For a richly detailed study

of this debate, see Bryant, *Quest for the Origins of Vedic Culture.*

6. For details of the independent identities of the two goddesses in the Vedic period, see Gonda, *Aspects of Early Viṣṇuism,* 176–225.

7. This linguistic factor may inform the concepts of "polytheism" and "kathenotheism" (or "henotheism") in fascinating new ways that are beyond the scope of our present discussion.

8. Gonda, *Aspects of Early Viṣṇuism,* 186–87.

9. Kane, *History of Dharmaśāstra,* Vol. II, Part II, 1215, and Vol. III, 79.

Chapter 2

1. Most accounts list eighteen classical Purāṇas, although there is also an expanded list of 108 Purāṇas, which includes works on yoga and other esoteric topics.

2. *Bṛhadāraṇyaka Upaniṣad* 3.9.1–9.

3. The term *Vaiṣṇava* refers to a worshiper or system of worship recognizing Viṣṇu as the Supreme Reality; dozens of rich and varied traditions (*sampradāya*) of Vaiṣṇavism have developed over the centuries. Those who recognize Śiva as the Supreme Reality are called Śaiva, and those who recognize the Goddess (Śakti) as the Supreme Reality are called Śākta. These categories, however, are not necessarily mutually exclusive.

4. The earliest and most complete version of this story occurs in *Viṣṇu Purāṇa.* It also appears in various other Purāṇas and in the *Mahābhārata.*

5. The Sanskrit word *amṛta* and the English word *immortal* are close cognates.

6. The long-*a* grammatical endings on the nouns *padmā, tulasī, ketakī,* and *mālatī,* for example, reiterate their feminine designations, as do the names of rivers.

7. *Song for the Glorious Lotus Goddess* (*Śrī Kamalā Stotram*) 12.

8. *The Heavenly Gods' Praise-Song for Lakṣmī* (*Śrī Daivakṛta Lakṣmī Stotram*) 3. "Emanation" is *kalā,* that is, an extension or a ray, as in the rays of the sun.

9. *Praise-Song for the Lotus Goddess* (*Kamalā Stotram*) 8. Though this song has been placed with the Tantric texts in our volume, it illustrates the same point.

10. *The Heavenly Gods' Praise-Song for Lakṣmī* (*Śrī Daivakṛta Lakṣmī Stotram*) 9. These designations are reiterated elsewhere.

11. For further discussion, see Bailly, "Śrī-Lakṣmī: Majesty of the Hindu King."

12. For brief overview, see Bailly, "Devadāsīs." For detailed study, see Marglin, *Wives of the God-King.*

13. *Song for the Glorious Lotus Goddess* (*Śrī Kamalā Stotram*) 7.

14. Women's *vratas* (vows and fasts) vary in length and complexity. For women's vows in Bengal (including some for Lakṣmī), see McDaniel, *Making*

Virtuous Daughters and Wives. For various contexts and applications of vows, see Raj and Harman, eds., *Dealing with Deities*, and Pearson, *"Because It Gives Me Peace of Mind."*

15. The four traditional stages of life are that of the student (*brahmācārya*), householder (*gṛhastha*), forest-dweller (*vānaprastha*), and renunciant (*samnyāsa*). The "householder stage" begins with the rite of marriage and ends with the death of the spouse or when the next generation is ready to take on the responsibilities of supporting and managing the household.

16. For extended discussion of Hestia and contemporary women, see Paris, *Pagan Meditations: The Worlds of Aphrodite, Artemis, and Hestia*, 168–169.

17. Qtd. in Eller, *Living in the Lap of the Godd.ss*, 108–109.

18. *Song for the Glorious Lotus Goddess* (*Śrī Kamalā Stotram*) 12.

19. Each of these broad categories has its own collection of literatures: The *Kāma Śāstra* (which includes Vatsyāyana's *Kāma Sūtra*) focuses on pleasure; Kautilya's *Artha Śāstra* focuses on material wealth; and Manu's *Dharma Śāstra* focuses on law and virtuous conduct. The literatures on *mokṣa*, or spiritual liberation, are by far the most extensive and constitute entire schools unto themselves.

20. *Song for Lakṣmī, Gracious Bestower of Blessings* (*Prasannavaradā Śrī Lakṣmī Stotram*) 10. Pradyumna is an incarnation of Kāmadeva, born to Lakṣmī and Viṣṇu in their forms as Rukmiṇī and Kṛṣṇa.

21. *The Heavenly Gods' Praise-Song for Lakṣmī* (*Śrī Daivakṛta Lakṣmī Stotram*) 6, 7.

22. Pattanaik, *Lakshmi*, 59.

23. Gonda, *Aspects of Early Viṣṇuism*, 190.

24. *Song for Lakṣmī, Gracious Bestower of Blessings* (*Prasannavaradā Śrī Lakṣmī Stotram*) 17.

25. Ponder, *Dynamic Laws of Prosperity*, 142–143.

26. Orman, *Women and Money*, 45.

27. *Ibid.*, 45–55.

28. Festival of India, University of South Florida, Tampa, Florida, October 1999.

29. Atulā and other aspects of Alakṣmī will be discussed later.

30. See, for example, *Song for Lakṣmī, Gracious Bestower of Blessings* (*Prasannavaradā Śrī Lakṣmī Stotram*) 21, where Lakṣmī is invoked as *dharmādhare* (Upholder of *Dharma*).

31. *Lord Indra's Song for Lakṣmī* (*Devarāja Indrakṛta Lakṣmī Stotram*) 9.

32. See, for example, *Eight Verses Praising Mahālakṣmī* (*Mahālakṣmyaṣṭakam Stotram*) 4.

33. *Lord Indra's Song for Lakṣmī* (*Devarāja Indrakṛta Lakṣmī Stotram*) 5, 6.

34. Ibid., 24.

35. Coomaraswamy, "Early Indian Iconography," 177.

36. *Gautamī-māhātmya* 67, 2–3 (part IV of the *Brahmā Purāṇa*).

37. *Liṅga Purāṇa* 6. 1–7, 15–18.

38. It is clear that Jyeṣṭhā's (i.e., Alakṣmī's) inauspicious nature is not conducive to the auspicious state of marriage. However, Lakṣmī's own marriage

cannot take place as long as her elder sister remains without a spouse, and therefore a match is arranged between Jyeṣṭhā and the sage Duḥsaha (whose name means "Unbearable"). See *Liṅga Purāṇa* 6.8–18.

39. *Liṅga Purāṇa* 6.8–14.

40. Ibid., 6.38–42. See verses 43–75 for a more extensive list.

41. Ibid., 6.69b–75.

42. *Lord Indra's Song for Lakṣmī* (*Devarāja Indrakṛta Lakṣmī Stotram*) 31, 32.

Chapter 3

1. *Song for the Lakṣmī of Spiritual Power* (*Siddhalakṣmī Stotram*) 15, 16.

2. I provide here only the briefest overview of Kuṇḍalinī as it serves the discussion of the Tantric Lakṣmī, for there is a rich literature available on the topic. See, for example, Kripananda, *Sacred Power*; or Brooks and Bailly, "Kuṇḍalinī," in *Meditation Revolution*, ed. Brooks et al., 445–496.

3. Seven is the standard recognized number, though various systems designate more, some of these existing in the auric field surrounding the physical body.

4. For discussion of *padmā* as a lotus seat or foundation, see discussion in ch. 1.

5. *Lakṣmī Tantra* 26.15 ff.

6. *The Secret Heart of Lakṣmī* (*Śrī Mahālakṣmī Hṛdayam*) 22.

7. In the concluding *maṅgala* (benediction) of his cycle of nine songs praising Kamalā, seventeenth-century South Indian poet Muttusvami Diksitar, for example, describes Kamalā as "flanked by Lakṣmī and Sarasvatī" and as "a friend of Lakṣmī and Sarasvatī" (Muttusvami Diksitar's *Kamalāmbikā Navavaraṇa Kīrtana*, second *āvaraṇa*, in Te Nijenhuis and Gupta, trans., 190).

8. *Song-Amulet of the Lotus Goddess* (*Kamalātmikā Kavacam*) 6–9. For discussion of Śiva's association with the *mahāvidyā*s, see Kinsley, *Tantric Visions*, 117 and passim.

9. We make the distinction regarding the householder, for it may be argued that Chinnamastā appears to be the most fearsome, least "worldly" of the group. However, Chinnamastā belongs to the category of goddesses who are to be worshiped solely by world-renunciants. Her image is forbidden from display in the homes of householders, for its marvelous and frightening power could well initiate the decay of the household, drawing the inhabitants' interests prematurely toward complete renunciation and abnegation of dharmic responsibilities. A more mundane interpretation, of course, is that householders of any culture might think twice before displaying such explicitly violent and sexual images in the home; these potent images, boldly illuminating the confluence of sex and death at its sacred core, necessarily deserve a domain separate from the realm of the "ordinary."

10. See, for example, Kinsley's reports of his varied informants (*Tantric Visions*, 232 ff.).

11. *Praise-Song for the Lotus Goddess* (*Kamalā Stotram*) 13–15.

12. *The Secret Heart of Lakṣmī* (*Śrī Mahālakṣmī Hṛdayam*) 13.

13. Ibid., 91.

14. Classical texts and Kashmiri ritual texts identify this goddess as Siddhalakṣmī, whereas Nepali ritual texts and contemporary priests call her Siddhilakṣmī (Timalsina, "Terrifying Beauty," 59).

15. *Song for the Lakṣmī of Spiritual Power* (*Śrī Siddhalakṣmī Stotram*) 1, 2.

16. Ibid., Meditation for Visualization of the Deity.

17. Timalsina, "Terrifying Beauty," 64.

18. *The Secret Heart of Lakṣmī* (*Śrī Mahālakṣmī Hṛdayam*) 88.

Chapter 4

1. *Hymn to Śrī* (*Śrī Sūktam)* 1.

2. Ibid., 4.

3. Ibid., 6.

4. Ibid. 4, 9.

5. Ibid., 2, 15.

6. Dhal, *Goddess Lakṣmī,* 57–58.

7. Note that the addressing of the inauspicious goddess by the name Jyeṣṭhā (rather than, for example, Nirṛti or Pāpī-lakṣmī) indicates the language of the late Vedic period.

8. Addressing the goddess as Mahālakṣmī and as the consort of Viṣṇu also indicates a later, perhaps post-Vedic designation of the goddess.

9. Dhal, *Goddess Lakṣmī,* 56–57.

10. *Ṛg Vidhāna* 2, 19, 3; qtd. in Dhal, *Goddess Lakṣmī,* 56–57.

Chapter 5

1. Over the centuries, some practitioners have questioned the relevancy of chanting in—or listening to—a language that they do not comprehend discursively, and thus their primary focus in the songs of praise is with their instrumentality as emotionally prayerful communications with the goddess. For discussion of this and related issues of women's involvement with worship of the goddess and devotional poetry in Sanskrit as well as translation into vernacular languages, see Humes, "Glorifying the Great Goddess or Great Woman?"

2. See, for example, *Song for Lakṣmī, Gracious Bestower of Blessings* (*Prasannavaradā Śrī Lakṣmī Stotram*) 24–27.

Chapter 6

1. *The Secret Heart of Lakṣmī* (*Śrī Mahālakṣmī Hṛdayam*) 92. *Hak!* is an onomatopoetic exclamation, used as a secret term among initiates as the sacred energy is being awakened.

2. Ibid., 89, 90.
3. Ibid., 108.
4. Ibid., 107.
5. Consider, for example, the words of the tenth-century Kashmiri *siddha* Utpaladeva:

> O Lord of the Universe!
> How lucky are your devotees,
> Worthy of being adored by you.
> For them, this turbulent ocean of the world
> Is like a great pleasure-lake
> For their amusement. (*Śivastotrāvalī* 3.15, trans. Bailly)

6. *Song-Formulary of the Glorious Mahālakṣmī* (*Śrī Mahālakṣmī Pañjara Stotram*), verses 1 and 6 of the *Six Verses on the Root Mantra* (*Mūlamantra Ṣaṭkam*).
7. *Song-Amulet of the Bestower of Wealth* (*Dhanadā Kavacam*) 3, 4.
8. *The Secret Heart of Lakṣmī* (*Śrī Mahālakṣmī Hṛdayam*) 99, 100.
9. *Bṛhannīla Tantra* 7.188–189; qtd. in Biernacki, *Renowned Goddess of Desire*, 46. Later in that volume (111–130), Biernacki provides detailed and fascinating discussion of how the goddess Nīlasarasvatī (Blue Goddess of Speech) gives birth to seed *mantras*, and how this action relates to the inherent power of women's speech.
10. *Song-Amulet of the Lotus Goddess* (*Kamalātmikā Kavacam*) 3–5.
11. For a rich discussion of the multivalent connotations of *mudrā*, see Muller-Ortega, "On the 'Seal of Śambhu,' " especially 576–580.
12. See, for example, *Song-Amulet of the Lotus Goddess* (*Kamalātmikā Kavacam*) 3–5, as well as the discussion in the section on "The Potency of a Woman's Recitations."

Introduction to Part Three

1. Bühnemann, *Pūjā*, 137.
2. This explains why some versions of the *Śrī Sūktam* contain sixteen verses.

Lakṣmī *Pūjā* Text

1. In estoteric *pūjā*, there is a form of preparatory meditation also called *bhūta-śuddhi* that entails visualizing the progressive dissolution (*śuddhi*) of the elements (*bhūta*) within one's body.
2. *Śrī Lakṣmī Upāsanā*, ed. Dixit, 15.
3. Keshavadas, *Gāyatrī*, 111.

4. *Verses for Meditation on Lakṣmī* 1, 2, 3, and 4 correspond with *Eight Verses Praising Mahālakṣmī (Mahālakṣmyaṣṭakam Stotram)* 1, 2, 7, and 8.

5. Kane notes that one may offer water for sipping (*ācamana*) after the end of each instance of bathing (*snāna*), clothing (*vastra*), and feeding (*naivedya*). *History of Dharmaśāstra*, Vol. II, Part II, 730.

6. *Pūjāprakāśa*, p. 34; qtd. in Kane, *History of Dharmaśāstra*, Vol. II, Part II, 731.

7. *Aitareya Brāhmaṇa* 8.20.1; qtd. in Bühnemann, *Pūjā*, 140.

8. For example, a bride's father welcomes the bridegroom to his home by offering *madhuparka*.

9. For further discussion of adornment and auspiciousness, see Bailly, "Ornamentation," 750–751.

10. Although some early texts suggest that, like their brothers, young girls received the sacrament of investiture, this is not widely known and in any case seems to have been discontinued well before the worship of Lakṣmī was expressed in the form of the *pūjā*.

11. *Viṣṇudharmaśāstra* 66.4 maintains that any ornaments of gold and precious gems offered should be authentic and not imitation (Kane, *History of Dharmaśāstra*, Vol. II, Part II, 729–731). Some texts acknowledge that if a person cannot afford to offer clothing or ornaments, he may perform a *pūjā* of ten, rather than sixteen, ritual attendances (ibid., 732).

12. *Lakṣmī Tantra* 48.15–17.

13. White, *Alchemical Body*, 247.

14. In the esoteric Buddhist and Taoist traditions of China, where it is called (in Mandarin) *ju-sha*, cinnabar carries the same significance as in India.

15. White, *Alchemical Body*, 194–197.

16. Some scholars identify *kumkuma* as saffron. See, for example, Monier-Williams, *Sanskrit-English Dictionary*; Apte, *Student's Sanskrit-English Dictionary*; Chaturvedi and Tiwari, *Practical Hindi-English Dictionary*. Others identify it as red turmeric. See, for example, Flood, *Introduction to Hinduism*, 208.

17. *Hymn to Śrī* (*Śrī Sūktam*) 9.

18. *Viṣṇudharmaśāstra* 66.2; qtd. in Kane, *History of Dharmaśāstra*, Vol. II, Part II, 732.

19. Ibid.

20. Monier-Williams, *Sanskrit-English Dictionary*. *Sub voce*.

21. Narrative cited in Courtright, "On This Holy Day in My Humble Way," 45.

22. The lord of the forest (*vanaspati*) is a type of tree.

23. As noted in the Introduction, Dīpāvalī is also known by its Indic vernacular name, Dīvālī.

24. Various texts cite as many as thirteen necessary ingredients of *tambula*. See Kane, *History of Dharmaśāstra*, Vol. II, Part II, 734–735.

25. Brahmanicide (*brahmahatya*) is considered the most heinous crime, incurring terrible karmic repercussions.

26. This being said, it should be noted that other texts cite yet other slight variations from this list.

27. According to several texts and worship manuals, circumambulation (*pradakṣinā*) and farewell (*namaskāra*) are often included together. For list of these, see Kane, Vol. II, Part II, 729.

Vedic Hymns to Lakṣmī

1. Kubera, a god of wealth, is lord of the *yakṣa*s, a type of nature spirit.

2. Alakṣmī is also known as Jyeṣṭhā, the inauspicious "elder sister" of Lakṣmī.

3. Kardama and Ciklīta are Vedic sages who were recognized as sons of Śrī and whose original embodiments were as the earth's fertile, primordial wetlands.

4. Mādhava and "imperishable lord" both refer to Viṣṇu.

5. Verse 10 constitutes the *Lakṣmī Gāyatrī mantra*, as discussed in ch. 4.

Purāṇic Songs to Lakṣmī

1. According to the sacred histories, Agastya was born to a Vedic god and a celestial nymph. He is known for his performance of lengthy austerities, which, according to legend, he carries on to this day. He is recognized as the celestial author of various works, particularly in the Pāñcarātra tradition, which acknowledges Śrī-Lakṣmī as the Supreme Reality.

2. The God of Love here is Pradyumna, born to Kṛṣṇa and Lakṣmī in her form as Rukmiṇī.

3. Rudra, an early form of Śiva, is an embodiment of storms and thunder; Ravi is the sun; Candra is the moon; and the Lord of the Gods is Indra.

4. Horses are a symbol of Lakṣmī's auspiciousness, particularly in the aspect of *aiśvarya*, which is majesty or royal sovereignty. Cows are also highly auspicious, as these gentle creatures have long been recognized as embodiments of Lakṣmī.

5. This song is said to have been composed and performed by Lord Indra to win back the favor of the goddess. It appears in the *Śrīmad Devī Bhāgavata Purāṇa*.

6. Nārāyaṇa, a form of Viṣṇu, is always depicted with Lakṣmī by his side.

7. Living death: *jīvanmṛtam*.

8. *Dharma* (virtuous conduct), *artha* (material wealth), *kāma* (pleasure), and *mokṣa* (liberation) are four cardinal "wealths," or goals; see discussion in ch. 2.

9. Īśana is an early name of Rudra-Śiva.

10. The three twilights are dawn, noon, and dusk.

11. At the conclusion of the Churning of the Ocean story, Indra, lord of the gods, sings this song to the goddess in gratitude for her restoring his kingdom and for harmony among the three worlds. This rendition of the song is from the *Viṣṇu Purāṇa*, considered to be the earliest version of the narrative.

12. The sage Parāśara is the narrator of the story. The Mighty One (*śakra*) is Indra.

13. This verse does not appear in either the *Viṣṇu Purāṇa* or the *Agni Purāṇa*.

14. Janārdana is Viṣṇu, who, like Indra, is also called lord of the gods. With the Churning of the Ocean story, Viṣṇu supersedes Indra in that role.

15. Son of Aditi: that is, as the dwarf.

16. Goloka, literally, "Cow Realm," is a heavenly realm where Kṛṣṇa reigns. The *rasa* dance is enjoyed by Kṛṣṇa and the *gopīs* (milkmaids) in the Vṛnda forest (Vṛndāvana).

17. "Single" (*abhāryo*) is masculine and literally means "unsupported." "Spouse" (*bhāryā*) is feminine and literally means "support."

Tantric Songs to Lakṣmī

1. Top back of the head: This is the *śikha*, a term that refers both to the top back of the head and to the "topknot," or tuft of long hair that grows on that spot, when the surrounding hair is shaved. The armor (*kavaca*) refers to the torso. The weapon (*astra*) refers to the hands. The preparatory securing of the cardinal directions (*digbandhana*) here is shifted from points on the earth and atmosphere to points on the body, thereby rendering the human form a cosmos unto itself.

2. This verse is identical to verse 1 of the *dhyāna* section of the *Song-Formulary of the Glorious Mahālakṣmī* (*Śrī Mahālakṣmī Pañjara Stotram*).

3. Madhu's foe is an epithet of Viṣṇu, who vanquished the demon Madhu.

4. The Thunder Beings (*rudrā*) are Vedic deities embodied as storms, thunder, and lightening. The Mighty One (*śakra*) is an epithet of Indra, lord of the Vedic gods.

5. Vaikuṇṭha is the heavenly abode of Lakṣmī and Viṣṇu. The White Island is located in the heavenly Ocean of Milk.

6. Ayodhyā is renowned as the home of Sītā, an incarnation of Lakṣmī.

7. The three qualities of nature are *rajas* (passion), *tamas* (lethargy), and *sattva* (equipoise).

8. *Hak!* is an onomatopoetic expression used by the spiritual masters of some esoteric traditions as a verbal confirmation of the disciple's interior state, especially when the sacred energy is being awakened.

9. *The Secret Heart of Primordial Lakṣmī, Source of All Sources*: This is simply an alternate title for the *Śrī Mahālakṣmī Hṛdayam*, also referred to as the *Śrī Mahālakṣmīhṛdaya Stotram* and the *Lakṣmī Hṛdayam*. The names vary so as to comply with the metrical cadence of the verses.

10. *Puraścaraṇa* is a preliminary ceremony in which the power within the *mantras* is awakened and made ready for use.

11. Bhārgavī translates as "Daughter of Bhṛgu," that is, Lakṣmī. Her sacred day (or night) may occur at various times throughout the lunar year. During the solar week it is on Friday, also the day sacred to Śukra, the constellation (and goddess) Venus.

12. The festival of Rāma refers to the *Rām Līlā*, celebrated during the bright half (i.e., waxing) of the lunar month of Āśvina (September–October).

13. Hari is a name of Viṣṇu.

14. Most Excellent of Men (*puruṣottama*) is an epithet of Viṣṇu.

15. Magical attainment: *siddhi*.

16. *Atharvaṇa* is emended from *Athayarvaṇa*.

17. Of all the songs compiled in his worship manual for Lakṣmī, this is the only one for which Pandit Dixit offers commentary. It reads almost as a disclaimer, and its words are most likely paraphrases of the song's original *phala* verses.

The commentary is as follows: "This 'Praise-Song for the Bestower of Wealth' is said to bear the desired fruit for the seeker. Whoever recites this song every day at the three twilights will acquire its power [*siddhi*] very quickly. It should not, therefore, be taken lightly. An extremely rare secret is embedded in this hymn. For this reason it should be held in utmost secrecy" (Dixit, 73; my translation from Hindi). Many Tantric texts include similar advisories, and though the potency of their mantras is indisputable, it is also true that the texts themselves have been made public without compromising the tradition, for the real power of their *mantras* is considered to be unleashed only when they have become *caitanya* (conscious or awakened).

18. The "five essential elements" (*pañcatattva*) and the "five practices" (*pañcācāra*) refer to a feature of left-handed Tantra most often called the "five *m*'s" (*pañcamakāra*), that is, a ritualized engagement with five transgressive elements beginning with the Sanksrit letter *m*: *madya* (wine), *māṃsa* (meat), *matsya* (fish), *mudrā* (fermented parched grain, according to some; ritual hand gestures, according to others), and *maithuna* (sexual union). "Spiritual practitioner": *sādhaka*, a term used mostly in the Tantric traditions.

19. For explication of the linguistic puzzles embedded in this song, see Ch. 6.

20. In a stylistic departure from most other Tantric songs, the initial verses here are presented in verse, rather than prose. The translation reflects this structure.

21. Virtue (*dharma*), wealth (*artha*), pleasure (*kāma*), and spiritual liberation (*mokṣa*) are known collectively as the four "wealths" or "goals" of a harmonious life. See discussion in ch. 2.

22. The Smṛti are the sacred narratives, such as in the Purāṇas.

23. Higher Self: *ātman*.

24. Heart: *cetas*, a faculty of consciousness seated in the heart.

25. Īśa, literally meaning "lord," refers to Lord Śiva.

26. In verses 21–24, the central sector plus ten directions refer to the cardinal directions, moving across the earth plane and then connecting upward to the heavens and downward to the netherworlds. In this text they are delineated as follows: the center; the space above [Vaikuṇṭha heaven]; the east; the west; the south; the north; the southeast; the southwest; the northwest; the space below [the netherworlds]; and the northeast. *Vāstu Śāstra*, the science of architecture and auspicious placement, reflects this cosmic configuration on a microcosmic level, dividing a building's floor-plan into sectors, each corresponding to a realm presided over by a deity (and consort). Students of *feng shui* will recognize similarities between the *ba-gua* and the nine lateral sectors of *vāstu*.

27. Beneath the earth are seven levels of netherworlds or hells, the lowest of which is Pātāla.

28. The Island of Gems (Maṇidvīpa) belongs to the goddess and is located in the Ocean of Milk. Īśana refers to Śiva as lord of the northeast.

29. The bridge leading toward Lanka: This is Setubandha, the causeway at Rāmeśvaram, the southernmost tip of India. Siṃhala is Sri Lanka.

30. Kalighatta is Kolkata (Calcutta). The Blue Hill, located in Assam, is the most powerful of the *śakti pīthas* (power-spots containing parts of the goddess's body), for it is here that the goddess's *yoni*, or vulva, fell to earth and became a cleft rock that periodically emits iron-laden, reddish secretions.

31. Vraja is a region in northeastern India well known as the location of the magnificent stories of Rādhā and Kṛṣṇa. Kurukṣetra and Dvāraka are also locations associated with Kṛṣṇa in his various forms. In verse 27, as in verse 24, the goddess is called Bhadrakālī, though the associated locations are different; this may be an erroneous duplication.

32. In a netherworld: *rasātala*, the sixth of the seven realms of the netherworlds.

33. One Goddess: *ekā devī*. This epithet usually describes Durgā.

34. This is true, O Pārvatī: Pārvatī is the consort of Śiva. Tantric texts known as Āgamas are structured as a dialogue in which Pārvatī poses questions about esoteric worship, and Śiva's responses constitute the core of the text. Texts known as Nigamas reverse this, where Śiva asks the questions and Pārvatī provides the discourse.

35. "O Lovely One" (*varānane*) refers to Pārvatī, whom Śiva addresses in sacred dialogue. See footnote to *Praise-Song for the Lotus Goddess* (*Kamalā Stotram*) 37.

36. Mother of the Great Boar: *mahāvarahajananī*. The great boar is Mahāvarāha, an *avatāra* of Viṣṇu.

37. The Lord of Vaikuṇṭha is Viṣṇu.

38. The Lord of the Cow Realm (Goloka) is Kṛṣṇa, an *avatāra* of Viṣṇu.

39. Rider of the Eagle: *garuḍāsanā*. Garuḍa is a majestic, heavenly bird who serves as a seat (*āsana*) or vehicle for Viṣṇu and Lakṣmī. Although he

has no exact earthly equivalent, Garuḍa is most closely associated with the eagle.

40. The Beautiful-Haired One is Kṛṣṇa.

41. Madhu, Kaitabha, Śumbha, and Niśumbha are among the *asura*s defeated by the goddess as described in the *Devīmāhātmyam*. Hari and Śaṅkara are names of Viṣṇu and Śiva, respectively.

42. Śambhu is a name of Śiva.

43. "Moon-faced" (*candramukhī*) suggests a round-shaped face, lauded as a sign of beauty in a woman.

44. Kamalātmikā, meaning "essence of the lotus," is a variant name of Kamalā as one of the Ten Great Wisdom Goddesses (*mahāvidyā*s).

45. "O Great Lady" (*maheśāni*) refers to Pārvatī, whom Śiva addresses in sacred dialogue; see footnote to *Praise-Song for the Lotus Goddess* (*Kamalā Stotram*) 37.

46. Feminine private parts: *guhye*.

47. Life-breath: *prāṇa*. Constituent elements: *dhātu*. Hair-part: *sīmante*.

48. This song invokes a large group of goddesses who are emanations of Lakṣmī. They express both the gentle and fierce forms of the goddess. In most cases I have retained their names rather than translating these names as epithets.

49. Hara is a name of Śiva.

50. Viṣṇu's mysterious creative power: *viṣṇumāyā*.

51. Legions of Divine Mothers: protective goddess-energies who emanate from eight core "mothers" (*mātṛs*): (1) Vaiṣṇavī, (2) Brāhmī or Brāhmaṇī, (3) Kārttikeyī or Māyurī, (4) Indrāṇī, (5) Yamī, (6) Vārāhī, (7) Īśānī or Devī, and (8) Lakṣmī. Female spirits of the sacred seals: *mudrāḥ*. These are formulations of the energies that seal and protect a sacred endeavor, and they are embodied as female spirits.

52. The admonition that a person with certain physical imperfections or other distinguishing characteristics be denied access to a sacred text also occurs elsewhere in the Hindu tradition.

53. "*Kula*" means "family" and it refers to a Tantric lineage of initiation.

54. The ritual use of sexual fluids is a feature of left-handed Tantra. Śrāvaṇa is the lunar month July–August, Āśvina is September–October, Kārttika is October–November, and Phālguṇa is February–March.

55. Bhādrapada is the lunar month August–September. This verse and the next few verses contain references to certain of the twenty-seven constellations (*nakṣatra*s) designated in Jyotiṣa, or the science of Vedic astrology.

56. Spiritual master: *gurudeva*.

57. Siddhalakṣmī is a form of the goddess embodying any type of success, mastery, prosperity, accomplishment, attainment, perfection, or power—whether spiritual or magical. The *Song for the Lakṣmī of Spiritual Power* (*Śrī Siddhalakṣmī Stotram*) demonstrates the crossing of categories between the "Purāṇic" and the "Tantric" songs in our collection. Technically, we might place it among the Purāṇic songs, for it shares certain qualities with the other

songs in that chapter: It is said to have been composed by the gods; it places thematic emphasis on royalty, brahmans, and material prosperity; the three aspects of the goddess who preside over the song—Mahākālī, Mahālakṣmī, and Mahāsarasvatī—are lauded in other Purāṇas; and, finally, the colophon places this work within the *Brahmā Purāṇa* (although I have not been able to locate this song within that text). It should be noted that it is not uncommon to encounter such discrepancies between what the colophon designates as the source of a text and whether the excerpt actually appears in that text.

I include this song in our Tantric chapter because of its emphasis on the mantric form of the goddess and on the ritual instructions that accompany the text, both being significant features of the Tantric works. Clearly, this is a work reflecting a Śākta worldview, for it recognizes the goddess as supreme reality, and as such, both its thematic content and its ritual application demonstrate that it cannot be contained by only one category. Most important, this aspect of the goddess is sought for *siddhi*, or spiritual power, the quintessential aspect of the Tantric goddess. For further discussion of the goddess Siddhalakṣmī, see ch. 3.

58. Brāhmaṇī, Vaiṣṇavī, and Rudrāṇī are Mahāsarasvatī, Mahālakṣmī, and Mahākālī, respectively. Brāhmaṇī is the feminine aspect/consort of Brahmā, the creator; Vaiṣṇavī is the feminine aspect/consort of Viṣṇu, the preserver; and Rudrāṇī is the feminine aspect/consort of Rudra-Śiva, the destroyer.

59. Securing the directions: *digbandhana mantra.*

60. Primordial sound (*praṇava*) refers to *oṃ*, whose actual transliteration is *a-u-m* or *a-u-ṃ*.

61. This verse refers to the written ligature of *oṃ*. The *anusvāra*, or aftertone, is written as a dot (thus, *sūryakoṭi*, the disk of the sun) and is nested within a crescent (thus, *candrakoṭi*, or moon crescent). Other texts have called this joint ligature the *candrabindu*, that is, the "moon" [and] the "drop."

62. Siddhalakṣmī is the Lakṣmī of spiritual and magical power; Mokṣalakṣmī is the Lakṣmī of spiritual liberation; and Ādyalakṣmī is the primordial Lakṣmī.

63. The pronunciations of the next twelve syllables refer to recitations of the three *mantra*s that preside over this text.

64. The rider of the swan is Sarasvatī.

65. Within the palace gates: This may be a literal reference to the use of this text for the protection of the royal court. As well, it may refer to the "gates," or apertures, of the practitioner's body.

66. Indrākṣī ("Eyes of Indra") is an epithet of Lakṣmī.

67. The Lord of the Thousand Eyes is Indra.

68. This is the first part of the sacred *Gāyatrī Mantra*, addressing the great spirit of Reality as it exists on the earth, in the atmosphere, and across space.

69. Here, the term *hundred* (*śatam*) is not meant literally but figuratively, to indicate many. In contrast, when an enumeration of the sacred number 108 is intended, the amount is specific. Compare, for example, the *108 Names of the Glorious Lotus Goddess* (*Śrī Kamalā Aṣṭottaraśatanāma Stotram*).

70. Note that the names Lakṣmī and Mahālakṣmī are used interchangeably.

71. Spiritual Power: *Siddhi.* The goddess of the sacred flame: Svāhā, personification of the sacred flame (*svāhā*) and the animating power (*śakti*) of this song.

72. This verse is identical to verse 1 of the Song of Praise section of the *The Secret Heart of Lakṣmī* (*Śrī Mahālakṣmī Hṛdayam*).

73. For discussion of how these six verses progress through the six *vargas*, or linguistic categories of the Sanskrit alphabet, see ch. 6.

74. The magical power of speech: *vāksiddhi.*

75. The one who surpasses all thought is Śiva.

76. Core essence: *mūlabhūtāyai.*

77. *Yantra:* a sacred geometric diagram. *Bilva* pedestal: The *bilva,* or wood-apple, is a tree sacred to Lakṣmī.

78. Rosary of turmeric: The golden-colored spice turmeric is sacred to Lakṣmī.

79. This song of praise in sixteen verses appears to have been abridged from a longer work and constructed to accompany worship using the sixteen *upacāras*, or ritual attendances (see previous section on ceremony). Eleven of its sixteen verses also appear in *The Secret Heart of Lakṣmī* (*Śrī Mahālakṣmī Hṛdayam*). Just as we have opened this chapter with *The Secret Heart of Lakṣmī,* we close with the *Secret Lakṣmī Incantation That Yields Immediate Results* as a reprise—a brief song that, as its title suggests, recapitulates the core essence of the longer, opening piece.

80. Verses 2–10 are identical to *The Secret Heart of Lakṣmī* (*Śrī Mahālakṣmī Hṛdayam*) 30–38.

81. Verse 12 is identical to the *The Secret Heart of Lakṣmī* (*Śrī Mahālakṣmī Hṛdayam*) 56.

82. Verse 13 is identical to the *The Secret Heart of Lakṣmī* (*Śrī Mahālakṣmī Hṛdayam*) 61.

83. Night sacred to Bhārgavī: Friday. See also note to *The Secret Heart of Lakṣmī* (*Śrī Mahālakṣmī Hṛdayam*) 98.

Transliterated Sanskrit Texts

1. Text from *Śrī Sūkta: Text with Translation and Explanation,* ed. Rao.

2. Rao's edition transposes some of the phrases in his Sanskrit rendering of verses 13 and 14; however, his romanized version adheres to the text as published in various other sources, and this is what I use here.

3. Text from *Pañcasūktam: Edited with the 'Siddhānta Dīpika' Sanskrit and Hindi Commentaries,* ed. Nārāyaṇadāsa Śāstrī.

4. I have added the verse numbers.

5. Text from *Śrī Lakṣmī Upāsanā,* ed. Dixit; it also appears in *Bṛhatstotraratnākaraḥ,* ed. Miśra Śāstrī.

6. Text from *Śrī Lakṣmī Upāsanā*, ed. Dixit. It also appears in *Bṛhatstotraratnākaraḥ* (*Sarvavidhadevānāṃ Stotrasaṃgraḥa*), ed. Miśra Śāstrī; *Bṛhatstotraratnākaraḥ* (*Stotrasaṃkhyā 464*), ed. Pāṇḍey; and numerous other sources.

7. I have added the verse numbers.

8. I have inserted verse numbers and section titles. Note that this text is in a nonstandard form of Sanskrit particular to Tantric texts of the Eastern transmission (as in Assam or Bengal). Most variations appear simply as minor idiosyncrasies, such as doubling of consonants to replace consonant clusters (*samāttam* for *samāptam*); or doubling of *v* (*sarvva* for *sarva*, *purvva* for *purva*, *pārvvatī* for *pārvatī*).

9. The *viniyoga* and the *stotra* are from *Śrī Lakṣmī Upāsanā*, ed. Pandit Rajesh Dixit. The *nyāsa* section has been inserted from the version in *Bṛhatstotraratnākaraḥ* (*Stotrasaṃkhyā 464*), ed. Paṇḍit Rāmateja Pāṇḍey.

Bibliography

Sanskrit Texts and Translations

Agni Purāṇa. Translated by N. Gangadharan. Ancient Indian Tradition and Mythology Series, vols. 27–30. Delhi: Motilal Banarsidass, 1984–1987.

Bhāgavata Purāṇa. Part III. Translated by Ganesh Vasudeo Tagare. Ancient Indian Tradition and Mythology Series, vol. 9. Delhi: Motilal Banarsidass, 1976.

Brahmā Purāṇa. Translated by a Board of Scholars. Ancient Indian Tradition and Mythology Series, vols. 33–36. Delhi: Motilal Banarsidass, 1985–1986.

Brahmāṇḍa Purāṇa. Translated by Ganesh Vasudeo Tagare. Ancient Indian Tradition and Mythology Series, vols. 22–25. Delhi: Motilal Banarsidass, 1983–1984.

Bṛhatstotraratnākaraḥ (*Sarvavidhadevānāṃ Stotrasaṃgraha*). Edited by Ācārya Paṇḍita Śrī Śivadatta Miśra Śāstrī Varanasi: Thakur Prasad and Sons Publishers, *saṃvat* 2035 [CE 1978].

Bṛhatstotraratnākaraḥ (*Stotrasaṃkhyā 464*). Edited by Paṇḍit Rāmateja Pāṇḍey. Kāśī [Varanasi]: Paṇḍitapustakālaya, *saṃvat* 2031 [CE 1975].

Devī-devatāon kī āratiyāṅ. Edited by Paṇḍit Sivanarayan Laksman Pandey and Paṇḍit Rajesh Dixit. Delhi: Dehati Pustak Bandar, n.d.

Garuḍa Purāṇa. Translated by a Board of Scholars. Ancient Indian Tradition and Mythology Series, vols. 12–14. Delhi: Motilal Banarsidass, 1978–1980.

Hymns of the Atharva-Veda. Together with Extracts from the Ritual Books and the Commentaries. Translated by Maurice Bloomfield. 1897. Reprint. Delhi: Motilal Banarsidass, 1967.

Kūrma Purāṇa. Translated by Ganesh Vasudeo Tagare. Ancient Indian Tradition and Mythology Series, vols. 20–21. Delhi: Motilal Banarsidass, 1981.

Lakṣmī-Tantra: A Pāñcarātra Agama. Edited by Pandit V. Krishnamacharya. Adyar Library Series, vol. 87. Adyar, Madras: Adyar Library and Research Centre, 1959.

Lakṣmī Tantra: A Pāñcarātra Text. Translated by Sanjukta Gupta. Leiden: Brill, 1972.

Liṅga Purāṇa. Translated by a Board of Scholars. Ancient Indian Tradition and Mythology Series, vols. 5–6. Delhi: Motilal Banarsidass, 1973.

Mahābhārata of Krishna-Dwaipayana Vyasa. 12 vols. Translated by Kisari Mohan Ganguli. 4th ed. Delhi: Munshiram Manoharlal , 1991–2001.
Nārada-Purāṇa. Translated by Ganesh Vasudeo Tagare. Ancient Indian Tradition and Mythology Series, vols. 15–19. Delhi: Motilal Banarsidass, 1980–1982.
Padmā-Purāṇa. Translated by N. A. Deshpande. Ancient Indian Tradition and Mythology Series, vols. 39–48. Delhi: Motilal Banarsidass, 1988–1992.
Pañcasūktam: Edited with the 'Siddhānta Dīpika' Sanskrit and Hindi Commentaries. Edited by Śrī Vaiṣṇavasvāmī Rāma Nārāyaṇadāsa Śāstrī. Haridās Sanskrit Series 290. Varanasi: Chowkhamba Sanskrit Series Office, 1971.
Śatapatha-Brāhmaṇa, According to the Text of the Mādhyandina School. Translated by Julius Eggeling. 1900. Reprint. 2d ed. Delhi: Motilal Banarsidass, 1966.
Śiva Purāṇa. Translated by a Board of Scholars. Ancient Indian Tradition and Mythology, Vols. 1–4. Delhi: Motilal Banarsidass, 1969–1970.
Śrī Lakṣmī Upāsanā. Edited by Pandit Rajesh Dixit. Delhi: Dehati Pustak Bhandar, *saṃvat* 2032 [CE 1974/1975].
Śrī Mad Devī Bhāgavatam. Translated by Swami Vijnanananda (Hari Prasanna Chatterji). Sacred Books of the Hindus, vol. 26. Reprint. Allahabad: Bhuvaneswari Asram, 1977.
Śrī Sūkta: Text with Translation and Explanation. Edited and translated by S. K. Ramachandra Rao. Bangalore: Kalpatharu Research Academy, 1985.
Thirteen Principal Upanishads, The. Translated by Robert Ernest Hume. 2d. rev. ed. London: Oxford University Press, 1931.
Vāmana Purāṇa, with English Translation. Edited by Anand Swarup Gupta. Translated by Satyamsu Mohan Mukhopadhyaya, Ahibhushan Bhattacharya, N. C. Nath, and V. K. Verma. Varanasi: All India Kashiraj Trust, 1968.
Vāstu-Śāstra: Hindu Canons of Iconography and Painting, Vol. II. Edited and translated by D. N. Shukla. New Delhi: Munshiram Manoharlal, 1993.
Vishnu Purāṇa: A System of Hindu Mythology and Tradition. Translated by H. H. Wilson. Calcutta: Punthi Pustak, 1961.
Viṣṇudharmottara (Part III): A Treatise on Indian Painting and Image-Making. Translated by Stella Kramrisch. Calcutta: Calcutta University Press, 1928.

Secondary Sources

Abbott, J. *The Keys of Power: A Study of Indian Ritual and Belief.* London: Methuen, 1932.
Apte, Vaman Shivaram. *The Student's Sanskrit-English Dictionary.* Delhi: Motilal Banarsidass, 1979.
Babb, Lawrence A. *The Divine Hierarchy: Popular Hinduism in Central India.* New York: Columbia University Press, 1975.
Bahadur, Om Lata. *The Book of Hindu Festivals and Ceremonies.* New Delhi: UBS, 1995.

Bailly, Constantina Rhodes. "Alchemy of the Goddess: An Introduction to the *Śrī Mahālakṣmī Hṛdayam*, an Apocryphal Sanskrit Text." Paper presented at the South Asia Seminar, University of Iowa, September 30, 2004.

———. "*Aṣṭa-Lakṣmī* (The 'Eight Lakṣmīs) and the Celebration of Dīvālī. Lecture presented at the SYDA Foundation, November 1991.

———. "Auspicious Glances: Decoding the Magnificent Paradox of Hindu 'Idol Worship.' " *Mythosphere: A Journal for Image, Myth, and Symbol* 2:3 (2000): 269–283.

———. "The Auspicious One and the Inauspicious: Didactic Tales of Lakṣmī and Alakṣmī from the Purāṇas." Lecture presented at the SYDA Foundation, June 1992.

———. "*Darśan* of the Goddess: Iconography of Aṣṭa-Lakṣmī." Lecture presented at the SYDA Foundation, June 1993.

———. Devadāsīs." In *Encyclopedia of Women and World Religions,* edited by Serinity Young, 1:250–251. New York: Macmillan, 1999.

———. "Discovering Lakṣmī in the Subtle Body of the Yogi: An Esoteric Reading of the *Śrī Sūkta* According to the *Lakṣmī Tantra*." Paper presented at the Society for Tantric Studies Conference, October 1997.

———. "The Domain of Mahālakṣmī." *Darshan* 116 (November 1996): 12–17.

———. "Four Arms, Three Eyes, and Endless Possibilities: How to Decode the Auspicious Images of Hindu Sacred Art." Presidential Address delivered at the American Academy of Religion/Southeast Annual Conference, March 1998.

———. "Invoking Lakṣmī/Conjuring Lakṣmī: Religious and Magical Practices in the *Lakṣmī Tantra*." Paper presented at the American Academy of Religion Annual Conference, November 23, 1998.

———. "Kamalā's Secret: How the *Saṃsārin* Obtains Outrageous Power through the Inconspicious Worship of the Hindu *Mahāvidyās*." Paper presented at the Society for Tantric Studies Conference, October 12, 2002.

———. "Lakṣmī, Alakṣmī, and the Practices of the Hindu Householder." Lecture presented at the SYDA Foundation, August 1991.

———. "Lakṣmī: Bestower of Beauty and Abundance." *Darshan* 66 (September 1992): 20–24.

———. "The Majestic Essence of Sweetness: Exploring the Rādhā-Lakṣmī Relationship." *Journal of Vaiṣṇava Studies* 10:1 (Fall 2001): 27–50.

———. "Marriage and Singleness: In Asian Religions." In *Encyclopedia of Women and World Religions,* edited by Serinity Young, 2:622–624. New York: Macmillan, 1999.

———. "Ornamentation." In *Encyclopedia of Women and World Religion,* edited by Serinity Young, 2:750–751. New York: Macmillan, 1999.

———. *Shaiva Devotional Songs of Kashmir: A Translation and Study of Utpaladeva's Shivastotravali*. Albany: State University of New York Press, 1987.

———. "*Śrī Lābha, Śrī Śubha:* Lakṣmī and the Concept of Auspiciousness." Lecture presented at the SYDA Foundation, June 1993.

———. "Śrī-Lakṣmī: Majesty of the Hindu King." In *Goddesses Who Rule*, edited by Elisabeth Benard and Beverly Moon, 133–145. New York: Oxford University Press, 2000.

———. "To Behold the Form of Auspiciousness: Popular Images of Mahālakṣmī." Paper presented at the American Academy of Religion Annual Conference, November 1992.

Bandyopadhyay, Pranab. *The Goddess of Tantra*. Revised edition. Calcutta: Punthi Pustak, 1990.

Benard, Elisabeth. *Chinnamastā: The Aweful Buddhist and Tantric Goddess*. Delhi: Motilal Banarsidass, 1994.

Bharati, Agehananda. *Tantric Traditions*. Rev. ed. Delhi: Motilal Banarsidass, 1993. [Original title: *The Tantric Tradition*. London: Rider and Co., 1965].

Bhattacharyya, N. N. *Indian Mother Goddess*. Calcutta: Indian Studies: Past & Present, 1971.

Biernacki, Loriliai. *Renowned Goddess of Desire: Women, Sex and Speech in Tantra*. New York: Oxford University Press, 2007.

Brooks, Douglas Renfrew. *Auspicious Wisdom: The Texts and Traditions of Śrīvidyā Śākta Tantrism in South India*. Albany: State University of New York Press, 1992.

———. *The Secret of the Three Cities: An Introduction to Hindu Sakta Tantrism*. Chicago: University of Chicago Press, 1990.

Brooks, Douglas Renfrew, and Constantina Rhodes Bailly. "Kuṇḍalinī." In *Meditation Revolution: A History and Theology of the Siddha Yoga Lineage*, by Douglas Renfrew Brooks, Swami Durgananda, Paul E. Muller-Ortega, William K. Mahony, Constantina Rhodes Bailly, and S. P. Sabharathnam, 445–496. South Fallsburg, NY: Agama Press, 1997.

Bryant, Edwin. *The Quest for the Origins of Vedic Culture: The Indo-Aryan Migration Debate*. New York: Oxford University Press, 2001.

Bühnemann, Gudrun. *Pūjā: A Study in Smārta Ritual*. Vienna: Gerold & Co., 1988.

Chaturvedi, Mahendra, and B. N. Tiwari, editors. *A Practical Hindi-English Dictionary*. 6th ed. New Delhi: National Publishing House, 1980.

Christ, Carol P. *Rebirth of the Goddess: Finding Meaning in Feminist Spirituality*. Reading, MA: Addison-Wesley, 1997.

Clark, Walter Eugene. "Śākadvīpa and Śvetadvīpa." *Journal of the American Oriental Society* 39 (1919): 209–242.

Clooney, Francis X., S.J. *Divine Mother, Blessed Mother: Hindu Goddesses and the Virgin Mary*. New York: Oxford University Press, 2005.

Coburn, Thomas B. *Devīmāhātmya: Crystallization of the Goddess Tradition*. Delhi: Motilal Banarsidass, 1984.

Coomaraswamy, Ananda K. "Early Indian Iconography: No. 2, Śrī-Lakṣmī," *Eastern Art* I (1928–1929): 175–189.

———. *Yakṣas: Essays in the Water Cosmology*. 1931. Rev. ed., edited by Paul Schroeder. Delhi: Oxford University Press, 1993.

Courtright, Paul B. "On This Holy Day in My Humble Way: Aspects of *Pūjā*." In *Gods of Flesh, Gods of Stone: The Embodiment of Divinity in India*, edited by Joanne Punzo Waghorne and Norman Cutler, with Vasudha Narayanan, 33–50. Chambersburg, PA: Anima Press, 1985.

Crooke, William. *The Popular Religion and Folk-Lore of Northern India.* 2 vols. 1896. 2d. ed., 4th reprint. New Delhi: Munshiram Manoharlal, 1978.

Davis, Richard H. *Ritual in an Oscillating Universe: Worshiping Siva in Medieval India.* Princeton: Princeton University Press, 1991.

Dhal, Upendra Nath. *Goddess Lakṣmī: Origin and Development.* 2d rev. ed. Delhi: Eastern Book Linkers, 1995.

Diehl, Carl Gustav. *Instrument and Purpose: Studies on Rites and Rituals in South India.* Lund: C. W. K. Gleerup, 1956.

Dyczkowski, Mark S. G. *The Canon of the Śaivāgama and the Kubjikā Tantras of the Western Kaula Tradition.* Albany: State University of New York Press, 1988.

———. *The Doctrine of Vibration: An Analysis of the Doctrines and Practices of Kashmir Shaivism.* Albany: State University of New York Press, 1987.

Eller, Cynthia. *Living in the Lap of the Goddess: The Feminist Spirituality Movement in America.* Boston: Beacon Press, 1993/1995.

Erndl, Kathleen M. *Victory to the Mother: The Hindu Goddess of Northwest India in Myth, Ritual, and Symbol.* New York: Oxford University Press, 1993.

Feldhaus, Anne. *Water and Womanhood: Religious Meanings of Rivers in Maharashtra.* New York: Oxford University Press, 1995.

Flood, Gavin. *An Introduction to Hinduism.* Cambridge: Cambridge University Press, 1996.

Fuller, C. J. *The Camphor Flame: Popular Hinduism and Society in India.* Princeton: Princeton University Press, 1992.

Gonda, Jan. *Aspects of Early Viṣṇuism.* 2d ed. Delhi: Motilal Banarsidass, 1969.

Ghosh, Niranjan. *Concept and Iconography of the Goddess of Abundance and Fortune in Three Religions of India.* Burdwan, University of Burdwan, 1979.

Goudriaan, Teun, and Sanjukta Gupta. *Hindu Tantric and Śākta Literature. A History of Indian Literature,* vol. II, fasc. 1. Ed. Jan Gonda. Wiesbaden: Otto Harrassowitz, 1981.

Gupta, Lina. "Hindu Women and Ritual Empowerment." In *Women and Goddess Traditions: In Antiquity and Today,* edited by Karen L. King, 85–110. Minneapolis: Fortress Press, 1997.

———. "Tantric Incantation in the *Devī Purāṇa: The Padamālā Mantra Vidyā.*" In *The Roots of Tantra,* edited by Katherine Anne Harper and Robert L. Brown, 231–249. Albany: State University of New York Press, 2002.

Gupta, S. K. *Elephant in Indian Art and Mythology.* Atlantic Highlands, NJ: Humanities Press, 1983.

Gupta, Sanjukta. "The Maṇḍala as an Image of Man." In *Indian Ritual and Its Exegesis,* edited by Richard F. Gombrich. Oxford University Papers on India, vol. 2, part 1. Delhi: Oxford University Press, 1988.

———. "The Pāñcarātra Attitude to Mantra." In *Mantra,* edited by Harvey P. Alper, 224–248. Albany: State University of New York Press, 1988.

Gupta, Sanjukta, Dirk Jan Hoens, and Teun Goudriaan. *Hindu Tantrism.* Leiden: Brill, 1979.

Hanchett, Suzanne. *Coloured Rice: Symbolic Structure in Hindu Family Festivals.* Delhi: Hindustan, 1988.

Hayes, Glen A. "The Necklace of Immortality: A Seventeenth-Century Vaiṣṇava Sahajīya Text." In *Tantra in Practice*, edited by David Gordon White, 308–325. Princeton: Princeton University Press, 2000.

Hiltebeitel, Alf. *The Ritual of Battle: Krishna in the Mahabharata.* Ithaca, NY: Cornell University Press, 1976.

Humes, Cynthia Ann. "Glorifying the Great Goddess or Great Woman? Hindu Women's Experience in Ritual Recitation of *Devī-Māhātmya.*" In *Women and Goddess Traditions in Antiquity and Today*, edited by Karen L. King, 39–63. Minneapolis: Fortress Press, 1997.

Jayakar, Pupul. *The Earth Mother: Legends, Ritual Arts, and Goddesses of India.* San Francisco, Harper & Row, 1990.

Kane, P[andurang] V[aman]. *History of Dharmaśāstra: Ancient and Medieval Religious and Civil Law.* 5 vols. Poona [Pune]: Bhandarkar Oriental Research Institute, 1930–1958.

Keith, Arthur Berriedale. *The Religion and Philosophy of the Veda and Upanishads.* 2 vols. 1925. 2nd reprint. Delhi: Motilal Banarsidass, 1976.

Keshavadas, Satguru Sant. *Gāyatrī: The Highest Meditation.* London and New York: Kegan Paul, 1978.

Kinsley, David. *The Goddesses' Mirror: Visions of the Divine from East and West.* Albany: State University of New York Press, 1989.

———. *Hindu Goddesses: Visions of the Divine Feminine in the Hindu Religious Tradition.* Berkeley: University of California Press, 1986.

———. *Tantric Visions of the Divine Feminine: The Ten Mahāvidyās.* Berkeley: University of California Press, 1997.

Kloppenburg, R., editor. *Selected Studies on Ritual in the Indian Religions.* Leiden: Brill, 1983.

Kripananda, Swami. *The Sacred Power: A Seeker's Guide to Kundalini.* South Fallsburg, NY: SYDA Foundation, 1995.

Kumar, P. Pratap. *The Goddess Lakṣmī: The Divine Consort in South Indian Vaiṣṇava Tradition.* Atlanta: Scholars Press, 1997.

Kumar, Pushpendra. *The Principle of Śakti.* Delhi: Eastern Book Linkers, 1986.

Larson, Gerald James, Pratapaditya Pal, and H. Daniel Smith. *Changing Myths and Images: Twentieth-Century Popular Art in India.* Bloomington: Indiana University India Studies Program in association with Indiana University Art Museum, 1997.

Leslie, Julia, editor. *Roles and Rituals for Hindu Women.* Rutherford, NJ: Fairleigh Dickinson University Press, 1991.

Long, Bruce. "Life Out of Death: A Structural Analysis of the Myth of the Churning of the Ocean of Milk." In *Hinduism: New Essays in the History of Religions*, edited by Bardwell Smith, 171–207. Leiden: Brill, 1976.

Lutgendorf, Philip. "Five Heads and No Tale: Hanumān and the Popularization of Tantra." *International Journal of Hindu Studies* 5, 3 (December 2001): 269–296.

Macdonell, Arthur A. *A History of Sanskrit Literature.* Delhi: Motilal Banarsidass, 1976 (1899).

Madan, T. N. "Concerning the Categories *Śubha* and *Śuddha* in Hindu Culture: An Exploratory Essay." In *Purity and Auspiciousness in Indian Society,* edited by John B. Carman and Frédérique Apffel Marglin, 11–29. Leiden: Brill, 1985.

Mahony, William K. *The Artful Universe: An Introduction to the Vedic Religious Imagination.* Albany: State University of New York Press, 1998.

Mani, Vettam. *Purāṇic Encyclopaedia: A Comprehensive Work with Special Reference to the Epic and Purāṇic Literature.* 1975. Reprint. Delhi: Motilal Banarsidass, 1993.

Marglin, Frédérique Apffel. "Types of Oppositions in Hindu Culture." In *Purity and Auspiciousness in Indian Society,* edited by John B. Carman and Frédérique Apffel Marglin, 65–83. Leiden: Brill, 1985.

———. *Wives of the God-King: The Rituals of the Devadasis of Pūri.* Delhi: Oxford University Press, 1985.

Maury, Curt. *Folk Origins of Indian Art.* New York: Columbia University Press, 1969.

McDaniel, June. *Making Virtuous Daughters and Wives: An Introduction to Women's Brata Rituals in Bengali Folk Religion.* Albany: State University of New York Press, 2003.

McDermott, Rachel Fell. *Singing to the Goddess: Poems to Kali and Uma from Bengal.* New York: Oxford University Press, 2001.

Monier-Williams, Monier. *A Sanskrit-English Dictionary.* Oxford: Clarendon Press, 1956.

Mookerjee, Ajit. *Tantra Āsana: A Way to Self-Realization.* New Delhi: Ravi Kumar, 1971.

Muller-Ortega, Paul E. "Becoming Bhairava: Meditative Vision in Abhinavagupta's *Parātrīśikā-laghuvṛtti.*" In *The Roots of Tantra,* edited by Katherine Anne Harper and Robert L. Brown, 213–230. Albany: State University of New York Press, 2002.

———. "On the Seal of Śambhu: A Poem by Abhinavagupta." In *Tantra in Practice,* edited by David Gordon White, 573–586. Princeton: Princeton University Press, 2000.

———. *The Triadic Heart of Śiva.* Albany: State University of New York Press, 1989.

Narayanan, Vasudha. "The Goddess Śrī: Blossoming Lotus and Breast Jewel of Viṣṇu." In *The Divine Consort: Rādhā and the Goddesses of India,* edited by John Stratton Hawley and Donna Marie Wulff, 224–237. Boston: Beacon Press, 1982.

———. "The Two Levels of Auspiciousness in Śrīvaiṣṇvava Literature." In *Purity and Auspiciousness in Indian Society,* edited by John B. Carman and Frédérique Apffel Marglin, 55–63. Leiden: Brill, 1985.

Orman, Suze. *Women and Money: Owning the Power to Control Your Destiny.* New York: Spiegel & Grau, 2007.

Padoux, André. "Tantrism: Hindu Tantrism." In *The Encyclopedia of Religion,* edited by Mircea Eliade, 14: 274–80. New York: Macmillan, 1987.

———. "What Do We Mean by Tantrism?" In *The Roots of Tantra*, edited by Katherine Anne Harper and Robert L. Brown, 17–24. Albany: State University of New York Press, 2002.

Paris, Ginette. *Pagan Meditations: The Worlds of Aphrodite, Artemis, and Hestia.* Translated from the French by Gwendolyn Moore. Woodstock, CT: Spring Publications, 1986.

Pattanaik, Devdutt. *Lakshmi, the Goddess of Wealth and Fortune: An Introduction.* Mumbai: Vakils, Feffer and Simons Private, 2002.

Pearson, Anne Mackenzie. *"Because It Gives Me Peace of Mind": Ritual Fasts in the Religious Lives of Hindu Women.* Albany: State University of New York Press, 1996.

Pintchman, Tracy. *Guests at God's Wedding: Celebrating Kartik Among the Women of Benares.* Albany: State University of New York Press, 2005.

———. *The Rise of the Goddess in the Hindu Tradition.* Albany: State University of New York Press, 1994.

Ponder, Catherine. *The Dynamic Laws of Prosperity.* Reprint. Marina del Rey, CA: DeVorss & Co., 1985 [1962].

Raj, Selva J., and William P. Harman, editors. *Dealing with Deities: The Ritual Vow in South Asia.* Albany: State University of New York Press, 2006.

Schrader, F. Otto. *Introduction to the Pāñcarātra and the Ahirbudhnya Saṃhitā.* Adyar, Madras: Adyar Library, 1916.

Shankaranarayanan, S. *The Ten Great Cosmic Powers* (*Daśa Mahāvidyās*). Chennai: Samata Books, 2008 [1972].

Shaw, Miranda. *Buddhist Goddesses of India.* Princeton: Princeton University Press, 2006.

———. *Passionate Enlightenment: Women in Tantric Buddhism.* Princeton: Princeton University Press, 1994.

Shukla, D. N. *Vāstu Śāstra. Vol. II: Hindu Canons of Iconography and Painting.* New Delhi: Munshiram Manoharlal, 1993.

Singh, O. P. *Iconography of Gaja-Lakshmī.* Varanasi: Bharati Prakashan, 1983.

Sircar, D. C. *Studies in the Religious Life of Ancient and Medieval India.* Delhi: Motilal Banarsidass, 1971.

Sircar, D. C., editor. *Foreignors in Ancient India AND Lakṣmī and Sarasvatī in Art and Literature.* Calcutta: University of Calcutta, 1970.

Sivaramamurti, C. *Śrī Lakshmī in Indian Art and Thought.* New Delhi: Kanak Publications, 1982.

Slocum, Perry D., and Peter Robinson. *Water Gardening: Water Lilies and Lotuses.* Portland, OR: Timber Press, 1990.

Smith, Frederick M. *The Self Possessed: Deity and Spirit Possession in South Asian Literature and Civilization.* New York: Columbia University Press, 2006.

Smith, H. Daniel, editor. *A Sourcebook of Vaiṣṇava Iconography According to Pāñcarātrāgama Texts.* Madras: Pancaratra Parisodhana Parisad, 1969.

Somayaji, Daivajna K. N., editor. *Pratima Kosha: Descriptive Glossary of Indian Iconography,* vols. 1–6. Bangalore: Kalpatharu Research Academy, 1989+.

Te Nijenhuis, Emmie, and Sanjukta Gupta, trans. *Sacred Songs of India: Dikṣitar's Cycle of Hymns to the Goddess Kamalā. Part I: Musicological and Religious Analysis, Text and Translation.* Forum Ethnomusicologicum 3. Winterthur: Amadeus Verlag, 1987.

Thieme, Paul. "Pūjā." *Journal of Oriental Research* 27 (1957–1958): 1–16.

Timalsina, Sthaneshwar. "Terrifying Beauty: Interplay of the Sanskritic and Vernacular Rituals of Siddhilakṣmī." *International Journal of Hindu Studies* 10:1 (2006): 59–73.

Vijay, Alahar. *Vaasthu Shastra: Indian Traditional Building Science.* Chennai: Sura Books, 2003.

White, David Gordon. *The Alchemical Body: Siddha Traditions in Medieval India.* Chicago: University of Chicago Press, 1996.

Winternitz, Maurice. *A History of Indian Literature.* Vol. 1. Translated by Mrs. S. Ketkar. Calcutta: University of Calcutta, 1927.

Woodroffe, Sir John (Arthur Avalon). *Hymns to the Goddess and Hymn to Kali.* Reprint. Wilmot, WI: Lotus Light Publications, 1981.

Zimmer, Heinrich. *Myths and Symbols in Indian Art and Civilization.* Edited by Joseph Campbell. Bollingen Series VI. Princeton: Princeton University Press, 1972.

Index

Page numbers for definitions are in boldface.

consciousness *(continued)*
transformation of, 7–8, 10, 72–73; undifferentiated state of pure, 203
cows, as embodiments of Lakṣmī, 17, 95, 106, 115, 256n4 (Purāṇic Hymns to Lakṣmī)

Daśamahāvidyās (Ten Great Wisdom Goddesses), 52–55, 58
devadāsī ("servant of the gods," sacred courtesan), 27, 29
devanāgarī script, 19
devas (deities), **5**, 25
devī (goddess), **5**, 19
devotional texts, origins of, 9–10
Dhanadā (Bestower of Wealth), 34, 36–38
dharma (virtuous conduct), 7, 27, 31, 74; as expression of Lakṣmī, 38–41; neglect of, 44
Dhūmāvatī, 55–56
Dīvālī (Festival of Lights), 1, 2, 33
Dixit, Pandit Rajesh, 8, 97, 116, 207, 254n2 (Lakṣmī *Pūjā* Text), 258n17, 262n5, 263n6, 263n9

elephants, in iconography of Lakṣmī, 15–16, 33, 47, 63
elixir, of immortality, 25–26, 76, 111; the goddess's marvelous, 74–76, 78

favor (*prasannā*) of the goddess, 8, 64, 68, 69, 75
flower offerings, 59, 110–111, 115–116, 117
fruit offerings, 59, 113–114

Gaṇeśa, 5, 94, 101–102
gaurī ("bright," beneficent goddess), 41, 52
ghee (clarified butter), 1, 2, 106, 112, 114, 115
"god-posters," 37
goddess of prosperity, 1–4, 15, 17, 31, 68, 203–204
gold coins, as forms of Lakṣmī, 17; in iconography of Lakṣmī, 33, 37; in Lakṣmī *pūjā*, 95, 114, 117
golden urn, as respository of immortal nectar, 111; as repository of seed-syllables, 76, 81; as symbol of woman's body, 81
Gonda, Jan, 35, 250n6, 250n8, 251n23
Gṛhya Lakṣmī (Lakṣmī of the Home), 27–30

Hestia, 30
horses, in iconography of Lakṣmī, 63, 256n4
hṛdayam, **82–83**

incense, 2, 44, 65, 95, 111–112, 117
Indra (lord of heaven), 24–26, 43, 99; as composer of praise-songs for Lakṣmī, 7, 26, 42, 133, 137, 146–147, 190–192
invoking Lakṣmī, as yogic discipline, 94; consistency of, 21, 36; for spiritual and material blessings, 7, 40, 80; study of, 3–5; to attract prosperity and auspiciousness, 3–5, 7–8, 43, 76, 68, 89; to awaken consciousness within, 27, 35–36, 79; to repel inauspiciousness, 20, 44, 65. *See also* chanting; *mantras*

Jones, Sir William, 16

Kālī, 41, 52–53
kāma (pleasure), 7, 27, 31, 41; as expression of Lakṣmī, 32–33, 39, 40
Kamalā, 16; as Tantric form of Lakṣmī, 52–55, 58, 70
karma, 23, 24; reversing the effects of, 67
Kashmir, worship of Lakṣmī in, 59, 253n14